Computer Accounting

a practical guide for Sage accounting courses

Michael Fardon

osborne
BOOKS

© Michael Fardon, 2002. Reprinted 2004, 2006.

Published by Osborne Books Limited
Unit 1B Everoak Estate
Bromyard Road
Worcester WR2 5HP
Tel 01905 748071
Email books@osbornebooks.co.uk
Website www.osbornebooks.co.uk

Graphic design by Richard Holt and Jon Moore

Printed by the Bath Press, Bath

British Library Cataloguing in Publication Data
A catalogue record for this book is available from the British Library

ISBN 1 872962 27 0

CONTENTS

ACKNOWLEDGEMENTS

The author wishes to thank the following for their help with the reading and production of the text: David Cox, Mike Gilbert, Pamela Green, Keith Hudson and Jon Moore. Particular thanks must go to Ann Fontbin of Herefordshire College of Technology for her help and advice and to her students Julie Reece, Kay Spencer and Glenda Witts for test running all the Sage Inputting Tasks and Extended Exercises in the book.

Thanks are also due to Microsoft UK for permission to use screen images of their software and to Sage PLC for their support for the project and permission to use screen images in the text.

THE AUTHOR

Michael Fardon has had extensive teaching experience on a wide range of banking, business and accountancy courses at Worcester College of Technology where he also set up and ran computer accounting courses, using Sage software. He now specialises in writing business and financial texts and is currently General Editor at Osborne Books.

INTRODUCTION

Computer Accounting has been written to provide a Sage-based practical study resource for students taking courses including:

- OCR Level 1 Certificate in Bookkeeping, Computer Accounting Units 4 and 5
- Pitman Computerised Accounts, Levels 1 and 2
- IAB Diploma in Computerised Book-keeping

The **text** of *Computer Accounting* contains clear and practical explanations of how to set up and run a Sage system. A Case Study – Pronto Supplies Limited – runs through the chapters and forms the basis of the processing activities and the first of the extended activities at the end of the book. Many of the teachers consulted in the writing process mentioned the need for an understanding by students of the theoretical background to computer accounting – in particular the use of financial documents and double-entry book-keeping. The documents are explained as they are encountered in the text and a chapter on double-entry book-keeping is included at the back of the book to help students who may not be studying it as part of their course.

The **processing activities** at the end of the chapters in this book have all been tried and tested a number of times, together with the screens in the explanatory text. Trial balances have been included periodically and also at the back of the book so that account balances can be checked. The end-of-chapter activities progressively build up the various processes needed to set up and run a Sage system. The two Extended Activities at the end of the book are designed for assessment purposes: the first follows on from the chapters, the second is standalone.

Invoicing has been treated flexibly in the text so that batch entry can be used if the teaching centre does not want to (or cannot) set up a full invoicing function. The OCR solution of using Service Invoices in their assessments is developed in Chapter 13 and in the second Extended Activity.

Sage Line 50 Version 7 has been used throughout, but the author asks the teacher's indulgence if he or she is using a different version, as some of the screens may vary. The basic principles, however, remain very much the same.

A supporting **Tutor Pack** is available from Osborne Books. Please call on 01905 748071 for further details.

1 INTRODUCTION TO COMPUTER ACCOUNTING

chapter introduction

- Computer systems involve
  - hardware – the equipment
  - software – the programs that run the computers
- There are a number of different types of computer programs used by businesses and other organisations:
  - word processing
  - databases
  - spreadsheets
  - email management
  - accounting packages
- Computers require input of data – which can either be carried out manually from sources such as financial documents or can be imported from other computer systems on disk or online.
- Computers also output data in the form of 'hard copy' printouts and electronic data which can be emailed or imported into other computer systems.

COMPUTER HARDWARE

Computer **hardware** is the equipment on which the programs will be run.

There are two main ways of setting up the hardware – a standalone system and a network.

standalone system

A typical standalone system uses a single computer with a screen, mouse, a hard disk for data storage and a printer and scanner. This computer is likely be linked to the internet by phone line. This type of system is useful for a small business when only one person needs to operate the computer at any one time.

networks (intranet)

A network comprises a number of computer workstations linked to a central server (which holds all the data) and other equipment such as printers and scanners – this type of system is likely to be used by a larger business or organisation (such as a College IT centre) where a number of operators need to access the system at the same time.

Data can be exchanged through the network and internal emails can be sent. This set up is also known as an **intranet**. The system can also be linked up by phone line to an external internet service provider (ISP) – eg AOL – so that the internet can be accessed and external emails sent and received.

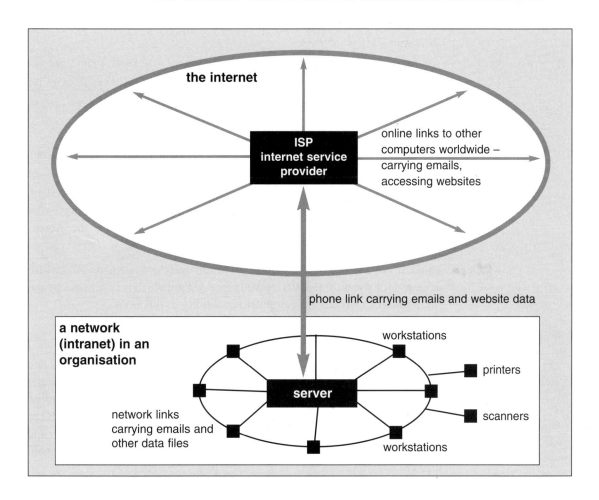

printers

All computer systems need a printer to produce 'hard copy' such as letters, financial documents and management reports. The old-fashioned form of printer is the dot matrix printer which prints text as a series of dots using a printer head with pins. This is useful if you need multiple copies of documents such as invoices: the pins strike the paper with some force and can print the characters through a number of sheets of paper. If better quality printing is required an inkjet or laser printer can be used, but these types only print one copy at a time. They are also less noisy!

data storage and backup

It is very important that the data held by the computer is backed up regularly and stored away from the premises or transmitted to another location. Data can be backed up onto a variety of storage media, eg floppy disk, Zip disk, tape and CD. All systems should therefore have some form of data storage facility or be able to transmit data to another location.

COMPUTER SOFTWARE

windows operating systems

The program – the **software** – that makes a computer work is known as the operating system. Most business computers are PCs (personal computers) which run the Windows operating system which is a Microsoft product. Another Microsoft product is the Office suite of programs which includes the Word word processing program, the Excel spreadsheet and the Access database.

Standard 'off-the-shelf' accounting programs such as Sage Line 50 are also designed for use on Windows, and it is this system which we will refer to and illustrate when explaining computer accounting in this book.

types of software

We will now outline the different types of software used in businesses and other organisations and then explain how they 'fit in' with computer accounting packages such as Sage. It may be that you are already familiar with these types of program. Even so it is a good idea to read through the next few pages to remind yourself of the exact function of the packages and see how they can be integrated with computer accounting software. The main types of program are:

- word processing
- databases
- spreadsheets
- email managers
- accounting packages

WORD PROCESSING

Word processing programs – including Microsoft Word – enable you to

- enter text
- format text, eg set it out in columns, add bullet points
- change and edit text
- set up tables

Word processed text can be saved and printed out in the form of letters, memos, reports, and notices. Word processed text can also be sent electronically either on disk or as an attachment file on an email. Some of the text in Osborne Books publications is first input in Word and sent to Osborne Books on disk or by email. It is then imported into a page set-up program.

Word processing programs can be linked up with other programs. For example the names and addresses from a computer accounting package can be imported to 'mailmerge' into a set of letters sent out to customers.

Similarly, names and addresses of customers entered in a word processing or spreadsheet program can be transferred into a computer accounting package to set up account details. The text format used is known as comma separated text (see page 9 for a practical illustration of this).

The screen below shows how the original version of some of the text on this page was set up in Word and then imported into a page set-up program.

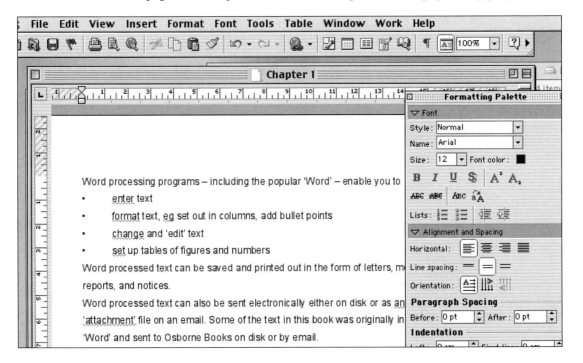

DATABASES

A computer database enables you to input and store information in an organised way so that it can be readily accessed, sorted and exported. A database is essentially an electronic filing system which takes all the hard work out of sorting and retrieving information.

Imagine, for example, your business does not have a computer database. It keeps the names and addresses of 250 customers on cards sorted alphabetically by surname and kept in a plastic box in the office. Suppose

- you drop the box on the floor and all the cards get out of order, or
- you are asked to identify all the customers who are based in Nottingham

These two situations will take a long time to sort out if the records are kept on cards. If this information were stored on a computer database . . .

- the records could automatically be sorted alphabetically by surname
- you could ask the computer could to search the field which contains the town or city name which is 'Nottingham'

Note that two terms are used here:

- a **record** is a set of information which corresponds to each card in a card index – here it is a customer record which is likely to contain the name of the customer, address, telephone number, and email
- a **field** is a part of the record (normally a box to fill in on the computer screen) which contains a specific piece of information, for example, customer surname, town, telephone number, email

A customer record is shown in the screen below. Note how the information is stored in different fields. In particular, note how the address is a series of fields. The 'Town/City' field is one of these.

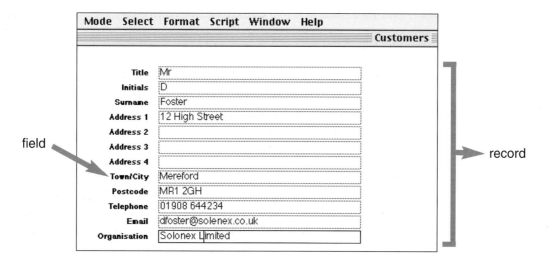

field / record

using data

Databases are very useful if you wish to record and make use of significant data relating to your business or organisation. For example, assume that the 'Customers' record shown on the previous page is part of a list of the people and organisations to whom a business sells its products. It could be expanded with further fields to record information such as:

■ date last contacted

■ status – eg target customers (those who have not ordered)

■ details of products sold

The 'Customers' file could then be accessed and searched to produce lists, for example, of customers not contacted within the last six months, target customers and customers who have bought a particular product.

The possibilities offered by a database apply in many areas. The index of this book, for example, was created by a database which sorts word fields alphabetically.

SPREADSHEETS

calculations

A spreadsheet is a grid of boxes – 'cells' – set up on the computer, organised in rows and columns into which you can enter text and numbers. It enables you to make calculations with the figures. The computer program will work out the calculations automatically once you have entered an appropriate formula in the cell where the result of the calculations is required.

The major advantage of a spreadsheet is that if you change any of the figures the computer will automatically recalculate the total, saving you much time and effort.

Spreadsheets are used for a variety of functions in organisations:

■ producing invoices – working out costs of products sold, calculating and adding on VAT and producing a sales total

■ working out budgets for future expenditure

■ working out sales figures for different products or areas

A commonly used spreadsheet program is Microsoft Excel. The example on the next page shows regional sales figures input into Excel. Note that the rows are numbered and the columns have letter references. The total sales figure appears in the cell (box) which therefore has the reference of B11.

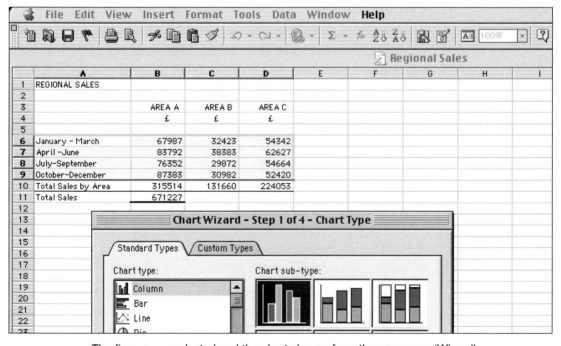

producing graphs and charts

Another function of the spreadsheet is its ability to produce graphs and charts from the figures in the spreadsheet grid. All that you need to do is to select the appropriate figures and the computer does the rest through its charting function. Look at the screens below and on the next page which use the Sales figures illustrated in the screen above. Note how the cells have been selected.

The figures are selected and the chart chosen from the on-screen 'Wizard'

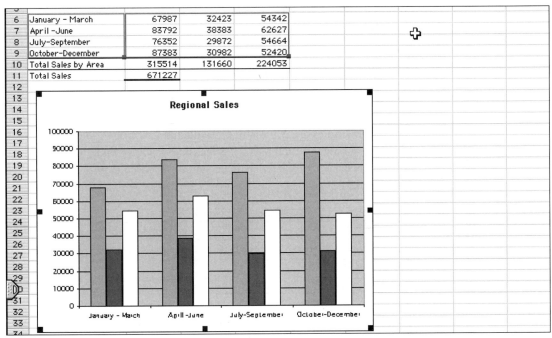

6	January – March	67987	32423	54342
7	April –June	83792	38383	62627
8	July–September	76352	29872	54664
9	October–December	87383	30982	52420
10	Total Sales by Area	315514	131660	224053
11	Total Sales	671227		

The computer produces a chart which can then be pasted into another program as required

EXPORTING DATA FROM A COMPUTER PROGRAM

It is sometimes useful to be able to export data such as names and addresses from one computer program to another.

If you had a file of customer names and addresses set up on a database you could export the data into a computer accounting package such as Sage to set up further Customer records using a text format known as Comma Separated Values (CSV). This is text from the originating file treated in the following way:

1 a comma is inserted after every field, including blank ones

2 a return is inserted after each record - this has the effect of turning each record into a continuous line of text

The customer record from the database on page 6 will look like this:

Mr,D,Foster,12 High Street,Mereford,MR1 2GH,01908 644234,dfoster@solenex.co.uk,Solonex Limited

Many programs, including word processing programs and spreadsheets will automatically set up a CSV file for you. All you need to do is open the appropriate file and save the data using the Save As function. You will not need to insert all the commas yourself!

EMAIL MANAGEMENT

Many businesses and other organisations are now online and can send and receive external emails. Some businesses and other organisations are also networked through an intranet and can send emails internally. Another important computer program is therefore the email management system. Common examples are Microsoft Outlook and Entourage. The screen below shows the outbox – which lists messages and enables you to access the texts sent. In this case a message has been sent to Osborne Books, the publishers of this book.

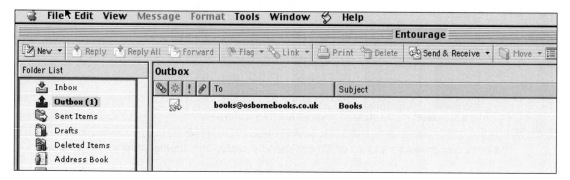

uses of email and attachments

Email is a very useful and inexpensive means of sending messages electronically not only within a business but also externally to customers and suppliers. Transmission is instantaneous. This can be an advantage, but can also be a disadvantage – it often demands a rapid reply.

Email acts as a link between many different types of computer program. Not only can a message be relayed in text form, email can also be used to transfer word processing, database and spreadsheet files from one computer to another in the form of an attachment file.

Documents – orders and invoices for example – can be generated on the computer and sent by email attachment to suppliers and customers.

electronic documents and EDI

Data and documents – eg financial documents such as orders and invoices – can also be sent electronically through Electronic Data Interchange (EDI) programs. This form of transfer – which has been in use for a number of years – employs software which is more specialised (ie expensive!) than the normal email management programs already mentioned. The principle, however, is the same – electronic documentation. The process is reliable, fast and efficient and often used by supermarket chains in ordering and paying for goods.

INTRODUCTION TO COMPUTER ACCOUNTING PACKAGES

a growth area

Although some organisations, particularly small businesses, still use paper-based accounting systems, an increasing number are now operating computerised accounting systems. Small and medium-sized businesses can buy 'off-the shelf' accounting programs from suppliers such as Sage while larger businesses often have custom-designed programs. Computer accounting programs are easy to use and can automate operations such as invoicing which take so much time and effort in a manual system.

links with traditional book-keeping

If you are studying on an AAT or similar course, your study of book-keeping and accounts concentrates largely on paper-based systems. The reason for this is that when you use a paper-based system you have to do all the work manually and so you can understand the theory that underlies the system: you prepare the documents, make entries in the accounts, balance the cash book, and so on. You know where all the figures are entered, and why they are entered. If you know how a paper-based system works, you will be in a much better position to be able to understand the operation of a computer-based system.

Important note: if you are not familiar with manual book-keeping systems and terms such as 'double-entry' and 'ledger' you should read **now** Chapter 14 on page 186 which provides an introduction to this important area.

comparison with other computer programs

Computer accounting packages – such as the Sage Line 50 series of products – make use of many of the functions of the other types of computer program already described in this chapter.

Most computer accounting packages contain:

- word processing functions – eg the facility to write memos and notes
- a series of databases – eg details of customers, stock items held
- built-in spreadsheets – eg invoices where the operator inputs figures and the program automatically generates VAT amounts and totals
- charting and graphing facilities – eg charting of activity on a customer account

FEATURES OF COMPUTER ACCOUNTING

facilities

A typical computer accounting program will offer a number of facilities:

- on-screen input and printout of sales invoices and credit notes
- automatic updating of customer accounts with sales transactions
- recording of suppliers' invoices
- automatic updating of supplier accounts with details of purchases
- recording of money paid into the bank
- recording of payments to suppliers and for expenses

Payroll can also be computerised – normally using a separate program.

management reports

A computer accounting program can provide instant reports for management, for example:

- an aged debtors' summary – showing who owes you what and for what periods of time
- activity reports on customer and supplier accounts
- activity reports on expenses accounts
- VAT Return

advantages of a computer accounting program

Computer accounting programs, like the other computer programs outlined in this chapter, are popular because they offer a number of distinct advantages over paper-based systems:

- they save time
- they save money
- they tend to be more accurate because they rely on single-entry input (one amount per transaction) rather than double-entry book-keeping
- they can provide the managers of the organisation with a clear and up-to-date picture of what is happening

computer accounting and ledgers

The 'ledgers' of a business are basically the books of the business. 'The ledgers' is a term used to describe the way the accounts of the business are grouped into different sections.

There are four main ledgers in a traditional accounting system:

- **sales ledger** contains the accounts of debtors (customers)
- **purchases ledger** contains the accounts of creditors (suppliers)
- **cash book** contains the main cash book and the petty cash book
- **nominal ledger** (also called general or main ledger) contains the remaining accounts, eg expenses (including purchases), income (including sales), assets, loans, stock, VAT

A diagram illustrating these ledgers is shown on the next page. The structure of a computer accounting system is based on these ledgers. It may also include stock control and be linked to a payroll processing program.

A ledger-based computer accounting system is designed to be user-friendly in Windows software. Look at the toolbar of the opening screen of a Sage Windows accounting system shown below and then read the notes printed underneath. Note that a toolbar is a series of icons (pictures) showing what the program can do; the icons can be 'clicked on' to access those activities. Many of these icons will be explained in detail in later chapters. Note that computer accounting packages vary in levels of sophistication; you may be working with one that does not include product records or invoice printing.

Please bear in mind that the screens shown in these chapters may not be exactly the same as those on your computer. The way a Windows accounting program works will, however, always be based on the principles shown in this book.

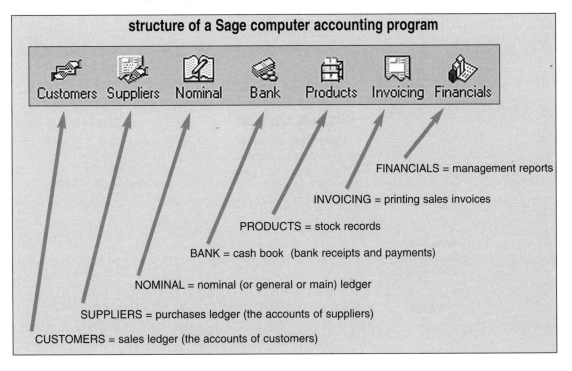

structure of a Sage computer accounting program

Customers Suppliers Nominal Bank Products Invoicing Financials

FINANCIALS = management reports

INVOICING = printing sales invoices

PRODUCTS = stock records

BANK = cash book (bank receipts and payments)

NOMINAL = nominal (or general or main) ledger

SUPPLIERS = purchases ledger (the accounts of suppliers)

CUSTOMERS = sales ledger (the accounts of customers)

computerised ledgers – an integrated system

Before we look at the various functions on the toolbar, it is important to appreciate that a computerised ledger system is **fully integrated.** This means that when a business transaction is input on the computer it is normally recorded in two accounts at the same time, although only one amount is entered. Take the three transactions shown in the diagram below:

■ a business buys from a supplier on credit (ie the business gets the goods but will pay later)

■ a business sells to a customer on credit (ie the business sells the goods but will receive payment later)

■ a business pays an advertising bill

At the centre of an integrated program is the nominal ledger which deals with all the accounts except customers' accounts and suppliers' accounts. It is affected one way or another by most transactions.

The diagram below shows how the three 'ledgers' link with the nominal ledger. Note in each case how an account in the nominal ledger is affected by each of the three transactions. This is the double-entry book-keeping system at work. The advantage of the computer system is that in each case only one entry has to be made. Life is made a great deal simpler this way!

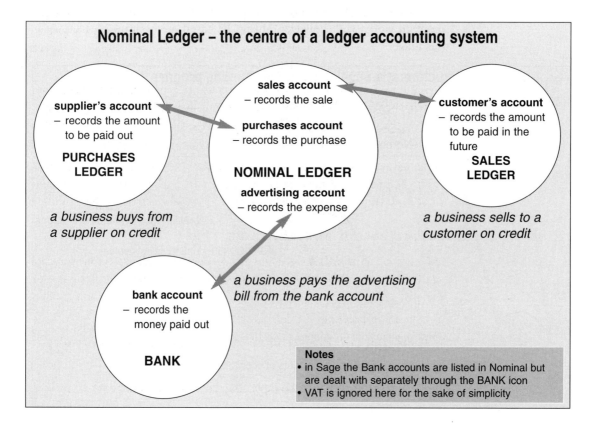

Nominal Ledger – the centre of a ledger accounting system

supplier's account
– records the amount to be paid out
PURCHASES LEDGER

a business buys from a supplier on credit

sales account
– records the sale

purchases account
– records the purchase

NOMINAL LEDGER

advertising account
– records the expense

customer's account
– records the amount to be paid in the future
SALES LEDGER

a business sells to a customer on credit

bank account
– records the money paid out

BANK

a business pays the advertising bill from the bank account

Notes
• in Sage the Bank accounts are listed in Nominal but are dealt with separately through the BANK icon
• VAT is ignored here for the sake of simplicity

INPUT INTO A COMPUTER ACCOUNTING PACKAGE

manual input

Input into a computer accounting package is normally made direct on screen from source documents or other data. You may by this stage be familiar with financial documents and the part they play in the accounting system; if you are not, please read pages 187 to 188 before proceeding any further.

Typical transactions which form the 'bread and butter' of computer accounting input include:

■ processing **sales invoices**, often in runs of several transactions known as 'batches' – the invoices are either written or typed out before input or, if a more advanced computer package is used, they can be input and printed out by the computer

■ inputting **credit notes** from customers' debit notes or from authorised documentation which says why the credit note has to be issued and a refund made – again the credit notes may be produced separately and used as a basis for input, or they may be printed out by the computer

■ inputting **bank receipts** (money paid into the bank) – for example cheques or BACS payments received from customers in settlement of accounts due; the source document in this case is the remittance advice which comes with the cheque or advises the BACS payment

■ inputting details of **new customer accounts** – this is the input of text onto what is effectively a database screen in the computer accounting package; this might happen if the sales team has been very successful and obtained a number of new sales

There are, of course, many other types of transactions which you will input on the computer, but these are common examples. We will cover the input procedures in much greater detail in the individual chapters of this book.

authorisation and checking

Each organisation will have its own procedures to make sure that the data input is accurate and authorised. Source documents – invoices received, for example – may have a stamp placed on them with boxes for the initials of

■ the person checking the document

■ the person authorising the input – often as part of a 'batch' of invoices

■ the computer operator

■ the person who checks the input against the source document

This ensures that accuracy is maintained. Each individual takes responsibility for a particular stage in the process. If there are any errors – and they do happen in the best regulated offices – they can be traced to an individual!

electronic input

Manual input is the most common form of input into a computer accounting package, but occasionally there may be the need to transfer data electronically. This can be done

- by disk

- by online transfer

Read through the following Case Study which explains how this is done.

CASE STUDY

ALEX HERON: DATA TRANSFER

Alex Heron is a sales rep working away from the office. He has obtained a new customer and taken an initial order. He wants the office – which uses a Sage accounting program – to open up an account for him so that a credit check can be made and the sales he has made can be invoiced.

Alex has a laptop computer with an Excel spreadsheet program he uses for various purposes, including logging customer details such as company name, address, telephone number and contact name.

The new customer is Optimus Limited, 45 Unicorn Way, Norwich, NR4 6TF, tel 01603 7773991.The contact is Mel Flower and the new account reference is 1011.

Alex enters the new customer details on a spreadsheet, using a column for each of the 'pieces' of information which will form a field in the Customer record in the Sage accounting program. He will then save the data as a CSV (comma separated) file. The spreadsheet file looks like this:

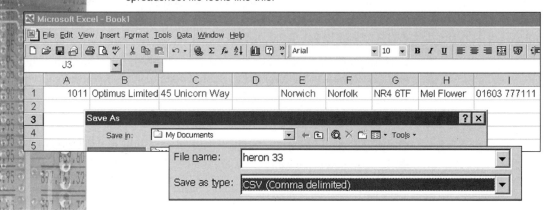

He will then send the file as an email attachment to his head office who will then import the data into the Sage program . . .

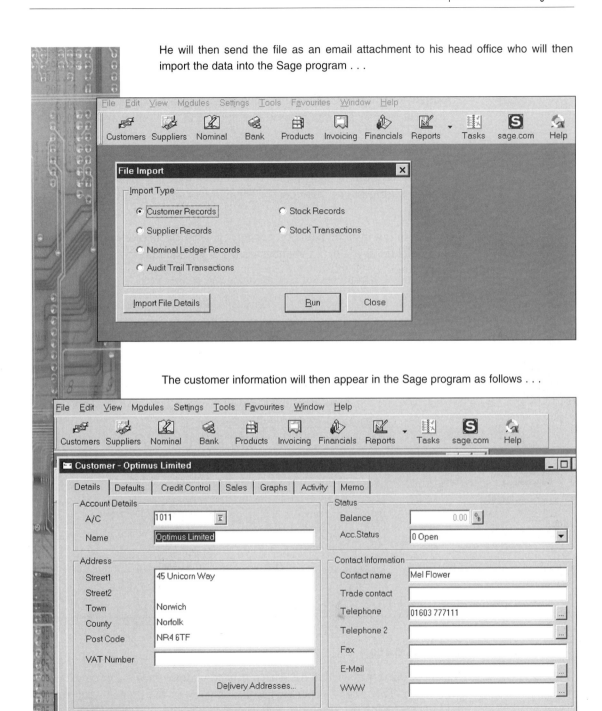

The customer information will then appear in the Sage program as follows . . .

This procedure is shown with one customer here for the sake of illustration and may seem a complex solution to a simple problem. In reality Alex may transfer electronically the details of ten or more customers, which will make the process more worthwhile.

OUTPUT FROM A COMPUTER ACCOUNTING PACKAGE

Output of data from a computer accounting package can take a number of different formats and can be used in a number of different ways.

printouts

The familiar form of data output from a computer is the paper printout. This is often referred to as 'hard copy'. There are a number of different forms of printout:

- day-to-day lists of items processed, eg a list of invoices produced on a particular day, a list of cheques issued to pay suppliers

- financial documents such as invoices and credit notes

- reports for management, eg activity reports on accounts, aged debtors analysis (a list of who owes what – highlighting overdue accounts)

A printout of sales invoices produced is shown below.

<u>**Pronto Supplies Limited**</u>   Page: 1

<u>**Day Books: Customer Invoices (Summary)**</u>

Transaction From: 1
Transaction To: 99999999

Tran No.	Items	Tp	Date	A/C Ref	Inv Ref	Details	Net Amount	Tax Amount	Gross Amount
54	1	SI	05/02/2001	JB001	10023	1 x 17" Monitor	400.00	70.00	470.00
55	1	SI	06/02/2001	CH001	10024	1 x printer lead	16.00	2.80	18.80
56	1	SI	06/02/2001	CR001	10025	1 x Macroworx	100.00	17.50	117.50
57	1	SI	08/02/2001	KD001	10026	2 hours consultancy	120.00	21.00	141.00
						Totals:	636.00	111.30	747.30

faxed data

Data or documents which have been printed out may in some circumstances be faxed. This often happens when it is a copy of the original data that is needed. When, for example, a business is chasing up its customers for overdue payments it may be given the classic lame excuse by the business that is late in paying:

'Oh - we didn't receive your invoice in the first place – can you fax us a copy please?'

emailed data

Most current computer accounting packages have the facility for data to be exported to an email management program so that it can be emailed direct to the person who needs the information. In the latest versions of Sage it is possible, for example, to send details of contacts kept on supplier or customer records to an email management program, as shown below.

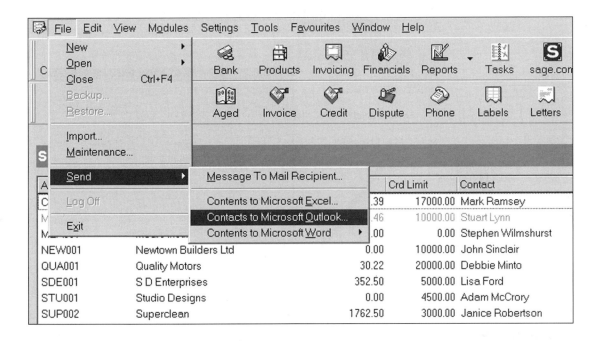

exporting data direct to other programs

Most current computer accounting packages also allow you to export data to spreadsheet and word processing programs.

Sage, for example, allows you to:

- export data to a Microsoft Excel spreadsheet, eg a list of the nominal accounts and their balances – this data will be placed direct into a spreadsheet grid from the Sage screen and can then be manipulated as required

- export data in the form of a mailmerge to a Microsoft Word word processing file – for example, if a business wants to send a letter advertising a new product to all its customers, it can export the names and addresses from the customer details in the computer accounting program to a letter file in Word which will then print out personalised letters to all the customers

Look at the illustrations on the next page.

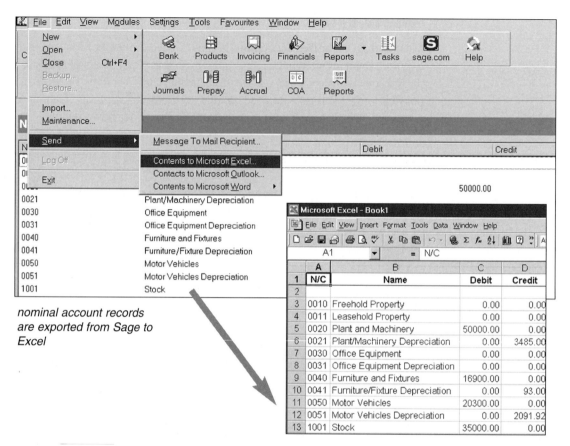

nominal account records
are exported from Sage to
Excel

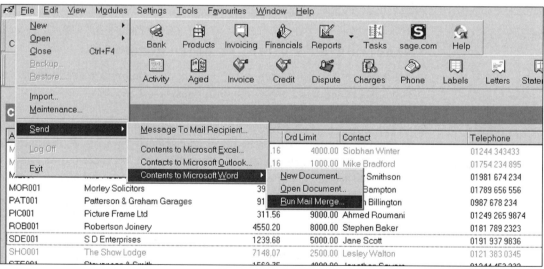

customer details are exported to produce a run of mailmerged letters in Word

exporting screengrabs

Another method of transferring data out of a computer accounting program is to perform a 'screen grab'.

A screen grab is a picture image of the computer screen as you see it. It is just like taking a photograph. You can normally copy the whole screen by pressing the 'print screen' key on the PC keyboard. (If this does not work, refer to your tutor for guidance). This image can then be imported into a program such as Paint (using the 'Paste' command) and copied into other programs as required. The point to remember about a screengrab is that it is just a picture of data – you cannot change figures or numbers as you can in a spreadsheet or wordprocessing package.

A screengrab could be useful if you wanted to export a chart showing activity on an account in an accounting program to, say, a Word memo for management reporting on that account. Look at the illustrations below showing the process. Incidentally, the main screen illustrated on this page is itself a screengrab produced using this simple process.

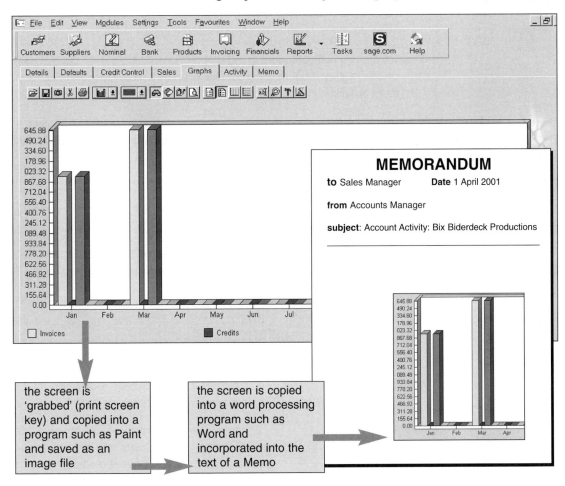

- Organisations using computer systems can either use a single standalone machine or a network of computers linked on an intranet. Many computer systems are now linked externally to the internet.

- Most computer programs – word processors, databases, spreadsheets, email managers and computer accounting packages – are designed so that you can interchange data from one to another.

- Computer accounting programs combine the functions of a number of different programs – they act as database and spreadsheet and can generate text and data for use in other programs.

- A computer accounting program can record financial transactions, generate financial documents, provide management with financial reports and generally make running and managing the finances of any organisation a more efficient process.

- Computer accounting programs are based on the ledger system of book-keeping and link together accounts for customers (sales ledger), suppliers (purchases ledger), bank (cash book) and other payments, receipts and items owned or owed by the organisation (nominal ledger).

- Input into a computer accounting program is normally carried out manually on the keyboard but many programs will now accept electronic data from disks or online.

- Output from a computer accounting program can be on paper (hard copy), can be faxed or sent by email or direct to other programs, a spreadsheet for example.

hardware	the computer equipment on which the computer programs run
software	the computer programs which enable the computer to work and carry out its functions
intranet	a linked network of computers within an organisation
internet	computers linked up externally by phone line with other computers on the worldwide web (www)
word processor	a computer program which allows text to be entered and manipulated on screen
database	a computer program which acts as an electronic filing system, storing data so that it can be sorted, searched and organised efficiently

record

a set of information stored in a computer database, eg a name and address

field

a part of a database record which contains a specific category of information, eg a postcode

spreadsheet

a computer program which stores text and numbers on a grid system of columns and rows and enables calculations to be performed on the numbers

CSV

Comma Separated Values is a special format of text used to transfer data from one computer program to another – the fields/pieces of data are separated by commas

email management

a program which enables the computer to send and receive emails and to organise messages sent and received

EDI

Electronic Data Interchange (EDI) is a system which enables data and financial documents to be sent electronically from computer to computer - eg from supermarket to supplier

ledgers

the books of the accounting system which contain individual accounts – the sales ledger, for example, contains the individual accounts of customers who buy on credit (ie they pay later)

integrated system

a computerised accounting system which links together all the ledgers and accounts so that a transaction on one account will always be mirrored in another account

double-entry book-keeping

the method of manual book-keeping from which the integrated system has been developed – it involves the making of two entries in the accounts for every financial transaction

hard copy

a paper document containing data – often a printout from a computer

data export

the transfer of data from one computer program to another

screengrab

capturing the image of a computer screen into an image file which can then be exported to another program – but only as an image

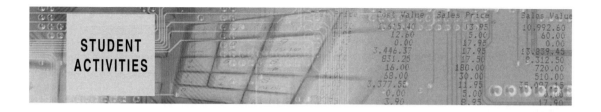

note

Many of the practical functions of computer programs described in this chapter will form the basis of tasks in activities in later chapters. The activities which follow here will develop your general understanding of the way computer programs work together.

1.1 What is the difference between computer hardware and computer software?

1.2 What is the difference between an intranet and the internet?

What are the advantages to an organisation of using an intranet?

Can you think of any disadvantages to an organisation of using an intranet?

1.3 Describe the main functions of the following programs (ie what they 'do'):

(a)   a word processing program

(b)   a database program

(c)   a spreadsheet program

(d)   an email management program

1.4 Give one example of the use of the four programs in 1.3 in all of the three businesses listed below. Try and think of different examples for each.

• (a)   a local car garage

(b)   a travel agency

(c)   an independent financial advisor

1.5 What is the difference between a field and a record in a database program?

1.6 Why is a spreadsheet program so useful if you want to

(a)   make a financial plan which involves inputting figures which might vary?

(b)   illustrate trends in figures that you have input?

1.7   How can you send an invoice electronically?

1.8   What are the main features of a typical computer accounting program?

1.9   Name the ledgers in an accounting system. Describe the type of accounts that they hold.

1.10   What is the main difference between a computer accounting system and the traditional double-entry book-keeping system? Why should this difference also be an advantage of a computer accounting system?

1.11   What are the two main methods of transferring data into a computer accounting system?

What methods of input are likely to be used in the following circumstances?

(a)   a business regularly receives cheques from its customers in settlement of invoices due and needs to enter the cheque amounts on the bank account kept on the computer accounting system

(b)   a business relies on a team of travelling sales representatives to generate new business and orders; the reps are rarely in the office but need regularly to set up customer accounts on the computer accounting system

1.12   What different forms of output are available to a computer accounting system?

What forms of output are likely to be used by a business from its computer accounting system in the following circumstances:

(a)   the business needs reports to be stored for at least six years so that they can be viewed by auditors, VAT inspectors or Inland Revenue investigators who may visit the business

(b)   a customer (who is not online) phones up to request an up-to-date statement of account which is needed that day

(c)   a sales rep who is online via her laptop emails to ask for an up-to-date list of customer contacts

(d)   the sales department wants to send out a standard letter announcing a new range of products to the customers who have accounts on the computer accounting system

(e)   the training department wants to set up some help sheets for staff starting work on the computer accounting system; they want to explain the different screens that computer operators will need to use

2 LOOKING AFTER THE COMPUTER AND THE DATA

chapter introduction

- Before looking in detail at the setting up of a computer accounting system it is important to establish the principles of good housekeeping for computers. In other words, knowing how to look after the computer hardware and software and avoid losing either the equipment or the data held on it.

- The issues we will look at in this chapter include;

  - general aspects of security of the equipment and the data held on it

  - the use of passwords and access rights to the computer accounting system

  - protection against computer viruses

  - the importance of using the correct date when inputting data

  - dealing with equipment and software failures

  - saving data regularly

  - closing down and backing up data

THE NEED FOR SECURITY

A business that has set up a computer accounting system will have invested thousands of pounds in buying equipment and in training staff to operate it. A business that neglects to look after the equipment and the data that it holds is potentially throwing this money down the drain.

What are the dangers? They relate both to the equipment and to the data.

dangers to the equipment

These dangers include:

- theft of the equipment through breaches of security at the premises
- damage to the equipment through slack Health & Safety observance – the well-known danger being the mug of coffee spilt into the computer

The way to avoid these dangers is to ensure that the area where the computer equipment is kept is well secured at night and is under supervision during the day when it is not being used. Some thieves practice what is literally daylight robbery.

Health & Safety rules should also be observed. For example, drinks should not be placed on the computer equipment. Electrical and other leads should not be allowed to trail in places where people can trip over them and pull computers and printers onto the floor.

dangers to the data

The data held on the computer is irreplacable once lost and so must be kept securely both on the computer system and also in the form of back ups. The data must be kept securely to prevent interference from outside and inside the business:

- people such as competitors or criminals outside the business may try to gain access to the data either directly (through 'hacking' if the computer is linked to the internet) or through an employee who can be persuaded to obtain the information
- employees of the business may try to access the data in order to work a fraud – through the payroll, for example, or by making bogus payments to external bank accounts which they control

Data Protection and confidentiality

A business has responsibility under the Data Protection Act 1998 to 'protect' data relating to people and organisations outside the business. The duty of **confidentiality** – not releasing information to third parties without authority – is implicit when a business keeps files on its customers, suppliers and employees.

PASSWORDS AND ACCESS RIGHTS

One solution to the problem of unauthorised employees gaining access to sensitive financial data is the use of **passwords** to gain access to the computer program. Many larger businesses will employ a number of people who need to operate the computer accounting system; they will be issued with an appropriate password.

Businesses can also set up **access rights** which restrict certain employees to certain activities and prevent them from accessing more sensitive areas such as the making of payments from the bank account.

passwords and access rights in action

When an employee comes to operate the computer accounting package, he or she will be asked to 'log on' in the same way that you 'log on' to the internet. In the example from Sage Line 50 shown below a person called Tom enters his log on name and a password (CRUISE).

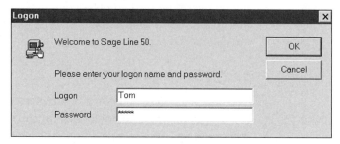

The next screens from Sage Line 50 (see below) shows that Tom and Britney are the two people authorised to access the program. Tom has full access, which means that he can access all the functions of the program. Britney, however, has partial access. She is only allowed to deal with Customers, Suppliers and the Nominal Ledger. She cannot access the Bank or other records.

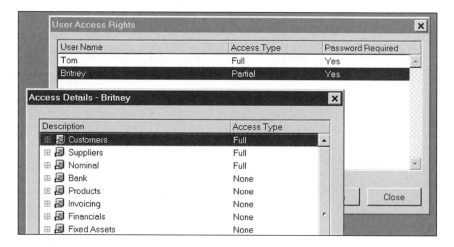

Sage operational note

Access rights and passwords can only be set up in Sage if the Access Rights box is ticked in COMPANY PREFERENCES (Parameters tab) reached through SETTINGS on the main menu bar.

ACCESS RIGHTS are themselves also reached through SETTINGS on the main menu bar. Access rights may be added, edited and deleted as appropriate to changes in the employees of a business.

VIRUS PROTECTION

Computers are vulnerable to viruses. A **virus** is a destructive program which can be introduced into the computer either from a disk or from another computer. If the computer or server which runs the computer accounting software is linked directly or indirectly to the internet, there is a danger that an incoming email with an attachment may introduce a virus.

Some viruses are relatively harmless and may merely display messages on the screen, others can be very damaging and destroy operating systems and data, putting the computer completely out of action.

Most computers are now sold already installed with virus protection software which will:

■ check for viruses

■ destroy known viruses

■ check for damage to files on the hard disk

■ repair damage to files on the hard disk where possible

This software should be run regularly, and updated regularly so that it can deal with the latest viruses.

The screen below shows a virus protection program scanning the hard disk of a computer. As you can see, it has not yet found any infected files.

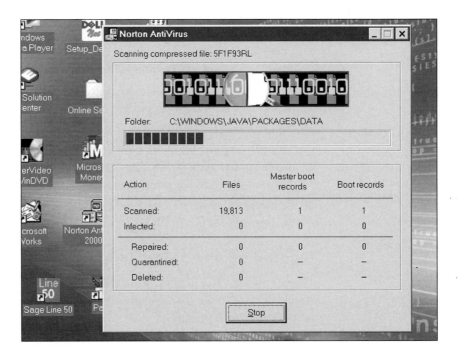

DEALING WITH EQUIPMENT AND SOFTWARE FAILURES

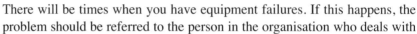

There will be times when you have equipment failures. If this happens, the problem should be referred to the person in the organisation who deals with the equipment. It is not advisable to 'have a go' yourself, unless it is a simple matter such as replacing a printer ribbon or cartridge. Many businesses will have back-up computers which can run the software and which can be loaded with your last back-up data disk. There may also be 'on-site' support provided under contract by the supplier of the hardware

Software problems can be more complex. If it is a case of not knowing how to carry out a particular operation, refer the matter to someone who does. Help is always at hand through HELP menus, on-line support or telephone technical support to which the business is likely to have subscribed. The rule is again, do not 'have a go' yourself unless you know what you are doing.

LOGGING ON AND DEALING WITH DATES

the different dates

One potential problem area for the operator of a computer accounting system is the use of dates when inputting. There are a number of dates that need to borne in mind:

■ the actual date – most people can manage this concept

■ the **system date** – this the date that the computer thinks is the actual date – the computer is normally right (unless its battery is running down!)

■ the **program date** – the date which you can instruct the accounting software to use as the actual date

■ the **financial year** start date – the month in which the financial year of the business starts – often January (but it does not have to be)

logging on and using dates

When you log on and start using the computer accounting software, you should check that the date shown at the bottom of the screen is the date you want to use for your input.

The date shown here will be allocated to any transactions that you input into the computer. Normally this is the **system date** (the date the computer thinks it is).

You should then ask yourself if you want your transactions to be allocated any other date. This might be the case if . . .

■ you are inputting a batch of transactions which went through last week – for example a run of cheques received from customers – and you want the transactions to show on the records as going through last week

■ you are in a training situation and you have been given a specific date for input

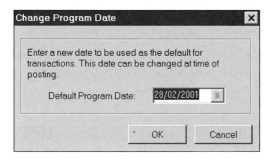

If you are using Sage software in these cases you should change the **program date** through the SETTINGS menu. The program date lets you set any date to be 'today's date'.

This new date will appear against every transaction you make and will remain in force until you exit from the program, after which it reverts to the system (actual) date.

financial year

A business will use a financial year for accounting purposes. The financial year, like the calendar year, may run from January through to December. But the financial year can start anytime during the year; some businesses end their financial year on 31 March or 30 June, for example. When setting up the data in a computer accounting program you have to state when the financial year starts. In Sage this is done from the SETTINGS menu:

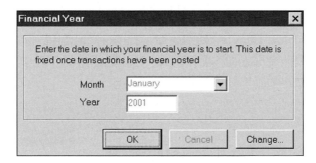

The financial year is important for the management of the business because it is then that the end-of-year routines are run on the computer. These provide the data to enable the business to produce end-of-year financial statements.

SAVING AND BACKUP

The computer accounting program you are using will tell you when to Save your work. This is normally done after inputting a group of transactions and before passing on to the next task.

You will also need to **backup** the data generated by the computer accounting program. There is no set rule about when you should do this, but it should be at least at the end of every day and preferably when you have completed a long run of inputting. Data is traditionally backed up onto floppy disks; often a number of disks are required each time. Data may also be backed up onto other storage media which nowadays hold far more data than the traditional floppy. Data may also be transmitted and kept secure at a remote location.

Backup in Sage is carried out from the FILE menu, or on the prompt when you close down. The screen gives you a choice of file name (you could use the date) and asks to which drive you want the data saved.

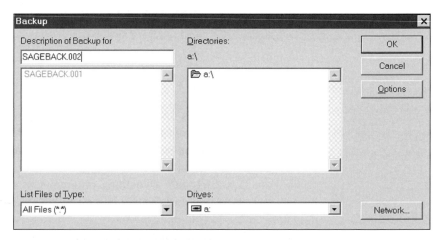

If you are using Sage you are recommended to run the ERROR CHECKING routine from MAINTENANCE (from the FILE menu) before backing up. This will check the data files and ensure that you do not backup any corrupted data. The screen after a check looks like this:

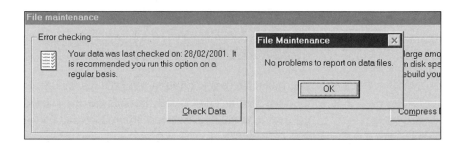

backup policy

It is important that a business works out a systematic policy for backup of its data. This could involve:

■ backup held on more than one set of disks

■ backup disks held off the premises

■ periodic backup (eg backups at the end of each month) stored securely

One solution is for the business to keep a set of disks for each working day labelled with the name of the day and the number of the disk (if there is more than one).

At the end of each working day the data is backed up on the appropriate disk(s), which is (are) kept securely on site.

As a further security measure a second set of disks could be kept as an off site backup. These would be backed up at the end of each day and taken off site by an employee.

With this system in place the business has double security for its accounting data.

It should also be mentioned that the disks should be replaced periodically (every three months, for example) as they wear out in time and their data becomes corrupted.

restoring data from a backup

In the unfortunate event that the accounting data on your computer has been corrupted, you can **restore** the data from an earlier date from the appropriate backup disk(s). This is carried out in Sage from RESTORE in the File menu. If there is more than one disk, the disks should be inserted in number order. Note that all the data is restored in this process; it is not possible to restore selected files. You should then run ERROR CHECKING routine from FILE MAINTENANCE to make sure the restored data is not corrupted.

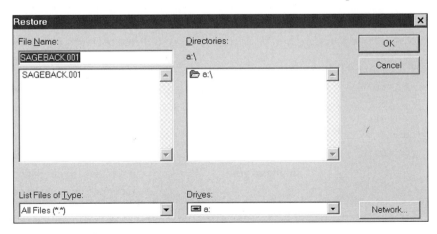

CHAPTER SUMMARY

■ A business which has invested in a computer accounting system needs to ensure that both the equipment and the data held on it are well maintained.

■ Computer equipment is vulnerable to theft and damage and should be kept secure during working hours and also after working hours. Equipment failure should be referred to the appropriate member of staff and dealt with in accordance with established guidelines.

■ Accounting data kept on a computer is valuable and vulnerable. Outsiders can use it to fraudulently obtain money and information about customers. Employees can log into the system to set up fraudulent money transfers. Accounting data can be protected with virus protection software.

■ Passwords and access rights can be set up on the computer system to restrict access to the data to authorised employees.

■ When the computer accounting system is in use, care should be taken with the use of dates. Data should be backed up regularly and a backup routine established. In the case of data corruption, data can be restored from the backup disks.

KEY TERMS

confidentiality	the duty of an organisation to prevent personal details of people with whom it has dealings falling to the hands of third parties
passwords	a code word used to allow an employee to access the computer accounting program
access rights	the right of an employee to access specified areas of the computer accounting program
virus	a computer program introduced into the computer system which then disrupts or destroys the operation of the system
system date	the date allocated by the operating system of the computer – normally the actual date
program date	the date which you can tell the computer accounting software to use as 'today's' date
financial year	the twelve month period used by the business to record its financial transactions

backup	to copy the computer data onto a separate storage medium in order to ensure that the data is not lost
restore	to copy the backup data back onto the computer when the original data has been lost or corrupted

STUDENT ACTIVITIES

2.1 List two potential dangers to computer equipment which a business must guard against.

Suggest ways in which the business can avoid these problems occurring. Draw up notices (to display in an office) which warn employees about these dangers.

2.2 Computer accounting data can be very vulnerable to unauthorised access.

(a) Why could this data be valuable to outsiders and employees?

(b) Which law protects personal data held by organisations such as businesses?

2.3 Explain how passwords and access rights to accounting software help protect computer data.

2.4 Explain the difference between a system date and a program date used on a computer accounting program such as Sage.

2.5 Write down a suggested backup policy for an office which runs a computer accounting system and which needs three disks for backing up all the data.

2.6 You are running a check on your computer accounting data at the end of the day before carrying out the backup routine. The message appears on screen that a number of your data files have become corrupted. You normally backup your data daily at the end of the day. Explain what you would do to rescue your data and bring the computer accounting records up-to-date.

2.7 You hear from a friend working for another business that their computer systems have had a catastrophic crash following infection by a virus which came in over the internet. Describe the measures you could take to safeguard against a similar catastrophe to your own systems.

3 SETTING UP THE COMPANY IN SAGE

chapter introduction

- Setting up a computer accounting program for a business or other organisation will take some time, but as long as the correct data is entered in the correct format there should be no problem.

- We will assume here that the organisation setting up the computer accounting program is a business. Sage software always calls a business a 'company' – so we will adopt that term.

- The chapter introduces a Case Study business – Pronto Supplies Limited – which will be used through this book to show how computer accounting works.

- There is plenty of help around when you are setting up accounts on the computer. In Sage, for example, there is the computer manual, the 'Help' function, on-screen step-by-step instruction procedures known as 'Wizards' and demonstration data (a 'sample' company) that is supplied with the Sage software.

- The data that will have to be input includes:

  - the 'company' details such as name and address and financial year

  - the customer details and any sales transactions already carried out

  - the supplier details and any purchases transactions already carried out

  - details of accounts for income and expenses, assets (items owned), liabilities (loans) and capital (money put in by the owner) – this is all contained in the nominal ledger

- This chapter concentrates on setting up the company details. The other data – customer and supplier details and balances and the nominal ledger– will be covered in the next two chapters.

WHERE ARE YOU STARTING FROM?

If you are reading this book you are likely to be in one of two situations:

1   You are in a real business and looking for guidance in setting up a computer accounting system.

2   You are a student in a training situation and will have the program already set up for you on a training centre network. You will be given exercises to practise the various functions of a computer accounting program.

In the first case – the real business – you will be starting from scratch and will have to go through the whole installation and set-up procedure. This is not at all difficult. The software itself will take you through the various steps.

In the second case – the training centre situation – much of the work of set-up will already have been done. What you will be faced with, however, is that the computer may already have accounting records already on it, possibly another student's work. What you must do here is to remove the data (making sure it is backed up first!) and then start again. This is done using a 'rebuild' procedure. There is more about this on page 160.

The Case Study which follows on the next page – Pronto Supplies Limited – assumes that you are in business setting up computer accounts for the first time using Sage software. It is important for your studies that you know how this is done, even if you may not carry out in the training centre all the procedures explained in the Case Study.

WHY SAGE AND WHICH SAGE?

Osborne Books (the publisher of this book) has chosen Sage software for this book for two very good reasons:

1   Sage software is widely used in business and is recognised as a user-friendly and reliable product.

2   Osborne Books has used Sage itself for over ten years and is well used to the way it works.

The Sage software used as a basis for this book is Sage Line 50 Accountant Plus (Version 7) for Windows. The screens displayed in this book are taken from this version by kind permission of Sage PLC.

screen illustrations

It should be appreciated that some training centres and businesses may be using older and slightly different versions and so some of the screens may look slightly different. This does not matter however: using Sage is like driving different models of car – the controls may be located in slightly different places and the dashboard may not look exactly the same, but the controls are still there and they still do the same thing. So if the screens shown here look unfamiliar, examine them carefully and you will see that they will contain the same (or very similar) Sage icons and functions as the version you are using.

CASE STUDY

PRONTO SUPPLIES LIMITED: SETTING UP THE COMPANY IN SAGE

the business

Pronto Supplies is a limited company run by Tom Cox who has worked as a computer consultant for over ten years. Pronto Supplies provides local businesses and other organisations with computer hardware, software and all the other computer 'bits and pieces' such as disks and ink cartridges needed in offices. It also provides consultancy for computer set-ups through its proprietor, Tom Cox. Pronto Supplies has eight employees in total. The business is situated on an industrial estate, at Unit 17 Severnvale Estate, Broadwater Road, Mereford, Wyvern, MR1 6TF.

the accounting system

Pronto Supplies Limited started business on 1 January 2001. The business is registered for VAT (ie it charges VAT on its sales) and after a month of using a manual accounting system Tom has decided to transfer the accounts to Sage Line 50 software and sign up for a year's telephone technical support. Tom has also decided to put his payroll onto the computer, but this will be run on a separate Sage program.

Tom has chosen Sage Line 50 because it will enable him to:

- record the invoices issued to his customers to whom he sells on credit

- pay his suppliers on the due date

- keep a record of his bank receipts and payments

- record his income and expenses, business assets and loans in a nominal ledger

In short he will have an integrated computer accounting package which will enable him to:

- record all his financial transactions

- print out reports

- manage his business finances

- save time (and money) in running his accounting system

getting started

Tom has decided to use just one machine in the office to run Sage and so he has bought a 'single user' package together with telephone technical support for a year.

He installs the program from his CD using the Express Install function and uses the Wizard to take him through the procedure . . .

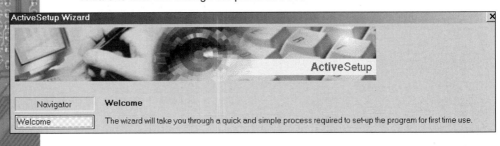

Tutor note

A Wizard is a series of dialogue boxes on the screen which take you step-by-step through a particular procedure. The ActiveSetup Wizard is only one of a number of Wizards in Sage. Wizards generally appear automatically on screen when you need to carry out a complicated procedure.

Tom will first have to enter his serial number and activation code supplied with the software. He will then be asked if he wants to create a new company and to adopt the standard list of accounts ('Chart of Accounts') or if he wants to create his own list. As Pronto Supplies is a fairly standard trading business he decides to adopt the 'General Business: Standard Accounts' as on the screen below. This 'Chart of Accounts' will be explained in more detail on page 67.

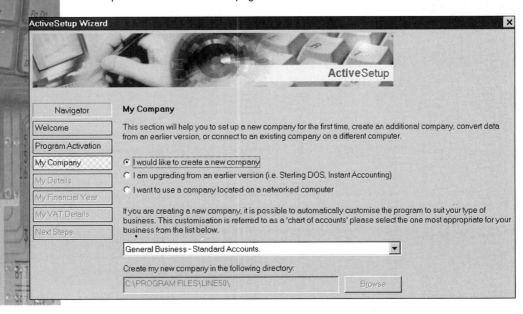

Tom then has to enter his VAT registration number and his business details . . .

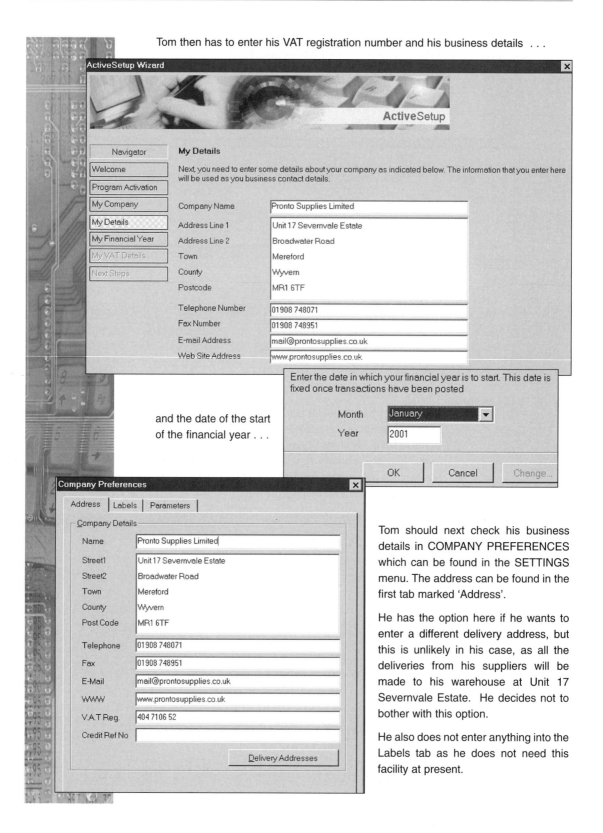

ActiveSetup Wizard

ActiveSetup

Navigator	**My Details**
Welcome	Next, you need to enter some details about your company as indicated below. The information that you enter here will be used as you business contact details.
Program Activation	
My Company	Company Name — Pronto Supplies Limited
My Details	Address Line 1 — Unit 17 Severnvale Estate
My Financial Year	Address Line 2 — Broadwater Road
My VAT Details	Town — Mereford
Next Steps	County — Wyvern
	Postcode — MR1 6TF

Telephone Number — 01908 748071
Fax Number — 01908 748951
E-mail Address — mail@prontosupplies.co.uk
Web Site Address — www.prontosupplies.co.uk

and the date of the start of the financial year . . .

Enter the date in which your financial year is to start. This date is fixed once transactions have been posted

Month — January
Year — 2001

OK   Cancel   Change...

Company Preferences

Address | Labels | Parameters

Company Details

Name	Pronto Supplies Limited
Street1	Unit 17 Severnvale Estate
Street2	Broadwater Road
Town	Mereford
County	Wyvern
Post Code	MR1 6TF
Telephone	01908 748071
Fax	01908 748951
E-Mail	mail@prontosupplies.co.uk
WWW	www.prontosupplies.co.uk
V.A.T Reg.	404 7106 52
Credit Ref No	

Delivery Addresses

Tom should next check his business details in COMPANY PREFERENCES which can be found in the SETTINGS menu. The address can be found in the first tab marked 'Address'.

He has the option here if he wants to enter a different delivery address, but this is unlikely in his case, as all the deliveries from his suppliers will be made to his warehouse at Unit 17 Severnvale Estate. He decides not to bother with this option.

He also does not enter anything into the Labels tab as he does not need this facility at present.

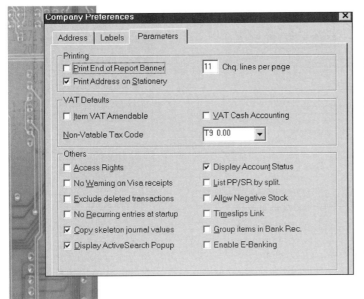

The third tab 'Parameters' provides Tom with a number of options. Most of these he will not have to worry about at the moment.

He should, however, check that the VAT Cash Accounting box is blank and that the Non-Vatable box shows the code T9 for transactions not involving VAT.

He should also check that the Access Rights box is blank, because otherwise he will have to set up passwords for anyone wanting to use the system (see page 27).

HELP!

Tom now has his business details set up on the computer but he still has to install his account balances and get to know how the system works. Sage provides a number of facilities which help the user when he or she needs information: wizards, a manual, an on-screen Help function and a demonstration company with records already set up.

wizards

Wizards, as seen in the Case Study, help the user step-by-step through difficult procedures. We will encounter wizards in later chapters. One particularly useful wizard is the one which takes you through the procedure for opening a customer account.

computer manual

The Sage manual supplied with the software is a useful reference source but the less experienced user may get better guidance on-screen.

F1 Help

The F1 function key opens up the Sage on-screen Help system. This works with three tabs, all of which will enable the user to access an entry on a down menu. When you click on an entry in the list, the Help text appears in a screen on the right. The index tab is probably the most useful of these. Look at the diagram at the top of the next page.

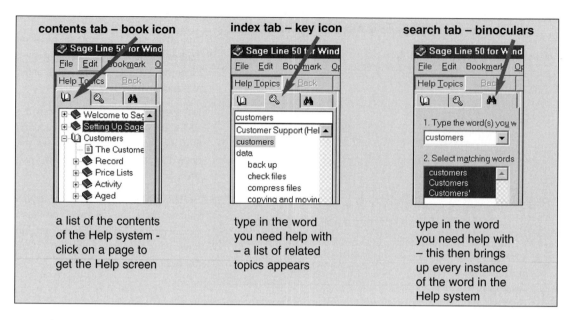

contents tab – book icon

a list of the contents
of the Help system –
click on a page to
get the Help screen

index tab – key icon

type in the word
you need help with
– a list of related
topics appears

search tab – binoculars

type in the word
you need help with
– this then brings
up every instance
of the word in the
Help system

on-screen demonstration company

When most versions of Sage are installed they provide the user with a set of company records already set up for use and experimentation. These records are quite separate from the 'real' company records and you can play around with them to see how the program works without endangering your data. This company can usually be reached by FILE, OPEN, OPEN DEMO DATA.

TRANSFERRING DATA INTO SAGE

When a business first sets up a computer accounting system a substantial amount of data will need to be transferred onto the computer, even if the business is in its first week of trading.

A summary of this data is shown in the diagram opposite. This transfer is normally done manually, but certain data, eg names addresses of customers and suppliers might already be held on a different computer program and can be transferred into Sage using CSV (comma separated data – see page 9).

The images shown below and in the diagram are the icons on the Sage desktop which represent the different operating areas of the program. As you can see they very much relate to the ledger structure of a manual book-keeping system . . .

transferring data from manual records to Sage - an overview

manual records		Sage records

Sales Ledger
(accounts of customers who are given credit)
- names
- addresses
- balances (amounts owed)

Customers
the computerised
Sales Ledger

Purchases Ledger
(accounts of suppliers who allow credit)
- names
- addresses
- balances (amounts owing)

Suppliers
the computerised
Purchases Ledger

Nominal Ledger
accounts which record:
- income
- expenses
- assets (items owned)
- liabilities (loans etc)
- capital invested by owner

Cash book
books which record:
- money paid into the bank
- money paid out of the bank
- petty cash (office cash)

Nominal
the computerised Nominal
Ledger

Note that the bank
accounts are listed in
Nominal Ledger but are
operated through a
separate icon

and topics not covered by this book . . .

Stock records
records of stock held:
- amounts of stock held
- valuation of stock

Products
the computerised Stock
records – not all versions
of Sage have this facility

Payroll records
pay, deductions and Inland
Revenue payments

Sage Payroll program
a separate program - which
can link with Sage Line 50

■ A business setting up a Sage computer accounting program for the first time will have to enter the details of the company on-screen, for example

- the program serial number and Activation Key code

- the start date of the financial year of the business

- the business VAT registration number (if applicable)

- the business name and address

- any passwords that are needed

■ The business will also be required to enter what 'chart of accounts' it requires – this is the list of Nominal accounts which will automatically be set up on the system.

■ The business can make use of the on-screen wizard and other 'Help' functions in the set-up process. The index is the most useful of these.

■ The business will need to enter details and balances of its customers, suppliers and its nominal accounts (the other accounts). These are covered in the next two chapters.

Wizard	on-screen dialogue boxes in a Sage program which take you step-by-step through complex procedures
sales ledger	the accounts of customers to whom a business sells on credit - in Sage this part of the accounting system is known as 'Customers'
purchases ledger	the accounts of suppliers from whom a business buys on credit - in Sage this part of the accounting system is known as 'Suppliers'
nominal ledger	the remaining accounts in the accounting system which are not Customers or Suppliers, eg income, expenses, assets, liabilities – in Sage this is known as 'Nominal'.
chart of accounts	the structure of the nominal accounts, which groups accounts into categories such as Sales, Purchases, Overheads . . . and so on

3.1 Describe the sources of assistance that are available to Alan Bramley who is setting up a Sage system for the first time.

3.2 Helen Egremont is setting up a Sage system for the first time. What details will have to be input before any account balances can be transferred?

3.3 James Greave has been trading for six months using a manual double-entry book-keeping system. Into what part of a Sage system will the following ledgers be transferred?

(a) Sales Ledger   (b) Purchases Ledger   (c) Nominal Ledger

3.4 Explain briefly what a chart of accounts is.

PRONTO SUPPLIES LIMITED INPUTTING TASK

warning note!

This activity involves you in setting up a new company in Sage and inputting live data into the computer. This activity is only suitable if you are in a supervised training environment.

Remember to Save your data and keep any printouts as you progress through the tasks.

Task 1

Set the program date as 1 February 2001. You may now have to enter the financial year start date (January 2001). Enter the company details of Pronto Supplies Limited into the computer. The details are:

Address/contact	Unit 17 Severnvale Estate, Broadwater Road, Mereford, Wyvern, MR1 6TF.
	Tel 01908 748071, Fax 01908 748951
	Email mail@prontosupplies.co.uk
	www.prontosupplies.co.uk
Financial year start:	January 2001 (if not already input)
VAT Registration number	404 7106 52
Chart of Accounts:	General Business – Standard Accounts

Task 2

Check the business details in the first tab of COMPANY PREFERENCES in SETTINGS. Save this screen as a screen grab and paste it into a suitable file (eg a Paint file) and print it out (in landscape format).

Now check that the Parameters tab in COMPANY PREFERENCES matches the screen on page 41. Make any amendments if you need to.

4 SETTING UP RECORDS FOR CUSTOMERS AND SUPPLIERS

chapter introduction

- The term 'Customers' is a word which in Sage means people to whom a business sells on credit. In other words the goods or services are supplied straightaway and the customer is allowed to pay at a specified later date – often a month or more later.

- A business keeps running accounts for the amounts owed by individual customers – much as a bank keeps accounts for its customers. The accounts are maintained by the business in the 'Sales Ledger'.

- The term 'Suppliers' is a word which in Sage means people from whom a business buys on credit. In other words the goods or services are supplied straightaway and the business is allowed to pay at a specified later date.

- A business keeps running accounts for the amounts owed to individual suppliers. The accounts are maintained by the business in the 'Purchases Ledger'.

- This chapter continues the Pronto Supplies Limited Case Study and shows how the business sets up its Customer and Supplier records on the computer.

- When the accounts have been set up on the computer the business will need to input the amounts owed by Customers and owing to Suppliers.

- The next step – dealt with in the next chapter – is to set up the Nominal ledger accounts. When this has been done, the set up is complete and the system will be ready for the input of transactions such as sales and purchases.

CASH AND CREDIT SALES

cash and credit – the difference

When businesses such as manufacturers, shops and travel agents sell their products, they will either get their money straightaway, or they will receive the money after an agreed time period. The first type of sale is a **cash sale**, the second is a **credit sale**. These can be defined further as:

cash sale   A sale of a product where the money is received straightaway – this can include payment in cash, or by cheque or by credit card and debit card. The word 'cash' means 'immediate' – it does not mean only notes and coins.

credit sale   A sale of a product where the sale is agreed and the goods or services are supplied but the buyer pays at a later date agreed at the time of the sale.

buying and selling for cash and on credit

Businesses are likely to get involved in cash and credit sales not only when they are selling their products but also when they are buying. Some goods and services will be bought for cash and some on credit. Buying and selling are just two sides of the same operation.

You will see from this that it is the nature of the business that will decide what type of sales and purchases it makes. A supermarket, for example, will sell almost entirely for cash – the cash and cheques and credit/debit card payments come in at the checkouts – and it will buy from its suppliers on credit and pay them later. It should therefore always have money in hand – which is a good situation to be in for a business.

SETTING UP CUSTOMER ACCOUNTS

accounting records for customers

You will first need to learn some accounting terminology.

Customers who buy from a business on credit are known as **debtors** because they owe money to the business.

The amounts owed by customers (debtors) are recorded in individual customer accounts in the **Sales Ledger**. In double-entry terms these customer account balances are **debit balances** (remember debtors = debits).

The total of all the customer (debtor) accounts in the Sales Ledger is recorded in an account known as **Debtors Control Account**. This is the total amount owing by the customers of a business.

accounting records for suppliers

When a business purchases goods and services from its suppliers on credit the suppliers are known as **creditors** because the business owes them money.

The amounts owed to suppliers (creditors) are recorded in individual supplier accounts in the **Purchases Ledger**. In double-entry terms these customer account balances are **credit balances** (remember creditors = credits).

The total of all the supplier (creditor) accounts in the Purchases Ledger is known as **Creditors Control Account**. This is the total amount owing to the suppliers of a business.

All this is summarised in the table set out below.

Customers	**Suppliers**
• buy from the business	• sell to the business
• have individual accounts in the Sales Ledger	• have individual accounts in the Purchases Ledger
• are also known as 'debtors'	• are also known as 'creditors'
• normally have debit balances on their accounts	• normally have credit balances on their accounts

credit references

A business is only likely to sell to customers on credit (ie receive the money at a later date) if it is reasonably sure that the money will come in. When an account is opened the seller should obtain credit references to make sure the customer can pay. These references can include:

bank reference can the business meet its financial obligations?

trade references references from other suppliers to this customer – does the customer have a good history of paying up on time?

credit bureau A reference from a business (a credit bureau) which specialises in assessing the credit risk of customers

credit limits

When a business is opening a new account it will need to establish a credit limit. A **credit limit** is the maximum amount of credit a seller is willing to grant to a customer. For example if a credit limit of £5,000 is set up by the seller, the customer can owe up to £5,000 at any one time – for example two invoices of £2,500. A well-managed business will keep an eye on situations where a credit limit might be exceeded.

credit terms

The seller will need to establish its **terms** of trading with its customers and the customer will have to agree. The terms are normally set out on the invoice (the invoice is the document issued when the goods or services are sold and supplied). They include:

- **trade discount** given to the customer based on the selling price, for example a customer with a 30% trade discount will pay £70 for goods costing £100, ie £100 minus £30 (30% discount)

- the **payment terms** – the length of credit allowed to the customer, ie the number of days the customer is allowed to wait before paying up – this is commonly 30 days after the invoice date

- **settlement discount** (also known as **cash discount**) sometimes given to a customer who settles up early within a specified number of days, for example a 2.5% reduction in the invoice total for settlement within 7 days

day-to-day customer/supplier information

A business will need information on file relating to its day-to-day dealings with customers and suppliers. For example:

- the name and address of the customer
- telephone, fax and email numbers and website address (if there is one)
- contact names
- credit limit, trade discount, payment terms and any settlement discount agreed
- warning markers – for example 'Account on hold - bad payer'

setting up the accounts in Sage

As you will see from the last three pages, there is a great deal of information that has to be input when setting up accounts for customers and suppliers on a computer accounting program such as Sage.

In the Case Study which follows on page 51 we will follow the steps taken by Pronto Supplies Limited in setting up its Customers and Suppliers records.

SETTING UP THE COMPUTER FILES

There are two methods in Sage for setting up new records for customers or suppliers. If, for example, you wanted to set up a new Customers account you could . . .

1   Go to the CUSTOMERS screen and click on NEW. You will be given a Wizard to take you through the procedure.

2   Go to the CUSTOMERS screen and click on RECORD. You will be given blank screens to complete, but with no Wizard guidance.

The Wizard screen is shown below and the second method is illustrated in the Case Study.

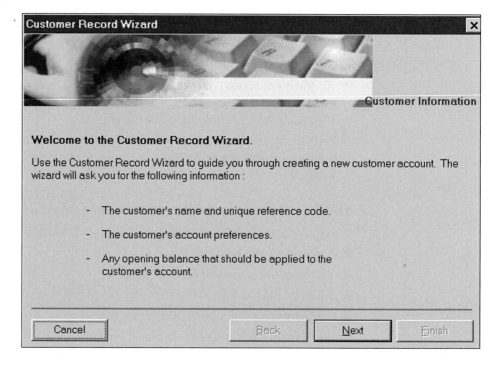

In both cases you will need to have to hand all the customer details you have on file. These are the type of details covered earlier in this chapter.

customer and supplier reference codes

You will see from the Wizard screen that you need to decide on a unique reference code for each customer and supplier account. This code can be numerical or a mixture of letters and numbers. If letters are used they are often an abbreviation of the account name. This process will be illustrated in the Case Study.

customer and supplier record defaults

If you are setting up a number of customer and supplier accounts it is possible that the terms agreed – discounts and payment periods – will be the same for each customer or supplier account. To save you entering these in each and every account (which can take a lot of time!) you can establish a default set of terms which will apply to all accounts. This can be set up from the CUSTOMER DEFAULTS or SUPPLIER DEFAULTS in SETTINGS (in the top menu bar).

In the illustration below the customer credit limit is set to £5,000 and the payment period to 30 days from the invoice date and the VAT rate set to T1, which is the standard rate. The 'Def N/C' is the default Sales Account in the Nominal Ledger and will be dealt with in the next chapter.

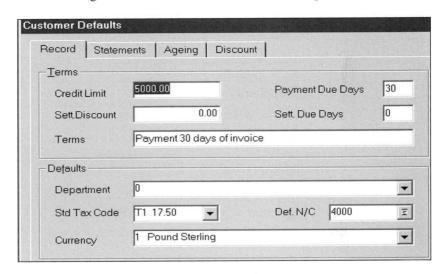

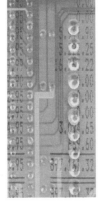

CASE STUDY

PRONTO SUPPLIES LIMITED: SETTING UP CUSTOMERS AND SUPPLIERS IN SAGE

Tom Cox at Pronto Supplies has decided to input his customer and supplier records into the computer first, and will then afterwards input the Nominal balances.

During the month of January Tom had set up accounts for customers and suppliers which now (on 1 February) have balances as follows:

Customers   10 accounts in the Sales Ledger   Total now outstanding £45,500

Suppliers   5 accounts in the Purchases Ledger   Total now outstanding £32,510

Tom has kept the relevant financial documents – sales and purchase invoices and purchase order forms – in two separate files marked 'Credit Sales' and 'Credit Purchases'. The accounts are as follows:

customers

account reference	account name	amount outstanding (£)
JB001	John Butler & Associates	5,500.00
CH001	Charisma Design	2,400.00
CR001	Crowmatic Ltd	3,234.00
DB001	David Boossey	3,400.00
KD001	Kay Denz	6,500.00
FE001	French Emporium	5,600.00
LG001	L Garr & Co	8,500.00
JG001	Jo Green Systems	3,480.00
ME001	Mendell & Son	4,300.00
PT001	Prism Trading Ltd	2,586.00
Total	(Debtors Control Account)	45,500.00

suppliers

account reference	account name	amount outstanding (£)
DE001	Delco PLC	5,750.00
EL001	Electron Supplies	8,500.00
MA001	MacCity	4,500.00
SY001	Synchromart	7,600.00
TY001	Tycomp Supplies	6,160.00
Total	(Creditors Control Account)	32,510.00

entering the customer defaults

Tom decides that he will save time by setting up in CUSTOMER DEFAULTS (reached through SETTINGS) his standard terms as follows:

Payment due days	30 days
Terms of payment	Payment 30 days of invoice
VAT rate	Standard rate of 17.5% (this is Tax Code T1)
Default nominal code	4000 (this is his computer hardware sales account, which accounts for most of his sales to customers)

Tom decides, however, not to set a default credit limit as this will vary from customer to customer and will be input with the individual customer details.

Note also that as Tom has not long been in business he does not allow **discounts** on his sales nor receive discounts on his purchases. These will be negotiated as time goes on.

entering customer details and opening balances

Tom will now enter the details and the opening balance for each customer. He does this by clicking on RECORD in CUSTOMERS. The first customer to input is John Butler Associates. The information he wants to input (including the invoice issued in January) is as follows:

Account name	John Butler & Associates
Account reference	JB001
Address	24 Shaw Street
	Mereford
	MR4 6KJ
Contact name	John Butler

Telephone 01908 824342, Fax 01908 824295, Email mail@jbutler.co.uk
www.jbutler.co.uk

Credit limit £10,000

Invoice reference 1001 for £5,500.00 issued on 05 01 01

Tom first inputs the data on the 'Details' screen . . .

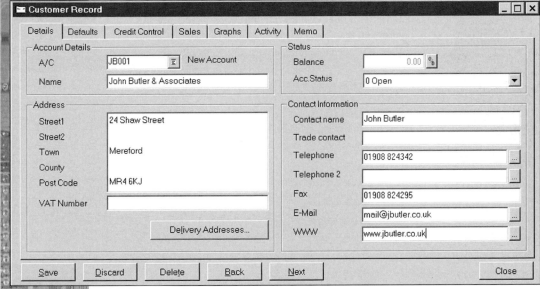

He now has to input the details of the invoice which he had issued on 5 January and which remains unpaid. He does this by clicking the O/B button which brings up the screen shown on the next page.

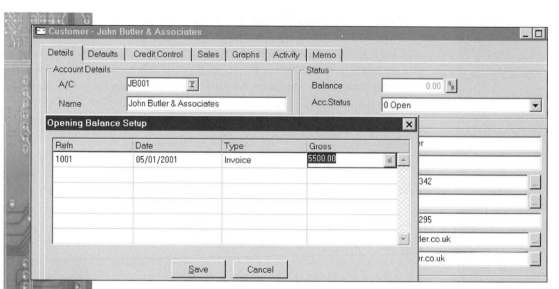

The data Tom inputs into the above screen are:

Refn: the invoice number

Date: the date the invoice was issued

Type: the transaction was the issue of an invoice

Gross: the total amount of the invoice, including the VAT element

Having saved this data, Tom will go to the CREDIT CONTROL screen and input the credit limit and tick the box marked 'Terms Agreed' and then Save again. The other details are already there on the screen because they are default details input beforehand (see page 51).

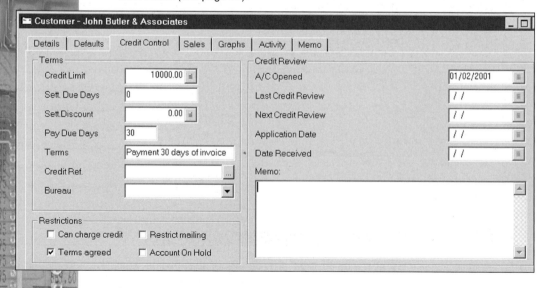

Tom will now repeat this process with the other nine customer records, checking carefully as he goes and saving each record as it is created.

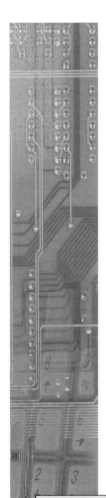

entering supplier details and opening balances

Tom can now carry out the same process for supplier details and opening balances. He will first ensure that the Supplier Defaults in SETTINGS include T1 as the default tax code and 5000 as the default Nominal Account number.

He sets up his Supplier accounts by clicking on RECORD in SUPPLIERS. The first supplier to input is Delco PLC. The information he wants to input (including the invoice issued by the supplier in January) is as follows:

Account name	Delco PLC
Account reference	DE001
Address	Delco House Otto Way New Milton SR1 6TF
Contact name	Nina Patel

Telephone 01722 295875, Fax 01722 295611, Email sales@delco.co.uk www.delco.co.uk

Credit limit granted £10,000, payment terms 30 days of invoice date

Invoice reference 4563 for £5,750.00 issued by Delco PLC on 04 01 01

Tom will now input the supplier details and opening balances, starting with Delco PLC. Note that the opening balance screen records the reference number, date and total amount of Delco's invoice.

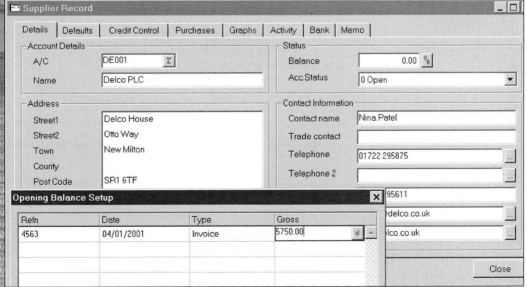

Tom will now input the credit limit and payment terms agreed on the credit control screen of the Supplier record. These are not held as defaults because they may well vary from supplier to supplier. The 'terms agreed' box will also be ticked.

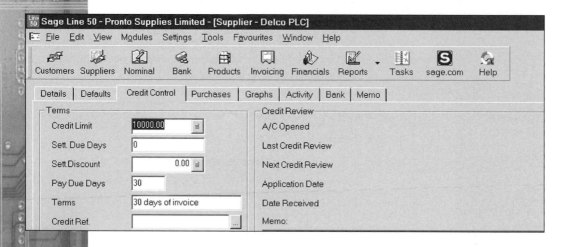

Tom will now repeat this process with the other supplier records, checking carefully as he goes and saving each record as it is created.

the final checks

Tom will need to ensure that his input is correct and that the customer and supplier accounts are accurate.

Tom will now check the individual account entries by comparing his original paper-based records with reports printed from CUSTOMERS and SUPPLIERS.

The input of customer invoices can be checked from the Day Books: Customer Invoices (Summary) report, which can be printed from the list of reports accessed through the REPORTS icon on the CUSTOMERS menu bar.

Pronto Supplies Limited   Page: 1
Day Books: Customer Invoices (Summary)

Date From: 01/01/2001
Date To: 01/02/2001

Transaction From: 1
Transaction To: 99999999

Tran No.	Item sTp	Date	A/C Ref	Inv Ref	Details	Net Amount	Tax Amount	Gross Amount
1	1	SI 05/01/2001	JB001	10013	Opening Balance	5,500.00	0.00	5,500.00
2	1	SI 05/01/2001	CH001	10014	Opening Balance	2,400.00	0.00	2,400.00
3	1	SI 09/01/2001	CR001	10015	Opening Balance	3,234.00	0.00	3,234.00
4	1	SI 10/01/2001	DB001	10016	Opening Balance	3,400.00	0.00	3,400.00
5	1	SI 10/01/2001	KD001	10017	Opening Balance	6,500.00	0.00	6,500.00
6	1	SI 17/01/2001	FE001	10018	Opening Balance	5,600.00	0.00	5,600.00
7	1	SI 17/01/2001	LG001	10019	Opening Balance	8,500.00	0.00	8,500.00
8	1	SI 23/01/2001	JG001	10020	Opening Balance	3,480.00	0.00	3,480.00
9	1	SI 23/01/2001	ME001	10021	Opening Balance	4,300.00	0.00	4,300.00
10	1	SI 26/01/2001	PT001	10022	Opening Balance	2,586.00	0.00	2,586.00
					Totals:	45,500.00	0.00	45,500.00

The input of supplier invoices can be checked from the Day Books: Supplier Invoices (Summary) report accessed through REPORTS on the SUPPLIERS menu bar.

Pronto Supplies Limited   Page: 1

Day Books: Supplier Invoices (Summary)

Date From: 01/01/2001
Date To: 01/02/2001

Transaction From: 1
Transaction To: 99999999

Tran No.	Item	Tp	Date	A/C Ref	Inv Ref	Details	Net Amount	Tax Amount	Gross Amount
11	1	PI	04/01/2001	DE001	4563	Opening Balance	5,750.00	0.00	5,750.00
12	1	PI	05/01/2001	EL001	81222	Opening Balance	8,500.00	0.00	8,500.00
13	1	PI	09/01/2001	MA001	9252	Opening Balance	4,500.00	0.00	4,500.00
14	1	PI	16/01/2001	SY001	1094	Opening Balance	7,600.00	0.00	7,600.00
15	1	PI	17/01/2001	TY001	3455	Opening Balance	6,160.00	0.00	6,160.00
						Totals	32,510.00	0.00	32,510.00

Lastly Tom will print out a **trial balance** which is accessed from the TRIAL icon on the FINANCIALS menu bar. A trial balance is a list of the account balances of the company. It shows the control (total) accounts as follows.

Debtors control account   £45,500 (the total of the customer invoices)

Creditors control account   £32,510 (the total of the supplier invoices)

The Suspense Account has been created automatically and shows the arithmetic difference (£12,990) between the two control accounts. It is put in automatically by the system to make the two columns balance.

Pronto Supplies Limited   Page: 1

Period Trial Balance

N/C	Name	Debit	Credit
1100	Debtors Control Account	45,500.00	
2100	Creditors Control Account		32,510.00
9998	Suspense Account		12,990.00
	Totals:	45,500.00	45,500.00

conclusion

The Customer and Supplier records are now installed and their account balances summarised in the two Control Accounts.

The trial balance is far from complete, however, and Tom's next task will be to input the Nominal Ledger balances – eg income received, expenses paid, loans, items purchased. When these items have all been entered the Trial Balance should 'balance' – the two columns will have the same total and the Suspense Account will disappear. This will be dealt with in the next chapter.

CHAPTER

SUMMARY

- Businesses buy and sell products either on a cash basis (immediate payment) or on credit (payment made later).

- The accounting records for selling on credit comprise the accounts of customers (debtors) contained in the Sales Ledger.

- The accounting records for buying on credit comprise the accounts of suppliers (creditors) contained in the Purchases Ledger.

- If a business is setting up an account for a customer it needs to ensure that the customer is a good credit risk, so it will take out references. It will also establish a credit limit which sets the maximum amount of credit that will be allowed.

- A business will also have to agree the terms of trading with a customer – basically the level of discounts and the payment period it allows.

- In the Sage accounting system the Sales Ledger is known as 'Customers' and the Purchases Ledger as 'Suppliers'.

- Setting up Customer and Supplier records in Sage involves the input of details such as names and addresses and past financial transactions.

- Records set up in this way should be carefully checked against printed out reports such as the Day Book report and the Trial Balance.

KEY

TERMS

cash sale	a sale where payment is immediate
credit sale	a sale where payment follows after an agreed period of time
debtors	customers who owe money to a business
creditors	suppliers who are owed money by a business
debtors control account	the total of the balances of debtors' accounts
creditors control account	the total of the the balances of creditors' accounts
credit terms	discounts and extended payment periods allowed to customers who make purchases
defaults	sets of data on the computer which are automatically applied

STUDENT ACTIVITIES

4.1   A cash sale is a sale where the only means of payment is notes and coins. True or false?

4.2   Define:

(a)   a debtor

(b)   a creditor

4.3   What books of the business (ledgers) contain:

(a)   debtors' accounts

(b)   creditors' accounts

4.4   What is shown in:

(a)   debtors control account

(b)   creditors control account

4.5   What is the difference between a trade discount and a settlement discount?

4.6   What report shows the debit and credit balances of the accounts in an accounting system?

4.7   There are two important pieces of information (excluding financial transactions) that are missing from the computer-held customer details shown below.

What are they, and why are they important?

Account name	John Butler & Associates
Address	24 Shaw Street
	Mereford
	MR4 6KJ
Contact name	John Butler

Telephone 01908 824342, Fax 01908 824295, Email mail@jbutler.co.uk
www.jbutler.co.uk

PRONTO SUPPLIES INPUTTING TASK

> **warning note!**
>
> This activity involves you in setting up Customer and Supplier records in Sage and inputting live data into the computer. This activity is only suitable if you are in a supervised training environment.
>
> Ensure that you have changed your program date to 1 February 2001 in SETTINGS.
>
> Also check that the Customer and Supplier Defaults are set to Nominal accounts 4000 and 5000 respectively. The default tax code should be T1 (standard rate). The Customer Defaults should also be set up for payment due days as 30 days and terms of payment 30 days of invoice.

Task 1

Enter the customer details into the Customers screens as indicated in the Case Study.

The ten customer records are as follows:

> **JB001**   **John Butler & Associates**
> 24 Shaw Street
> Mereford
> MR4 6KJ
> Contact name: John Butler
> Telephone 01908 824342, Fax 01908 824295, Email mail@jbutler.co.uk
> www.jbutler.co.uk
> Credit limit £10,000
> Invoice 10013 issued, 05 01 01, £5,500.00

> **CH001**   **Charisma Design**
> 36 Dingle Road
> Mereford
> MR2 8GF
> Contact name: Lindsay Foster
> Telephone 01908 345287, Fax 01908 345983, Email mail@charisma.co.uk
> www.charisma.co.uk
> Credit limit £5,000
> Invoice 10014 issued, 05 01 01, £2,400.00

> **CR001**   **Crowmatic Ltd**
> Unit 12 Severnside Estate
> Mereford
> MR3 6FD
> Contact name: John Crow
> Telephone 01908 674237, Fax 01908 674345, Email mail@crowmatic.co.uk
> www.crowmatic.co.uk
> Credit limit £5,000
> Invoice 10015 issued, 09 01 01, £3,234.00

DB001   **David Boossey**
17 Harebell Road
Mereford Green
MR6 4NB
Telephone 01908 333981, Fax 01908 333761, Email dboossey@swoopwing.com
Credit limit £5,000
Invoice 10016 issued, 10 01 01, £3,400.00

KD001   **Kay Denz**
The Stables
Martley Hillside
MR6 4FV
Telephone 01908 624945, Fax 01908 624945, Email kdenz@centra.com
Credit limit £10,000
Invoice 10017 issued,10 01 01 , £6,500.00

FE001   **French Emporium**
76 Canal Street
Stourminster
ST2 9FN
Contact name: Henri Fevrier
Telephone 01621 444342, Fax 01621 444976, Email mail@frenchemporium.co.uk
www.frenchemporium.co.uk
Credit limit £10,000
Invoice 10018 issued, 17 01 01, £5,600.00

LG001   **L Garr & Co**
17 Broadheath Chambers
Stourminster
ST1 6MX
Contact name: Ted Nigma
Telephone 01621 333691, Fax 01621 333982, Email mail@lgarr.co.uk
www.lgarr.co.uk
Credit limit £15,000
Invoice 10019 issued, 17 01 01, £8,500.00

JG001   **Jo Green Systems**
19 High Street
Mereford
MR1 2JF
Contact name: Jo Green
Telephone 01908 234974, Fax 01908 234956, Email jgreen@cadenza.com
Credit limit £5,000
Invoice 10020 issued, 23 01 01, £3,480.00

        ME001   **Mendell & Son**
                          26 Broad Street
                          Mereford
                          MR1 8VB

Contact name: Felix Mendell

Telephone 01908 234116, Fax 01908 234387, Email mail@mendellson.co.uk

www.mendellson.co.uk

Credit limit £5,000

Invoice 10021 issued, 23 01 01, £4,300.00

        PT001   **Prism Trading Ltd**
                          Unit 2 Everbeech Estate
                          Mereford
                          MR2 5HP

Contact name: Helen Lenz

Telephone 01908 748083, Fax 01908 748423, Email mail@prismtrading.co.uk

www.prismtrading.co.uk

Credit limit £5,000

Invoice 10022 issued, 26 01 01, £2,586.00

Task 2

Enter the supplier details into the Suppliers screens as indicated in the Case Study.

The five supplier records are as follows:

        DE001   **Delco PLC**
                          Delco House
                          Otto Way
                          New Milton
                          SR1 6TF

Contact name: Nina Patel

Telephone 01722 295875, Fax 01722 295611, Email sales@delco.co.uk

www.delco.co.uk

Credit limit £10,000, payment period 30 days.

Invoice 4563 issued, 04 01 01, £5,750.00

        EL001   **Electron Supplies**
                          17 Maxim Way
                          Manchester
                          M1 5TF

Contact name: Jon Summers

Telephone 0161 6282151, Fax 0161 628161, Email sales@electronsupplies.co.uk

www.electronsupplies.co.uk

Credit limit £15,000, payment period 30 days.

Invoice 81222 issued 05 01 01, £8,500.00

MA001   **MacCity**
Unit 15 Elmwood Trading Estate
Roughway
RM2 9TG
Contact name: Josh Masters
Telephone 01899 949233, Fax 01899 949331, Email sales@maccity.co.uk
www.maccity.co.uk
Credit limit £10,000, payment period 30 days.
Invoice 9252 issued 09 01 01, £4,500.00

SY001   **Synchromart**
Synchro House
Elstree Way
St Albans
AL3 6YG
Contact name: Lauren Dee
Telephone 01727 616851, Fax 01727 616344, Email sales@synchromart.co.uk
www.synchromart.co.uk
Credit limit £15,000, payment period 30 days.
Invoice 1094 issued 16 01 01, £7,600.00

TY001   **Tycomp Supplies**
10, Tybridge Street
Worcester
WR2 7GH
Contact name: Alan Lucas
Telephone 01905 743263, Fax 01905 743244, Email sales@tycomp.co.uk
www.tycomp.co.uk
Credit limit £10,000, payment period 30 days.
Invoice 3455 issued 17 01 01, £6,160.00

Task 3

Print out a Day Books: Customer Invoices (Summary) report for the new Customer accounts and check and agree the amounts you have input.

Task 4

Print out a Day Books: Supplier Invoices (Summary) report for the new Supplier accounts and check and agree the amounts you have input.

Task 5

Print out a Trial Balance and check that the Debtors and Creditors Control account balances agree with the figures on page 57 and the totals shown on the Day Book reports produced in Tasks 3 and 4.

Reminder! Have you made a backup?

5 SETTING UP THE NOMINAL LEDGER

chapter introduction

■ In the last two chapters we have set up the company in Sage and entered details of Customers and Suppliers. All that remains to be done is to set up the Nominal Ledger on the computer.

■ The Nominal Ledger contains all the other accounts in the accounting system:

  - income accounts, including Sales

  - purchases accounts for goods that the company trades in

  - expenses and overheads accounts

  - asset accounts (items the business owns)

  - liability accounts (items the business owes)

  - capital accounts (the investment of the business owner)

■ The Nominal Ledger lists the bank accounts of the business, but they are operated from a separate BANK icon, just as in a manual accounting system the bank accounts are recorded in a Cash Book, kept separately from the Nominal Ledger accounts.

■ The accounts in the nominal ledger are set up in Sage using the structure of a 'Chart of Accounts' provided by the program. This allocates suitable reference numbers to the various accounts which are grouped in categories (eg expenses, assets, liabilities) so that the computer program knows where to find them in the system and can then provide suitable reports to management.

■ One of the reports produced by the computer is the Trial Balance, which lists the nominal account balances in two balancing columns. When the nominal accounts have all been entered on the computer, the two columns should balance and the Suspense Account (which records any difference) should disappear.

NOMINAL ACCOUNTS

nominal accounts

An account in an accounting system works in the same way as a bank 'account' – it records financial transactions and has a running balance of what is left in the account at the end of each day. The **nominal ledger** accounts in any accounting system are the accounts which are not Customer accounts (sales ledger) or Supplier accounts (purchases ledger). They record income and expenses, assets, liabilities and capital.

bank accounts

In a manual accounting system the bank accounts are kept in a separate Cash Book and are not strictly speaking part of the Nominal Ledger. In Sage the bank accounts of the business are *listed* in NOMINAL, but they are *operated* from a separate BANK icon, just as in a manual accounting system the bank transactions are recorded in a separate Cash Book.

the default Nominal accounts

When Tom in the Case Study set up his company he chose the set of nominal accounts automatically provided by the Sage program. These 'default' accounts are common to most Sage systems.

If you click on the NOMINAL icon in the Sage opening screen the accounts are to be found in the NOMINAL opening screen (see below). You can scroll down this screen to see the whole list (reproduced on the next page).

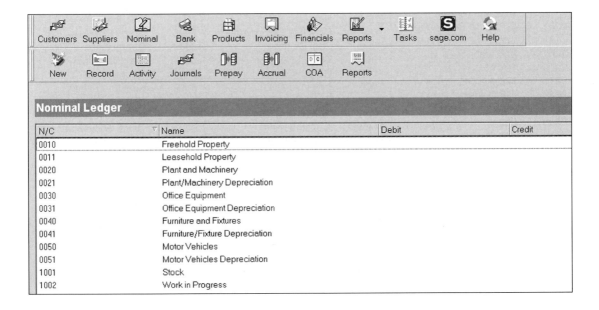

N/C	Name	Debit	Credit
0010	Freehold Property		
0011	Leasehold Property		
0020	Plant and Machinery		
0021	Plant/Machinery Depreciation		
0030	Office Equipment		
0031	Office Equipment Depreciation		
0040	Furniture and Fixtures		
0041	Furniture/Fixture Depreciation		
0050	Motor Vehicles		
0051	Motor Vehicles Depreciation		
1001	Stock		
1002	Work in Progress		

Nominal Account List

0010	Freehold Property	4009	Discounts Allowed	7301	Repairs and Servicing
0011	Leasehold Property	4100	Sales Type D	7302	Licences
0020	Plant and Machinery	4101	Sales Type E	7303	Vehicle Insurance
0021	Plant/Machinery Depreciation	4200	Sales of Assets	7304	Miscellaneous Motor Expenses
0030	Office Equipment	4400	Credit Charges (Late Payments)	7350	Scale Charges
0031	Office Equipment Depreciation	4900	Miscellaneous Income	7400	Travelling
0040	Furniture and Fixtures	4901	Royalties Received	7401	Car Hire
0041	Furniture/Fixture Depreciation	4902	Commissions Received	7402	Hotels
0050	Motor Vehicles	4903	Insurance Claims	7403	U.K. Entertainment
0051	Motor Vehicles Depreciation	4904	Rent Income	7404	Overseas Entertainment
1001	Stock	4905	Distribution and Carriage	7405	Overseas Travelling
1002	Work in Progress	5000	Materials Purchased	7406	Subsistence
1003	Finished Goods	5001	Materials Imported	7500	Printing
1100	Debtors Control Account	5002	Miscellaneous Purchases	7501	Postage and Carriage
1101	Sundry Debtors	5003	Packaging	7502	Telephone
1102	Other Debtors	5009	Discounts Taken	7503	Telex/Telegram/Facsimile
1103	Prepayments	5100	Carriage	7504	Office Stationery
1200	Bank Current Account	5101	Import Duty	7505	Books etc.
1210	Bank Deposit Account	5102	Transport Insurance	7600	Legal Fees
1220	Building Society Account	5200	Opening Stock	7601	Audit and Accountancy Fees
1230	Petty Cash	5201	Closing Stock	7602	Consultancy Fees
1240	Company Credit Card	6000	Productive Labour	7603	Professional Fees
1250	Credit Card Receipts	6001	Cost of Sales Labour	7700	Equipment Hire
2100	Creditors Control Account	6002	Sub-Contractors	7701	Office Machine Maintenance
2101	Sundry Creditors	6100	Sales Commissions	7800	Repairs and Renewals
2102	Other Creditors	6200	Sales Promotions	7801	Cleaning
2109	Accruals	6201	Advertising	7802	Laundry
2200	Sales Tax Control Account	6202	Gifts and Samples	7803	Premises Expenses
2201	Purchase Tax Control Account	6203	P.R.(Literature & Brochures)	7900	Bank Interest Paid
2202	VAT Liability	6900	Miscellaneous Expenses	7901	Bank Charges
2210	P.A.Y.E.	7000	Gross Wages	7902	Currency Charges
2211	National Insurance	7001	Directors Salaries	7903	Loan Interest Paid
2220	Net Wages	7002	Directors Remuneration	7904	H.P. Interest
2230	Pension Fund	7003	Staff Salaries	7905	Credit Charges
2300	Loans	7004	Wages-Regular	8000	Depreciation
2310	Hire Purchase	7005	Wages-Casual	8001	Plant/Machinery Depreciation
2320	Corporation Tax	7006	Employers N.I.	8002	Furniture/Fitting Depreciation
2330	Mortgages	7007	Employers Pensions	8003	Vehicle Depreciation
3000	Ordinary Shares	7008	Recruitment Expenses	8004	Office Equipment Depreciation
3010	Preference Shares	7009	Adjustments	8100	Bad Debt Write Off
3100	Reserves	7010	SSP Reclaimed	8102	Bad Debt Provision
3101	Undistributed Reserves	7011	SMP Reclaimed	8200	Donations
3200	Profit and Loss Account	7100	Rent	8201	Subscriptions
4000	Sales Type A	7102	Water Rates	8202	Clothing Costs
4001	Sales Type B	7103	General Rates	8203	Training Costs
4002	Sales Type C	7104	Premises Insurance	8204	Insurance
		7200	Electricity	8205	Refreshments
		7201	Gas	9998	Suspense Account
		7202	Oil	9999	Mispostings Account
		7203	Other Heating Costs		
		7300	Fuel and Oil		

CHART OF ACCOUNTS

If you look at the nominal account list you will see that a four digit code is assigned to each nominal account in the nominal ledger. These account number codes range from 0010 to 9999. Tom is very unlikely to use all these accounts and may even want to change some.

What is important, however, is that Tom – or any user of Sage – must appreciate that these accounts are organised into categories by account number. These categories are set out in the **chart of accounts.** They can be accessed in NOMINAL by clicking on the COA (chart of accounts) icon and then EDIT . . .

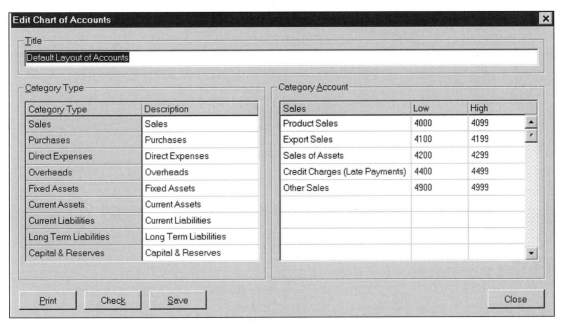

The left hand panel shows the **categories** of account, eg Sales, Purchases. If you click on a category you will see the ranges of accounts and account numbers covered by that category displayed in the right-hand panel.

In this case the Sales category has been selected and the types of Sales listed on the right. This panel tells you that all Product Sales should have an account number between 4000 and 4099. When you set up the Customer records in the last chapter you chose 4000 as the default number (see page 51) for sales to customers.

But if you wanted to categorise customer sales (by area or type of product, for example) you could choose to have three accounts running for Product Sales: 4000 Sales Type A, 4001 Sales Type B, 4002 Sales Type C.

reports from Nominal

The Sage Nominal accounts are used as the basis for a number of computer-generated management reports telling the owner about subjects such as the profit and the value of the business. If accounts get into the wrong category, the reports will also be wrong.

a summary of categories

It may be that a new business will adopt all the default nominal accounts (see list on page 66) because it does not need any others, but if a new account has to be set up it is critical that the new account is in the right category. The business owner will therefore need to understand what the categories mean and what they include.

The nominal categories and account number ranges are:

Sales	4000 - 4999	income from sales of goods or services
Purchases	5000 - 5999	items bought bought to produce goods to sell
Direct Expenses	6000 - 6999	expenses directly related to producing goods
Overheads	7000 - 9999	expenses the business has to pay anyway

These are used to produce the **profit and loss statement** *which shows what profit (or loss) the business has made.*

Fixed Assets	0001 - 0999	items bought to keep in the business long-term
Current Assets	1000 - 1999	items owned by the business in the short-term
Current Liabilities	2000 - 2299	items owed by the business in the short-term
Long Term Liabilities	2300 - 2999	items owed by the business in the long-term
Capital & Reserves	3000 - 3999	the financial investment of the owner(s)

These are used to produce the **balance sheet** *which gives an idea of the value of the business and shows the owner what is represented by the capital investment (the money put in by the owner).*

If this all seems very theoretical we will now put theory into practice with a continuation of the Pronto Supplies Limited Case Study.

CASE STUDY

PRONTO SUPPLIES LIMITED: SETTING UP THE NOMINAL ACCOUNTS

Pronto Supplies Limited was set up in January 2001 and during that month operated a **manual** book-keeping system using hand-written double-entry ledger accounts.

It was a busy month for Tom Cox . . .

financing   Tom paid £75,000 into the bank as ordinary share capital to start up the business.

Tom also raised a £35,000 business loan from the bank.

assets   The finance raised enabled Tom to buy:

office computers	£35,000
office equipment	£15,000
furniture for the office	£25,000

purchases   Tom bought in a substantial amount of stock during January for £69,100.

All of this stock was for resale by Pronto Supplies Limited.

sales   Tom divided his sales into three types:

Computer hardware sales
Computer software sales
Computer consultancy

overheads   Tom also had to pay fixed expenses including:

Wages	£16,230
Advertising	£12,400
Rent	£4,500
Rates	£450
Electricity	£150
Telephone	£275
Stationery	£175

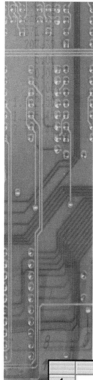

Pronto Supplies Trial Balance

Tom at the end of January listed all the balances of his accounts in two columns, using a spreadsheet. This is his **trial balance** and will form the basis of the entries to the Sage system. The columns are headed up Debit (Dr) and Credit (Cr) and they have the same total. In double-entry book-keeping each debit entry in the accounts is mirrored by a credit entry. (Refer to page 191 if you are not sure about this). If the book-keeping is correct, the total of debits should be the same as the total of the credits. The spreadsheet is shown below. Note that:

- **debits** = assets and expenses   **credits** = liabilities, capital and income

- the control (total) account for debtors shows the total amount owed by all Toms' customers; it is a debit balance because it is money owed to the business

- the control (total) account for creditors shows the total amount owed by Tom to his suppliers: it is a credit balance because it is money owed by the business

- Tom is registered with HM Customs & Excise for Value Added Tax (VAT). This means that he has to quote his registration number on all his documents and also

  - charge VAT on his sales – this is due to HM Customs & Excise and so is a credit balance - Sales tax control account

  - reclaim VAT on what he has bought – this is due from HM Customs & Excise and so is a debit balance - Purchase tax control account

	A	B	C	D	E	F
1		Dr	Cr			
2						
3						
4	Plant and machinery	35000				
5	Office equipment	15000				
6	Furniture and fixtures	25000				
7	Debtors control account	45500				
8	Bank current account	12450				
9	Creditors control account		32510			
10	Sales tax control account		17920			
11	Purchase tax control account	26600				
12	Loans		35000			
13	Ordinary Shares		75000			
14	Hardware sales		85000			
15	Software sales		15000			
16	Computer consultancy		2400			
17	Materials purchased	69100				
18	Advertising	12400				
19	Gross wages	16230				
20	Rent	4500				
21	General rates	450				
22	Electricity	150				
23	Telephone	275				
24	Stationery	175				
25						
26						
27	Total	262830	262830			
28						

inputting the accounts into Sage Nominal

The date is 1 February 2001.

Tom uses his trial balance as the source document for inputting his nominal account balances. The procedure he adopts is:

1 He clicks on the NOMINAL icon on the opening screen and examines the nominal accounts list which appears on the NOMINAL screen. He allocates the accounts in his existing books with computer account numbers as follows:

Plant and machinery (his computers)	0020
Office equipment (photocopiers, phones etc)	0030
Furniture and fixtures	0040
Debtors control account	1100
Bank current account	1200
Creditors control account	2100
Sales tax control account	2200
Purchase tax control account	2201
Loans	2300
Ordinary Shares	3000
Sales type A (hardware)	4000
Sales type B (software)	4001
Sales type C (consultancy)	4002
Materials purchased	5000
Advertising	6201
Gross wages	7000
Rent	7100
General rates	7103
Electricity	7200
Telephone	7502
Stationery	7504

2 Tom scrolls down the screen and clicks on all the accounts that he is going to need – they then show as selected.

But – importantly – he does not click on the following two accounts:

Debtors Control Account - the total of the Customers' accounts

Creditors Control Account - the total of the Suppliers' accounts

This is because he has already input the debtors' (Customers') and creditors' (Suppliers') balances (see the last chapter). If he inputs these totals now they will be entered into the computer twice and cause havoc with the accounting records!

The NOMINAL screen is shown at the top of the next page.

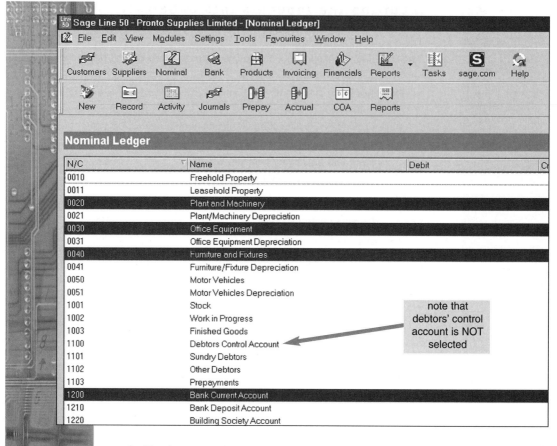

3   Tom is now ready to input the balances of these accounts. To do this he will

- Select the RECORD icon which will bring up a RECORD window.

- Click on O/B on the balance box which asks him to enter the date (01/02/2001) and the balance which must go in the correct box: debits on the left, credits on the right. He should ignore the 'ref' box. The first account entry will look like this;

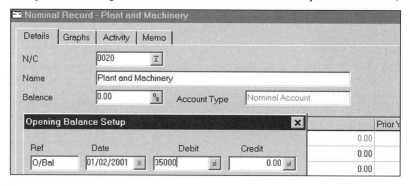

This record should then be saved.

Tom should repeat this for all the selected accounts, making sure that he is saving all the data as he goes along.

checking the input – the trial balance

Tom needs to check that what he has input is accurate. He needs to check his original list of balances – his trial balance (see page 70) – against the computer trial balance.

The trial balance is produced through FINANCIALS by clicking on the TRIAL icon. The printout produced is shown below.

Pronto Supplies Limited
Period Trial Balance

Page:

To Period: Month 2, February 2001

N/C	Name	Debit	Credit
0020	Plant and Machinery	35,000.00	
0030	Office Equipment	15,000.00	
0040	Furniture and Fixtures	25,000.00	
1100	Debtors Control Account	45,500.00	
1200	Bank Current Account	12,450.00	
2100	Creditors Control Account		32,510.00
2200	Sales Tax Control Account		17,920.00
2201	Purchase Tax Control Account	26,600.00	
2300	Loans		35,000.00
3000	Ordinary Shares		75,000.00
4000	Sales Type A		85,000.00
4001	Sales Type B		15,000.00
4002	Sales Type C		2,400.00
5000	Materials Purchased	69,100.00	
6201	Advertising	12,400.00	
7000	Gross Wages	16,230.00	
7100	Rent	4,500.00	
7103	General Rates	450.00	
7200	Electricity	150.00	
7502	Telephone	275.00	
7504	Office Stationery	175.00	
	Totals:	262,830.00	262,830.00

Is the input accurate? Yes, because all the figures agree with the original trial balance figures and they are all in the correct column.

You will see that the Suspense Account which the system created in the last chapter (see page 57) has now disappeared because the total of the debits now equals the total of the credits, as on Tom's spreadsheet shown on page 70.

Tom is now ready to input February's transactions – new sales invoices, new purchase invoices and payments in and out of the bank. These will be dealt with in the chapters that follow.

CHANGING NOMINAL ACCOUNT NAMES

It is possible to change the names of accounts in NOMINAL if they do not fit in with the nature of your business. If, for example, you run a travel agency your NOMINAL account names may be very different from the names used by an insurance broker.

The important point to remember is that if you change your account names they must fit in with the categories in the Chart of Accounts. You should not, for example, include an insurance premium received account in the Purchases category. Much of this should be common sense!

In the Case Study continuation below, Tom changes the names of his Sales accounts to reflect more accurately what is going on in his business.

CASE STUDY

PRONTO SUPPLIES LIMITED: CHANGING NOMINAL ACCOUNT NAMES

Tom looks at his Trial Balance (see page 73) and realises that his Sales Accounts are named 'Type A' and 'Type B' and Type C'. This does not really tell him much about what he is actually selling, so he decides that he will change the names as follows:

account number	old name	new name
4000	Sales Type A	Computer hardware sales
4001	Sales Type B	Computer software sales
4002	Sales Type C	Computer consultancy

He selects the three accounts in the NOMINAL screen, goes to RECORD in NOMINAL and overwrites the old name in the name box for each account . . .

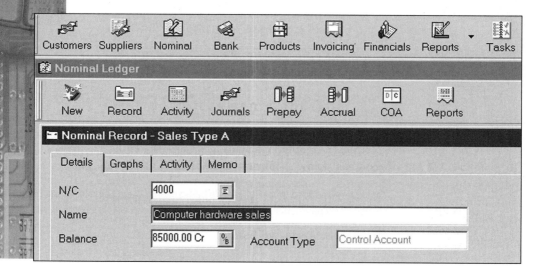

CHAPTER SUMMARY

- When a business sets up its accounts on a Sage computer accounting package it will normally set up its Customer and Supplier records first.

- The next stage will be for the business to set up its nominal accounts, adopting the default list of accounts supplied by Sage in its 'chart of accounts' structure.

- If the business has already started trading it should input all its nominal account balances (except for the Debtors and Creditors control accounts).

- The input balances should be checked carefully against the source figures. The Sage program can produce a trial balance which will show the balances that have been input.

- Account names can be changed to suit the nature of the business – but it is important that the type of account should be consistent with the appropriate category in the 'chart of accounts'.

KEY TERMS

nominal ledger	the remaining accounts in the accounting system which are not Customers or Suppliers, eg income, expenses, assets, liabilities – in Sage this is known as 'Nominal'
chart of accounts	the structure of the nominal accounts, which groups accounts into categories such as Sales, Purchases, Overheads . . . and so on
categories	subdivisions of the chart of accounts (eg Sales, Purchases) each of which is allocated a range of account numbers by the computer
trial balance	a list of the accounts of a business divided into two columns: *debits* – mostly assets and expenses *credits* – mostly income and liabilities The two columns should have the same total, reflecting the workings of the double-entry book-keeping system

5.1 Explain briefly what a chart of accounts is.

5.2 List the categories of account in a chart of accounts and write a sentence for each category, explaining what type of account that category includes.

5.3 You are transfering the manual accounting records of a company into a Sage system. The account names listed below are included in those used in the manual system. Refer to the nominal account list on page 66.

(a) What account numbers will you allocate to these accounts?

(b) In what categories in the chart of accounts will these accounts appear?

Complete the table below (or draw up your own table).

account name	account number	category
Freehold Property		
Office Equipment		
Motor Vehicles		
Materials Purchased		
Bank current account		
Creditors Control		
Directors Salaries		
Electricity		
Share Capital		

PRONTO SUPPLIES INPUTTING TASK

warning note!
This activity involves inputting live data into the computer. This activity is only suitable if you are in a supervised training environment.
Remember to Save your data and keep your printouts as you progress through the tasks.

Task 1

Make sure the program date is set to 1 February 2001.

Open up NOMINAL and select accounts in the computer nominal ledger screen for the accounts listed on the spreadsheet trial balance (see page 70).

But do *not* select Debtors Control Account or Creditors Control Account as they already have balances on them.

Task 2

Enter the balances from the spreadsheet trial balance (see page 70) into the appropriate nominal accounts as opening balances – but do not input the debtors control account and the creditors control account.

Make sure that debits are entered as debits and credits as credits.

Task 3

Print out a trial balance from the computer and have it checked by your Tutor. The suspense account should have disappeared.

Task 4

Change the names of the three sales accounts you have chosen as follows:

number	old name	new name
4000	Sales Type A	Computer hardware sales
4001	Sales Type B	Computer software sales
4002	Sales Type C	Computer consultancy

Reminder! Have you made a backup?

6 SELLING TO CUSTOMERS ON CREDIT

chapter introduction

- A business that sells on credit will invoice the goods or services supplied and then receive payment at a later date.

- The invoice is an important document because it sets out the details of the goods or services supplied, the amount owing, and the date by which payment should be made.

- It is therefore essential that details of the invoice are entered in the computer accounting records so that the sale can be recorded and the amount owed by the customer logged into the accounting system.

- Some Sage computer accounting programs contain an invoicing function which will enable the business to input and print out invoices on a printer linked to the computer. Other more basic programs do not actually print out the invoice but require the business to enter details of each invoice.

- In this chapter we look at the more basic programs which require invoice details to be entered but which do not print out the invoices. If you are working with a program that will print out invoices, the principles are just the same and you should relate them to the way your program works.

- A business that sells on credit may have to issue a refund for some or all of the goods or services supplied. They may be faulty or the sale may be cancelled. As payment has not yet been made, the 'refund' takes the form of a deduction from the amount owing. The document that the seller issues in this case is a credit note.

- A credit note is dealt with by a computer accounting program in much the same way as an invoice: some programs will print out credit notes, some more basic programs do not print them out but require the details to be input. This chapter deals with the input of credit note details into the computer accounting records.

- This chapter continues the Pronto Supplies Case Study and shows how details of invoices and credit notes are entered into the computer accounting records.

- The next chapter looks at how the invoices and credit notes issued by suppliers are dealt with by a computer accounting program.

BACKGROUND TO FINANCIAL DOCUMENTS

When a business sells goods or services it will use a number of different financial documents. A single sales transaction involves both seller and buyer. In this chapter we look at the situation from the point of view of the seller of the goods or services. Documents which are often used in the selling process for goods include:

- **purchase order** which the seller receives from the buyer
- **delivery note** which goes with the goods from the seller to the buyer
- **invoice** which lists the goods and tells the buyer what is owed
- **credit note** which is sent to the buyer if any refund is due
- **statement** sent by the seller to remind the buyer what is owed
- **remittance advice** sent by the buyer with the **cheque** to make payment

Study the diagram below which shows how the documents 'flow' between buyer and seller.

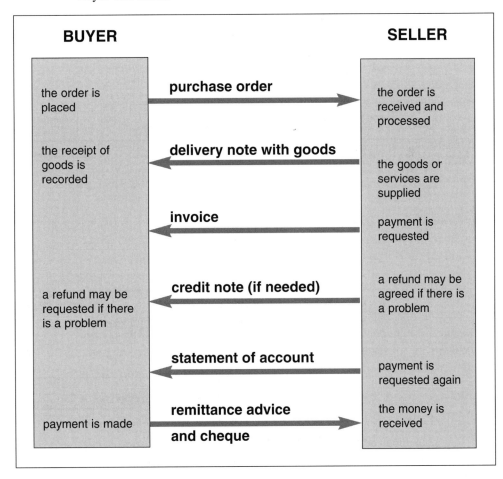

INVOICE

The main document we will deal with in this chapter is the **invoice** which is sent by the seller to the buyer to state what is owing and when it has to be paid. An invoice is illustrated below and explained on the next page.

INVOICE

DELCO PLC

Delco House, Otto Way, New Milton SR1 6TF
Tel 01722 295875 Fax 01722 295611 Email sales@delco.co..uk
VAT Reg GB 0745 4672 76

invoice to

Pronto Supplies Limited Unit 17 Severnvale Estate Broadwater Road Mereford MR1 6TF		

invoice no	12309
account	3993
your reference	47609
date	02 10 01

product code	description	quantity	price	unit	total	discount %	net
Z324	Zap storage disks	10	40.00	box of 10	400.00	0.00	400.00

terms
30 days

goods total	400.00
VAT	70.00
TOTAL	470.00

The invoice here has been issued by Delco PLC for some Zap computer disks ordered by Pronto Supplies on a purchase order.

The reference number quoted here is the order number on Pronto Supplies' original purchase order.

The date here is the date on which the goods have been sent. It is known as the 'invoice date'.

The date is important for calculating when the invoice is due to be paid. In this case the 'terms' (see the bottom left-hand corner of the invoice) are 30 days. This means the invoice is due to be paid within 30 days of the invoice date.

The arithmetic and details in this line must be checked very carefully by Pronto Supplies to make sure that they pay the correct amount:

- *product code* – this is the catalogue number for the disks which Pronto put on the original purchase order
- *description* – this describes the goods ordered – the disks
- *quantity* – this should be the same as the quantity on the purchase order
- *price* – this is the price of each unit shown in the next column
- *unit* is the way in which the unit is counted up and charged for, eg units (single items), or 10s, boxes (as here)
- *total* is the price multiplied by the number of units
- *discount %* is the percentage allowance (known as trade discount) given to customers who regularly deal with the supplier, ie they receive a certain percentage (eg 10%) deducted from their bill
- *net* is the amount due to the seller after deduction of trade discount, and before VAT is added on

The Goods Total is the total of the column above it. It is the final amount due to the seller before VAT is added on.

Value Added Tax (VAT) is calculated and added on – here it is 17.5% of the Goods Total, ie £400.00 x $\frac{17.5}{100}$ = £70.00

The VAT is then added to the Goods Total to produce the actual amount owing:
£400.00 + £70.00 = £470.00

The 'terms' explain the conditions on which the goods are supplied. Here '30 days' mean that Pronto has to pay within 30 days of 2 October.

CREDIT NOTE

The other document we will deal with in this chapter is the **credit note**.

The **credit note** is issued when some form of refund has to be given to the buyer of goods or services. As payment has not yet been made the credit note allows the buyer to deduct an amount from the invoice when settlement is finally made.

Note that it is never acceptable practice to change the amounts on an invoice; a credit note is always required.

The credit note illustrated below has been issued by Delco PLC because one of the boxes of Zap computer disks ordered by Pronto Supplies was faulty. Pronto Supplies has returned the box, asking for a reduction in the amount owing.

Study the document below and read the notes which follow.

CREDIT NOTE

DELCO PLC

Delco House, Otto Way, New Milton SR1 6TF
Tel 01722 295875 Fax 01722 295611 Email sales@delco.co..uk
VAT Reg GB 0745 4672 76

to

Pronto Supplies Limited Unit 17 Severnvale Estate Broadwater Road Mereford MR1 6TF		
credit note no		12157
account		3993
your reference		47609
our invoice		12309
date/tax point		10 10 01

product code	description	quantity	price	unit	total	discount %	net
Z324	Zap storage disks	1	40.00	box	40.00	0.00	40.00

Reason for credit
1 box of Zap disks received faulty and returned.

GOODS TOTAL	40.00
VAT	7.00
TOTAL	47.00

notes on the credit note

You will see from the credit note on the previous page that the credit note total is £47. This can be deducted from the invoice total (see page 80) of £470. In other words, Pronto Supplies now owes £470 minus £47 = £423.

Note in particular from the credit note opposite:

■ The format of the credit note is very much the same as the invoice.

■ The reference quoted is Pronto Supplies' purchase order number.

■ The columns (eg 'product code') are identical to those used on the invoice and work in exactly the same way.

■ VAT is also included – it has to be refunded because the goods have not now been supplied.

■ If there was any discount this should also be refunded – but there is no discount here.

■ The reason for the credit note (the 'reason for credit') is stated at the bottom of the document. Here it is a box of faulty disks that has been returned to Delco PLC by Pronto Supplies.

INVOICES, CREDIT NOTES AND SAGE

the book-keeping background

The totals of invoices and credit notes have to be entered into the accounting records of a business. They record the sales and refunds made to customers who have bought on credit – the **debtors** of the business' (known in Sage as Customers). The amounts from these documents combine to provide the total of the **Sales Ledger**, which is the section of the accounting records which contains all the debtor (Customer) balances. This is recorded in the **Debtors Control Account** which tells the business how much in total is owing from customers who have bought on credit.

methods of recording invoices and credit notes

When a business uses a computer accounting program such as Sage, it will have to make sure that the details of each invoice and credit note issued are entered into the computer accounting records. Businesses using Sage accounting programs have two alternatives: batch entry and computer printed invoices.

batch entry

The business produces the invoices independently of the computer program (ie it types or writes them out) and then enters the invoice details into the computer accounting program on a **batch invoice** screen. A 'batch' is simply a group of items (eg a 'batch' of cakes in the oven). The term is used in this context to describe a group of invoices which are all input at one time. This may not be the day that each invoice is produced – it may be the end of the week, or even the month.

It is normal practice to add up the totals of all the actual invoices that are being input – the 'batch total' – and check this total against the invoice total calculated by the computer from the actual input. This will pick up any errors.

A batch invoice entry screen with three invoices input is shown below.

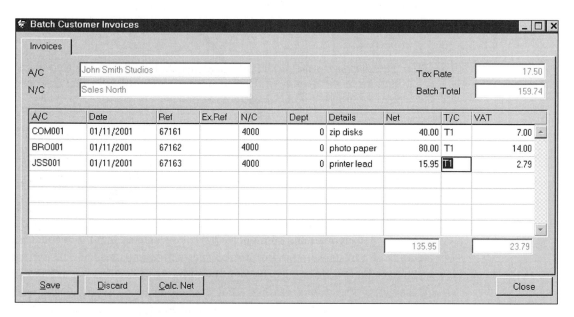

notes on the data entry columns:

- ■ 'A/C' column contains the customer account reference
- ■ 'Date' is the date on which each invoice was issued
- ■ 'Ref' column is the invoice number (note that they are consecutive)
- ■ 'Ex.Ref' is optional – it could be used for the purchase order number
- ■ 'N/C' column is the nominal account code which specifies which type of sale is involved
- ■ 'Dept' is optional and is not used here
- ■ 'Details' describes the goods that have been sold

■ 'Net' is the amount of the invoice before VAT is added on

■ 'T/C' is the tax code which sets up the VAT rate that applies – here T1 refers to Standard Rate VAT, and is the default rate set up in Customer Preferences in SETTINGS.

■ 'VAT' is calculated automatically

When the operator has completed the input and checked the batch totals with the computer totals, the batched invoices can be saved.

computer printed invoices

Most versions of Sage include an invoicing function which requires the business to input the details of each invoice on screen. The computer system will then print out the invoices on the office printer – exactly as input. The invoices can either be for stock or for a service provided. If the invoice is for stock, 'product' records with product codes will normally have to be set up in Sage, and the product code used each time stock is invoiced.

Service invoices do not require a product code, because no stock is involved in the transaction. A invoice input screen is shown below.

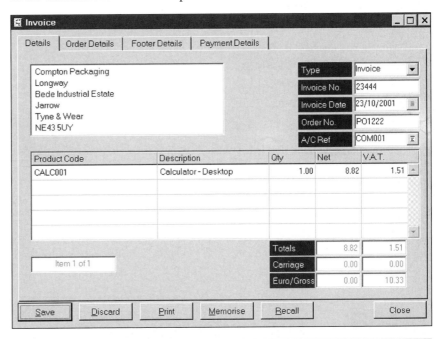

---

important note: treatment of invoicing in this book

In this book we will initially concentrate on the batch entry method of recording invoices and credit notes. It is far simpler to operate and is common to all versions of Sage. If your system can print out its own invoices and you want to use this facility in the exercises that follow, turn to Chapter 13 (pages 171 to 175) which will explain how to do this – even without having to set up product codes.

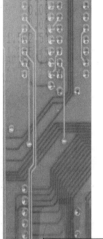

CASE STUDY

PRONTO SUPPLIES LIMITED:
PROCESSING SALES INVOICES AND CREDIT NOTES

Tom Cox runs Pronto Supplies Limited which provides computer hardware, software and consultancy services. At the beginning of February he input his Nominal accounts and his Customer and Supplier details and balances into his Sage accounting program. He has set up three Sales Accounts in his Nominal Ledger:

Computer hardware sales	Account number 4000
Computer software sales	Account number 4001
Computer consultancy	Account number 4002

It is now February 9, the end of the first full trading week. Tom needs to input

- the sales invoices he has issued to his customers
- the credit notes he has issued to his customers

He has the documents on file and has collected them in two batches . . .

SALES INVOICES ISSUED

invoice	name	date	details	net amount	VAT
10023	John Butler & Associates	5/02/01	1 x 17" monitor	400.00	70.00
10024	Charisma Design	6/02/01	1 x printer lead	16.00	2.80
10025	Crowmatic Ltd	6/02/01	1 x MacroWorx software	100.00	17.50
10026	Kay Denz	8/02/01	2 hours consultancy	120.00	21.00
Subtotals				636.00	111.30
Batch total					747.30

CREDIT NOTES ISSUED

credit note	name	date	details	net amount	VAT
551	David Boosey	6/02/01	Software returned	200.00	35.00
552	French Emporium	6/02/01	Disks returned (hardware)	40.00	7.00
Subtotals				240.00	42.00
Batch total					282.00

batch invoice entry

Tom will start by opening up the CUSTOMERS screen in Sage and clicking on the INVOICE icon. This will show the screen shown on the next page. He will then

- identify the account references for each of the four customers
- enter each invoice on a new line
- take the data from the invoice: date, invoice no ('Ref'), product details and amounts
- enter the appropriate Sales account number ('N/C') for the type of sale

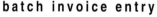

- enter the T1 tax code for standard rate VAT and check that the VAT amount calculated on screen is the same as on the invoice

When the input is complete Tom should check his original totals (Net, VAT and Batch total) against the computer totals. Once he is happy that his input is correct he should SAVE.

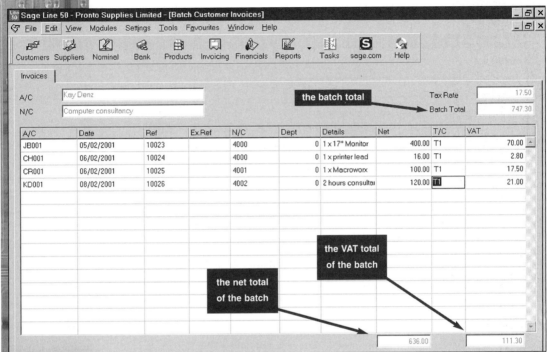

checking the invoices are on the system

As a further check Tom could print out a Day Book Report. This can be obtained through the REPORTS icon on the CUSTOMER menu bar. The title of the report is 'Day Books: Customer Invoices (Summary)'. The report appears as follows:

Pronto Supplies Limited   Page: 1

Day Books: Customer Invoices (Summary)

Transaction From: 1
Transaction To: 99999999

Tran No.	Item s	Tp	Date	A/C Ref	Inv Ref	Details	Net Amount	Tax Amount	Gross Amount
54	1	SI	05/02/2001	JB001	10023	1 x 17" Monitor	400.00	70.00	470.00
55	1	SI	06/02/2001	CH001	10024	1 x printer lead	16.00	2.80	18.80
56	1	SI	06/02/2001	CR001	10025	1 x Macrow orx	100.00	17.50	117.50
57	1	SI	08/02/2001	KD001	10026	2 hours consultancy	120.00	21.00	141.00
						Totals:	636.00	111.30	747.30

batch credit note entry

Tom will input the details from the two credit notes in much the same way as he processed the invoices. He will start by opening up the CUSTOMERS screen in Sage and clicking on the CREDIT icon. This will show the screen shown below. He will then identify the account references for each of the two customers and the Sales account numbers and input the credit note details as shown on the screen. When the input is complete he should again check his original totals (Net, VAT and Batch total) against the computer totals. Once he is happy that his input is correct he should SAVE.

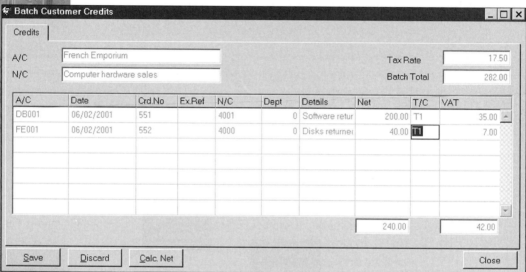

checking the credit notes are on the system

As a further check Tom could print out a Day Book Report for Credit notes. This can be obtained through the REPORTS icon on the CUSTOMER toolbar. The title of the report is 'Day Books: Customer Credits (Summary)'.

The report appears as follows:

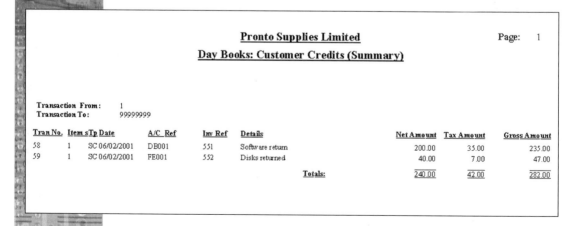

Pronto Supplies Limited   Page: 1

Day Books: Customer Credits (Summary)

Transaction From: 1
Transaction To: 99999999

Tran No.	Item s	Tp	Date	A/C Ref	Inv Ref	Details	Net Amount	Tax Amount	Gross Amount
58	1	SC	06/02/2001	DB001	551	Software return	200.00	35.00	235.00
59	1	SC	06/02/2001	FE001	552	Disks returned	40.00	7.00	47.00
						Totals:	240.00	42.00	282.00

CHAPTER SUMMARY

KEY TERMS

- When a business sells on credit it will issue an invoice to the buyer. This sets out the amount owing and the date by which it has to be paid.

- When a business has to make a refund to a customer to whom it sells on credit it will issue a credit note to the customer. This sets out the amount by which the amount owing is reduced.

- Sales invoices and credit notes are part of the 'flow of documents' which occurs when a sale is made on credit. The full list is purchase order, delivery note, invoice, credit note, statement, remittance advice and cheque. Not all of these will be used all of the time.

- The details of invoices and credit notes must be entered into the accounting records of a business. If a computer program is used the details will be input on screen.

- Computer accounting programs will either print out the invoices after input, or will need to have the details of existing invoices input, commonly in batches.

- It is essential to check the details of invoices and credit notes which have been input. This can be done by printing out a daybook report.

credit sale	a sale made where payment is due at a later date
debtors	customers who owe money to a business
sales ledger	the part of the accounting system where the debtors' accounts are kept – it records the amounts that are owed to the business
purchase order	the financial document which requests the supply of goods or services and specifies exactly what is required
invoice	the financial document which sets out the details of the goods sold or services provided, the amount owing and the date by which the amount is due
credit note	the financial document – normally issued when goods are returned – which reduces the amount owing by the customer
batch	a group of documents, eg invoices or credit notes
batch entry	the input of a number of documents in a group

6.1 Place the following documents in the order in which they are likely to be used in a transaction in which goods are sold on credit.

statement

invoice

purchase order

delivery note

cheque

credit note

6.2 A delivery note will always be used in a sale made on credit. True or false?

6.3 A credit note will always be used in a sale made on credit. True or false?

6.4 List two important pieces of information that the invoice will provide to the purchaser of goods or services.

6.5 Give a definition of the 'debtors' of a business.

6.6 Where in the accounting records of a business will the debtor balances be found?

6.7 What are the two ways in which computer accounting programs deal with the recording of invoices and credit notes?

6.8 What arithmetic checks should be made when inputting details of invoices and credit notes into a computer accounting system?

6.9 What two main references would you expect to enter when inputting details of each invoice into a computer accounting system?

6.10 What difference does the tax code make when inputting details of an invoice or credit note into a computer accounting system?

PRONTO SUPPLIES INPUTTING TASK

warning note!
This activity involves you in inputting live data into the computer. This activity is only suitable if you are in a supervised training environment.

Task 1

Making sure that you have set the program date to 9 February 2001, enter the following invoice details into the computer. Check your totals before saving and print out a Day Books: Customer Invoices (Summary) Report to confirm the data that you have saved.

SALES INVOICES ISSUED					
invoice	name	date	details	net amount	VAT
10023	John Butler & Associates	5/02/01	1 x 17" monitor	400.00	70.00
10024	Charisma Design	6/02/01	1 x printer lead	16.00	2.80
10025	Crowmatic Ltd	6/02/01	1 x MacroWorx software	100.00	17.50
10026	Kay Denz	8/02/01	2 hours consultancy	120.00	21.00
Subtotals				636.00	111.30
Batch total					747.30

Task 2 *(check with Trial Balance on page 240 when you have finished this Task)*

Enter the following credit note details into the computer. Check your totals before saving and print out a Day Books: Customer Credits (Summary) Report to confirm the data that you have saved.

CREDIT NOTES ISSUED					
credit note	name	date	details	net amount	VAT
551	David Boosey	6/02/01	Software returned	200.00	35.00
552	French Emporium	6/02/01	Disks returned (hardware)	40.00	7.00
Subtotals				240.00	42.00
Batch total					282.00

Task 3

It is now a week later and the date is now 16 February 2001. Change your program date setting. You have a further batch of invoices to process. Enter the details into the computer. Check your totals before saving and print out a Day Books Summary Report to confirm the data that you have saved.

account	invoice date	number	details	net	VAT
John Butler & Associates	12/02/01	10027	2 hours consultancy	120.00	21.00
David Boossey	13/02/01	10028	1 x EF102 printer	200.00	35.00
French Emporium	14/02/01	10029	1 x QuorkEdit software	400.00	70.00
L Garr & Co	16/02/01	10030	2 x Zap drive	180.00	31.50
Jo Green Systems	16/02/01	10031	1 x Fileperfect software	264.00	46.20
Prism Trading Ltd	16/02/01	10032	1 x 15" monitor	320.00	56.00

Task 4 *(check with Trial Balance on page 241 when you have finished this Task)*

You also on the same date have two credit notes to process. Enter the details into the computer. Check your totals before saving and print out a Day Books Summary Report to confirm the data that you have saved.

account	date	reference	details	net	VAT
Jo Green Systems	12/02/01	553	1 x printer lead	16.00	2.80
Mendell & Son	13/02/01	554	Zap disks (hardware)	20.00	3.50

Reminder! Have you made a backup?

- This chapter should be read in conjunction with the last chapter 'Selling to customers on credit' as it represents 'the other side of the coin' – the invoice and the credit note as they are dealt with by the purchaser.

- A business purchaser that buys on credit will receive an invoice for the goods or services supplied and will then have to pay at a later date.

- Details of invoices and any credit notes received are entered by the purchaser into the account of the supplier in the computer accounting records. In this way the credit purchase and any credit due are recorded and the total amount owing by the purchaser logged into the accounting system.

- This chapter continues the Pronto Supplies Case Study and shows how details of invoices and credit notes received are entered into supplier accounts in the computer accounting records.

INVOICES AND CREDIT NOTES

Make sure that you are familiar with the two types of financial document we will be dealing with – the invoice and the credit note. Read the descriptions below and remind yourself of the 'flow of documents' by studying the diagram on the opposite page.

invoice

The main document we will deal with in this chapter is the **invoice** which is sent by the seller to the buyer to state the amount that is owing and the date by which it has to be paid. See page 80 for an illustration.

credit note

The **credit note** is issued by the seller when some form of refund has to be given to the buyer of goods or services. As payment has not yet been made the credit note allows the buyer to deduct an amount from the invoice when settlement is finally made. See page 82 for an illustration.

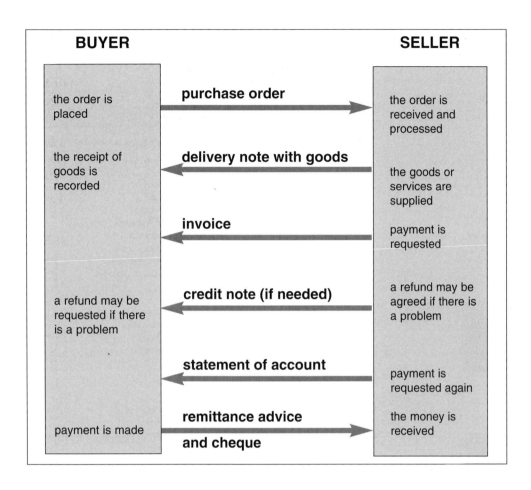

THE BOOK-KEEPING BACKGROUND

Details of invoices and credit notes have to be entered into the accounting records of a business that buys on credit. They record the sales and refunds made by suppliers who have sold on credit – the **creditors** of the business, known in Sage as 'Suppliers'.

The amounts from these documents combine to provide the total of the **Purchases Ledger**, which is the section of the accounting records which contains all the supplier accounts and their balances. The total of the **Purchases Ledger** (recorded in the **Creditors Control Account**) tells the business how much in total it owes to suppliers.

The documents received from the suppliers – invoices and credit notes – are recorded in the computer accounting system on the **batch** basis illustrated in the Case Study in the last chapter. The important point about receiving documents from a seller is that they have to be checked very carefully before input – is the buyer being overcharged, for example?

PURCHASES AND EXPENSES AND CAPITAL ITEMS

One point that is very important to bear in mind is the difference between **purchases** and **expenses** and **capital items**, as it affects the nominal account codes used when inputting invoices and credit notes on the computer. Look at the Pronto Supplies account list (with account numbers) shown below.

N/C	Name
0020	Plant and Machinery
0030	Office Equipment
0040	Furniture and Fixtures
1100	Debtors Control Account
1200	Bank Current Account
2100	Creditors Control Account
2200	Sales Tax Control Account
2201	Purchase Tax Control Account
2300	Loans
3000	Ordinary Shares
4000	Computer hardware sales
4001	Computer software sales
4002	Computer consultancy
5000	Materials Purchased
6201	Advertising
7000	Gross Wages
7100	Rent
7103	General Rates
7200	Electricity

Purchases are items a business buys which it expects to turn into a product or sell as part of its day-to-day business. For example:

- a business that makes cheese will buy milk to make the cheese
- a supermarket will buy food and clothes to sell to the public

All these items are bought because they will be sold or turned into a product that will be sold. In Sage these purchases will be recorded in a **purchases account**, normally 5000, or a number in that category. In the list shown above Pronto Supplies uses account 5000 for 'Materials Purchased'.

Expenses, on the other hand, are items which the business pays for which form part of the business running expenses (overheads), eg rent and electricity. They all have separate nominal account numbers.

Capital items are 'one off' items that the business buys and intends to keep for a number of years, for example office equipment and furniture. They all also have separate nominal account numbers.

conclusion

The important point here is that all of these items may be bought on credit and will have to be entered into the computer accounting records, **but with the correct nominal account number.**

CASE STUDY

PRONTO SUPPLIES LIMITED: PROCESSING PURCHASES INVOICES AND CREDIT NOTES

It is now February 16 2001. Tom has a number of supplier invoices and supplier credit notes to enter into the computer accounting system.

He has the documents on file and has collected them in two batches.

PURCHASES INVOICES RECEIVED

invoice	name	date	details	net amount	VAT
11365	Delco PLC	9/02/01	Desktop computers	3,600.00	630.00
8576	Electron Supplies	9/02/01	Peripherals	2,000.00	350.00
2947	MacCity	12/02/01	Powerbooks	2,400.00	420.00
34983	Synchromart	14/02/01	Software	1,280.00	224.00
Subtotals				9,280.00	1624.00
Batch total					10,904.00

CREDIT NOTES RECEIVED

credit note	name	date	details	net amount	VAT
7223	Delco PLC	6/02/01	1 x Computer	480.00	84.00
552	MacCity	8/02/01	1 x optical mouse	38.00	6.65
Subtotals				518.00	90.65
Batch total					608.65

batch invoice entry

Tom will start by opening up the SUPPLIERS screen in Sage and clicking on the INVOICE icon. This will show the screen shown on the next page. He will then

- identify the account references for each of the four customers
- enter each invoice on a new line
- take the data from the invoice: date, invoice no ('Ref'), product details and amounts
- enter the Materials Purchased account number 5000 under 'N/C'
- enter the T1 tax code for standard rate VAT and check that the VAT amount calculated on screen is the same as on the invoice – if there is a difference it should be queried (there could, for example, be a calculation mistake on the original invoice or a 'rounding' difference might occur)

When the input is complete Tom should check his original totals (Net, VAT and Batch total) against the computer totals. Once he is happy that his input is correct he can SAVE.

The batch suppliers' invoice screen will appear like this:

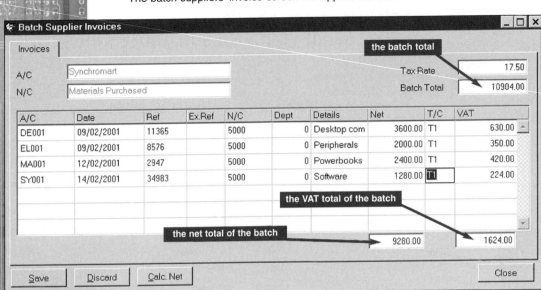

checking the invoices are on the system

As a further check Tom could print out a Day Book Report. This can be obtained through the REPORTS icon on the SUPPLIER menu bar. The title of the report is 'Day Books: Supplier Invoices (Summary)'. The report appears as follows:

Pronto Supplies Limited   Page: 1

Day Books: Supplier Invoices (Summary)

Date From: 01/02/2001
Date To: 31/12/2019

Transaction From: 1
Transaction To: 99999999

Tran No.	Item	Tp	Date	A/C Ref	Inv Ref	Details	Net Amount	Tax Amount	Gross Amount
68	1	PI	09/02/2001	DE001	11365	Desktop computers	3,600.00	630.00	4,230.00
69	1	PI	09/02/2001	EL001	8576	Peripherals	2,000.00	350.00	2,350.00
70	1	PI	12/02/2001	MA001	2947	Powerbooks	2,400.00	420.00	2,820.00
71	1	PI	14/02/2001	SY001	34983	Software	1,280.00	224.00	1,504.00
						Totals	9,280.00	1,624.00	10,904.00

batch credit note entry

Tom will input the details from the two credit notes in much the same way as he processed the invoices. He will open up the SUPPLIERS screen in Sage and click on the CREDIT icon. This will show the screen shown on the next page. He will then identify the account references for each of the two customers and input the credit note details as shown on the screen. He will use the Materials Purchased account number 5000. When the input is complete he should again check his original totals (Net, VAT and Batch total) against the computer totals. Once he is happy that his input is correct he should SAVE.

The batch suppliers' credit note screen will appear like this:

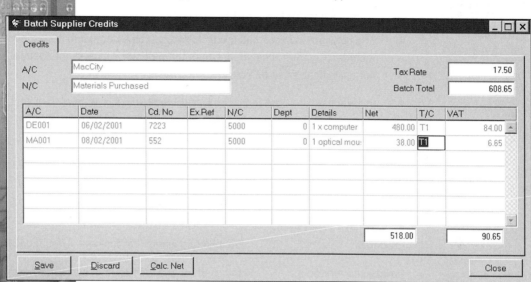

checking the credit notes are on the system

As a further check Tom could print out a Day Book Report for Supplier Credit notes. This can be obtained through the REPORTS icon on the SUPPLIERS toolbar. The title of the report is 'Day Books: Supplier Credits (Summary)'. The report appears as follows:

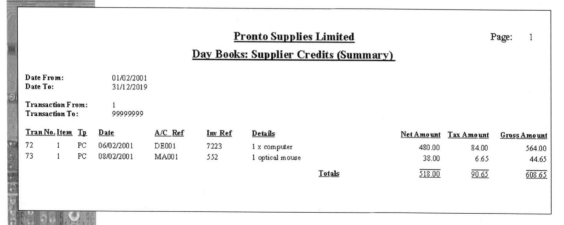

what next?

Tom has now entered into his computer:

- his company details and nominal accounts and balances
- customer and supplier details
- customer and supplier invoices
- customer and supplier credit notes

The next chapter shows how he enters details of payments made to suppliers and payments received from customers. The 'flow of documents' will be complete.

■ When a business buys on credit it will receive invoices and possibly credit notes from its suppliers as part of the 'flow of documents'.

■ The details of invoices and credit notes must be entered into the accounting records of a business. If a computer program is used the details are normally input on screen on the batch basis.

■ In the case of supplier invoices and credit notes it is important that the correct Nominal account number is used to describe whether the transaction relates to purchases, expenses or capital items.

■ It is essential to check the details of invoices and credit notes before input and the details of input by printing out, for example, a day book report.

credit sale	a sale made where payment is due at a later date
creditors	suppliers to whom the business owes money
purchases ledger	the part of the accounting system where the suppliers' accounts are kept
purchases	items bought which will be turned into a product or be sold as part of day-to-day-trading
expenses	payments made which relate to the running of the business – also known as overheads
capital items	items bought which the business intends to keep
batch	a group of documents, eg invoices or credit notes

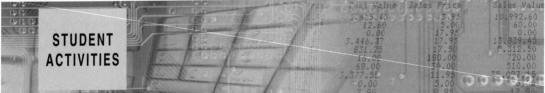

7.1 Define the term 'creditors'.

7.2 In what section of the accounting system are supplier balances kept? What information does this provide for the owner of the business?

7.3 What is the difference between purchases, expenses and capital items? Why is it important to identify these types of transaction before entering a supplier invoice on the computer?

7.4 Write a list of instructions for a person entering supplier invoices into a batch screen on a computer accounting program. Explain what data is entered in each of the columns and what checks should be made before and after input.

PRONTO SUPPLIES INPUTTING TASK

warning note!
This activity involves you in inputting live data into the computer. This activity is only suitable if you are in a supervised training environment.

Task 1

Set the program date to 16 February 2001. Enter the following invoice details into the computer. Check your totals before saving and print out a Day Books: Supplier Invoice (Summary) Report to confirm the data that you have saved.

PURCHASES INVOICES RECEIVED					
invoice	name	date	details	net amount	VAT
11365	Delco PLC	9/02/01	Desktop computers	3,600.00	630.00
8576	Electron Supplies	9/02/01	Peripherals	2,000.00	350.00
2947	MacCity	12/02/01	Powerbooks	2,400.00	420.00
34983	Synchromart	14/02/01	Software	1,280.00	224.00
Subtotals				9,280.00	1624.00
Batch total					10,904.00

Task 2

Enter the following credit note details into the computer. Check your totals before saving and print out a Day Books: Supplier Credits (Summary) Report to confirm the data that you have saved.

CREDIT NOTES RECEIVED					
credit note	name	date	details	net amount	VAT
7223	Delco PLC	6/02/01	1 x Computer	480.00	84.00
552	MacCity	8/02/01	1 x optical mouse	38.00	6.65
Subtotals				518.00	90.65
Batch total					608.65

Task 3 *(check with Trial Balance on page 242 when you have finished this Task)*

On the same day Tom receives two further supplier invoices in the post. He wants them to be input straightaway while the computer is up and running. He checks all the documentation and finds that the invoices are both correct. You are to input them, taking care to use the correct nominal code (the Pronto codes are listed on page 66). The computer and printer purchased are not for resale to customers but are to be used as office equipment at Pronto Supplies. When the input is complete the totals should be checked and a Day Book Summary Report printed (showing just the last two invoices, if possible).

invoice	name	date	details	net amount	VAT
11377	Delco PLC	14/02/01	Desktop computer	400.00	70.00
8603	Electron Supplies	14/02/01	Laser Printer	360.00	63.00
Subtotals				760.00	133.00
Batch total					893.00

Reminder! Have you made a backup?

chapter introduction

■ So far in this book we have set up accounts for customers and suppliers and entered details of financial documents. But we have not covered the way in which the accounting system records the payment of money by customers to the business or by the business to suppliers.

■ The bank account is central to any accounting system as the payment of money is vital to all business transactions.

■ The bank account will be used not only for payments by customers and to suppliers (credit transactions), but also for transactions for which settlement is made straightaway (cash transactions), for example payment of telephone bills and wages.

■ A computer accounting system may maintain more than one 'bank' account in its Nominal Ledger. For example, it may also keep a petty cash account for purchases made from the office petty cash tin and a credit card account for purchases made with its company credit card.

■ This chapter concentrates on the use of the bank account for credit transactions, ie when a business receives payment of its customers' invoices and when it makes payments of its suppliers' invoices.

The 'cash' transactions mentioned above are covered in detail in the next two chapters.

THE BANK ACCOUNTS IN COMPUTER ACCOUNTING

The bank accounts and all the functions associated with them are found in Sage by clicking on the BANK icon in the main menu bar . . .

The BANK screen then appears as shown on the next page.

Study the screen below and read the notes that follow. The most important icons are explained by the text with the arrows.

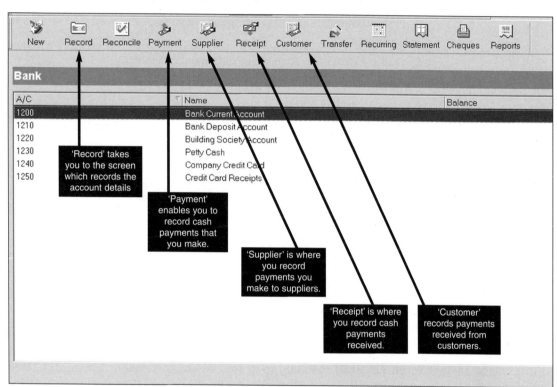

types of bank account

The accounts listed above come from the default list in the chart of accounts (see page 66 if you need reminding about this). The business does not have to adopt all the accounts listed here, but may use some of them if it needs them:

- **bank current account** records all payments in and out of the bank 'cheque' account used for everyday purposes – it is the most commonly used account

- **bank deposit account** and **Building Society account** can be used if the business maintains interest-paying accounts for savings and money that is not needed in the short term

- **petty cash account** can be used if the business keeps a petty cash tin in the office for small business purchases such as stationery and stamps

- **company credit card account** can be used if the business uses credit cards for its employees to pay for expenses

- **credit card receipts account** can be used if the business receives a significant number of credit card payments by its customers

cash or credit payments?

The number of icons on the menu bar record payments which are either:

- **cash payments** – ie made straightaway without the need for invoices or credit notes
- **credit payments** – ie made in settlement of invoices

The problem is, which is which? The rule is:

= **cash payments** (not involving credit customers or suppliers)

= **credit payments** (payments from customers and to suppliers in settlement of accounts)

bank account details

It must be stressed that if a Sage computer account number is listed on the BANK screen it does not *have* to be used. It is there so that it can be used if the business needs it. The Bank Current Account (here number 1200), for example, is always going to be used, assuming businesses always have bank current accounts!

When a business is setting up its bank accounts it should click on RECORD on the BANK screen to produce the bank account DETAILS screen . . .

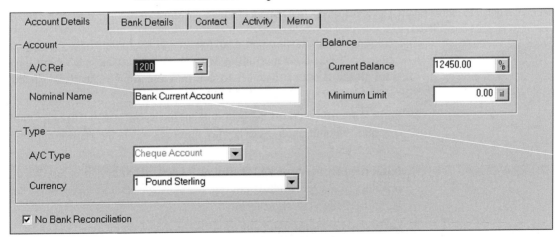

This screen enables the business to input details of the account, the bank and bank contact and to see the activity on the account.

The checked box at the bottom in this example means that the business will not use the program to reconcile (tally up) the computer bank account with the bank statement when it is received. This is not needed at this stage.

RECORDING PAYMENTS FROM CUSTOMERS

how do payments arrive?

When a payment arrives from a customer who has bought on credit it will normally arrive at the business in one of two ways:

- A cheque and **remittance advice**. A remittance advice is a document stating what the payment relates to – eg which invoices and credit notes.

- A remittance advice stating that the money has been sent direct to the business bank account in the form of a **BACS payment** (a BACS [Bankers Automated Clearing Services] payment is a payment sent direct between the banks' computers and does not involve a cheque).

Examples of cheque and BACS remittance advices are shown below:

TO	REMITTANCE ADVICE	FROM

TO
A B Supplies Limited
Unit 45 Elgar Estate,
Broadfield, BR7 4ER

Compsync
4 Friar Street
Broadfield
BR1 3RF
Tel 01908 761234 Fax 01908 761987
VAT REG GB 0745 8383 56

Account 3993   6 November 2001

date	your reference	our reference	payment amount
01 10 01	INVOICE 787923	47609	277.30
10 10 01	CREDIT NOTE 12157	47609	(27.73)
		CHEQUE TOTAL	249.57

BACS REMITTANCE ADVICE

FROM: Excelsior Services
17 Gatley Way
Bristol BS1 9GH

TO
A B Supplies Ltd
Unit 45 Elgar Estate, Broadfield, BR7 4ER

06 12 01

Your ref	Our ref		Amount
788102	3323	BACS TRANSFER	465.00
		TOTAL	465.00

THIS HAS BEEN PAID BY BACS CREDIT TRANSFER DIRECTLY INTO YOUR BANK ACCOUNT AT ALBION BANK NO 11451226 SORT CODE 90 47 17

customer payments and the accounting system

An incoming payment from a customer settling one or more invoices (less any credit notes) needs to be recorded in the accounting system:

■ the balance in the bank account will increase (a debit in double-entry)

■ the balance in the customer's account (and the Debtors Control Account) will decrease because the customer will owe less (a credit in double-entry accounting)

In computer accounting the payment is input once and the two entries will be automatically made from the same screen.

the practicalities

The business will normally input a number (a 'batch') of payments at one time on a regular basis, eg every week, using the remittance advice as the source document. The remittance advice will have all the details on it (date, amount, invoices paid) and in the case of a BACS payment it is the only document from the customer relating to the payment the business will have.

The appropriate bank account should first be selected on the BANK screen and then the CUSTOMER icon selected to access the Customer Receipt input screen:

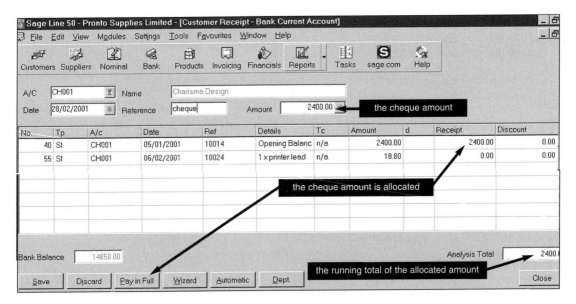

processing the payments received

The procedure for recording the customer payment on this screen is to:

■ input the customer account reference – this will bring up on screen the account name and all the outstanding amounts due on invoices

- input a reference if required – for example you might type 'cheque' or 'BACS' or the numerical reference relating to the payment

- input the amount of the payment in the Amount box

- click on the 'Receipt' box of the invoice that is being paid

- click on the 'Pay in Full' button at the bottom

- if there is more than one invoice being paid click on the items being paid as appropriate; the Analysis Total box at the bottom will shown a running total of the money allocated

- if there is a long list of invoices and a payment to cover them, click on 'Automatic' at the bottom and the computer will allocate the payment down the invoice list until it runs out

- check that what you have done is correct and SAVE; details to check are:

  - customer, amount, invoices being paid and amount received

  - the amounts in the Amount box and the Analysis Total box should be the same (but see next point)

- if the amount received by way of payment is greater than the amount allocated to outstanding invoices the extra payment will show as a 'Payment on Account' after you have saved

- if the amount received by way of payment is less than the amount of the invoice(s) it is settling, the amount received will be allocated to the appropriate invoice(s) and the unpaid amount will show as outstanding on the Customer's account

- you should print out a Day Books: Customer Receipts (Summary) for these transactions from REPORTS in BANK to check that the total of the cheques (or BACS payments) received equals the total input

RECORDING PAYMENTS TO SUPPLIERS

what documents are involved?

A business usually pays its suppliers after it receives a **statement** setting out the amounts due from invoices and any deductions made following the issue of credit notes.

Payment is often made by cheque, although some payments may be made by BACS transfer between the banks' computers. Payment is normally made in full, but occasionally a part payment may be made.

A typical payment cheque, together with a completed counterfoil (cheque stub) is shown on the next page.

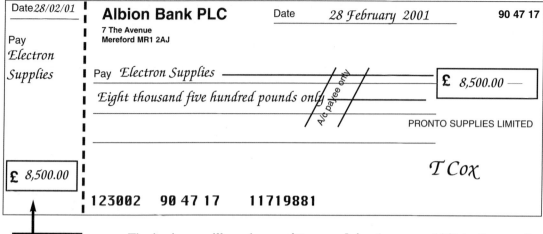

counterfoil

The business will send a **remittance advice** (see page 103) to the supplier with the cheque, or, if a BACS payment is being made, on its own. This, together with the cheque, will often provide the details for the input of the payment details on the computer.

Some programs can print remittance advices on the computer when the payment is processed. If the business decides to do this, the payment details are likely to be taken from the completed cheque and counterfoil. Some computer accounting programs which deal with long 'cheque runs' will also print the cheques themselves on special preprinted cheque stationery.

supplier payments and the accounting system

Payment to a supplier settling one or more invoices (less any credit notes) needs to be recorded in the accounting system:

• the balance in the bank account will decrease (a credit in double-entry)

• the balance in the supplier's account (and the Creditors Control Account) will decrease because the supplier will be owed less (a debit in double-entry accounting)

In computer accounting the payment is input once and the two entries will be automatically made from the same screen.

processing the payments

As with customer receipts, the business will normally input a number (a 'batch') of payments at one time on a regular basis, for example just after the cheques have been written out or the BACS payment instructions prepared.

The payments are input in Sage from the SUPPLIER icon on the BANK screen – after the appropriate bank account has been selected.

The procedure for recording the supplier payment is to:

- input the supplier reference in the box next to the word 'Payee' on the 'cheque' – this will bring up on screen the account name and all the outstanding amounts due on invoices

- input the cheque number on the cheque and alter the date if the cheque date is different

- input the amount of the payment in the amount box on the cheque; if it is a part payment the same procedure will be followed

- click on the Payment box of the invoice that is being paid – here it is the first one – and click on the 'Pay in full' icon at the bottom; if there is more than one invoice being paid click on the items being paid as appropriate; any part payment will be allocated to the appropriate invoice(s) in the same way

- check that what you have done is correct (ie supplier, amount, invoices being paid), print out a remittance advice if you want one by clicking on REMITTANCE, and SAVE

- print out a Day Books: Customer Payments (Summary) from REPORTS in BANK to check that the total of the cheques (or BACS payments) issued equals the total input on the computer

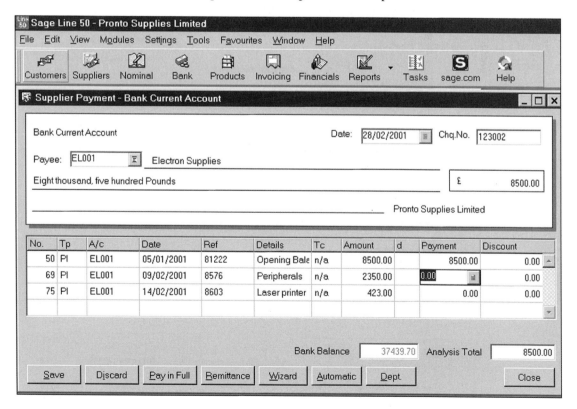

printing remittance advices

As we have already seen, you can print out remittance advices to accompany cheques, or to advise BACS payments to the supplier.

The printing should be done when you have checked the payment details and before you Save the payment transaction. It is important to note that this is your only chance to do this. Once the input details have been Saved, the screen disappears!

In order to print a remittance advice you should click on the Remittance button at the bottom of the screen. This will bring up a screen for you to select a suitable remittance advice:

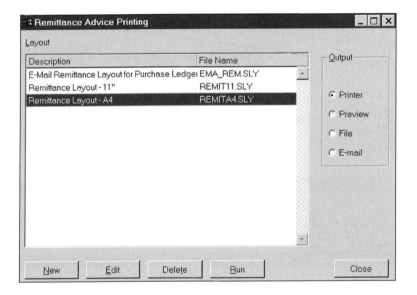

To print the remittance advice click on Run at the bottom of the screen. A printed remittance advice (extract) is shown below.

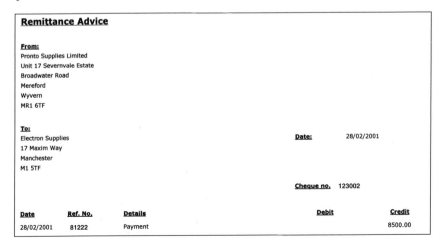

We will now look at the way in which Tom Cox's business, Pronto Supplies Limited, inputs its payments from customers and payments to suppliers on the computer.

CASE STUDY

PRONTO SUPPLIES LIMITED: PROCESSING PAYMENTS FROM CUSTOMERS AND TO SUPPLIERS

It is February 28 2001. Tom has received a number of cheques (with remittance advices) from his customers in settlement of invoices sent out in January.

Some of the cheques also take into account the credit notes issued by Pronto Supplies.

Tom also has a list of supplier invoices to pay, the money being due at the end of the month.

receipts from customers

The list of cheques received is shown below.

John Butler & Associates	£5,500.00
Charisma Design	£2,400.00
Crowmatic Limited	£3,234.00
David Boossey	£3,165.00
French Emporium	£5,553.00
Jo Green Systems	£3,461.20
L Garr & Co	£8,500.00
Mendell & Son	£4,276.50
Prism Trading Limited	£2,586.00
Batch total of payments received	£38,675.70

These cheques are entered into the computer accounting system under CUSTOMERS in the BANK section as shown on the screen shown at the top of the next page.

Tom then prints out a report 'Day Books: Customer Receipts (Summary)' which shows the transactions he has processed. This is also shown on the next page. He checks the total on the report against the batch total of the cheques (or remittance advices) he has received.

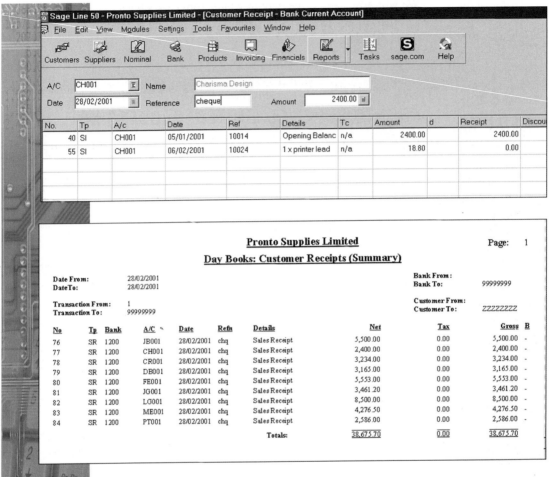

payments to suppliers

Tom has made a list of the amounts he owes to his suppliers for goods sent to Pronto Supplies Limited in January.

The documents he has for this are his original purchase orders, invoices received and any credit notes issued by his suppliers.

The cheques and remittance advices are then typed out. The data is now ready for input. The details are:

Delco PLC	£5,186.00	Cheque 123001
Electron Supplies	£8,500.00	Cheque 123002
MacCity	£4,455.35	Cheque 123003
Synchromart	£7,600.00	Cheque 123004
Tycomp Supplies	£6,160.00	Cheque 123005
Batch total of payments made	£31,901.35	

These cheques are entered into the computer accounting system under SUPPLIERS in the BANK section as shown below. Tom also decides to print out remittance advices as he goes along.

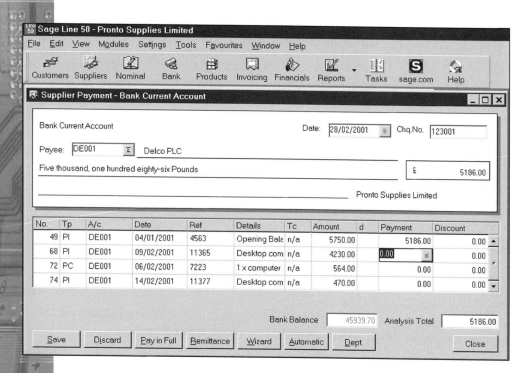

Tom then prints out a report Day Books: Supplier Receipts (Summary) which shows the transactions he has processed. He checks the total on the report against the total of the cheques he has issued.

Pronto Supplies Limited

Day Books: Supplier Payments (Summary)

Page:

Date From:	28/02/2001					Bank From:		
Date To:	28/02/2001					Bank To:	99999999	
Transaction From:	1					Supplier From:		
Transaction To:	99999999					Supplier To:	ZZZZZZZZ	

No	Tp	Bank	A/C	Date	Refn	Details	Net	Tax	Gross
85	PP	1200	DE001	28/02/2001	123001	Purchase Payment	5,186.00	0.00	5,186.00
86	PP	1200	EL001	28/02/2001	123002	Purchase Payment	8,500.00	0.00	8,500.00
87	PP	1200	MA001	28/02/2001	123003	Purchase Payment	4,455.35	0.00	4,455.35
88	PP	1200	SY001	28/02/2001	123004	Purchase Payment	7,600.00	0.00	7,600.00
89	PP	1200	TY001	28/02/2001	123005	Purchase Payment	6,160.00	0.00	6,160.00
						Totals:	31,901.35	0.00	31,901.35

DEALING WITH CREDIT NOTES

When inputting payments from customers and to suppliers in a program like Sage, you may encounter the situation where the amount received (or paid out) is not the same as the amount of the invoice being settled.

For example, if a customer is issued with an invoice for £1,000 and then issued with a credit note for £100 because some of the goods are faulty, the customer will only owe – and pay – £900. The computer screen, however, will show this £900 as two separate lines: an invoice for £1,000 and a credit note for £100. If the £900 cheque received is allocated against the £1,000, the computer will think a balance of £100 still needs to be paid against this invoice, even though the account balance is nil!

the solution

The credit note, which is also outstanding on the computer screen needs to be allocated to the balance of the invoice. This is done by:

■ clicking on the Receipt box on the credit note line

■ clicking on 'Pay in Full' so that the analysis total shows a minus amount

■ clicking on the Receipt box on the invoice line and then 'Pay in Full' so that the analysis box shows a nil balance

This tidying up procedure can be carried out before, during or after the payments received routine.

The procedure for allocating supplier credit notes to invoices works on exactly the same principles.

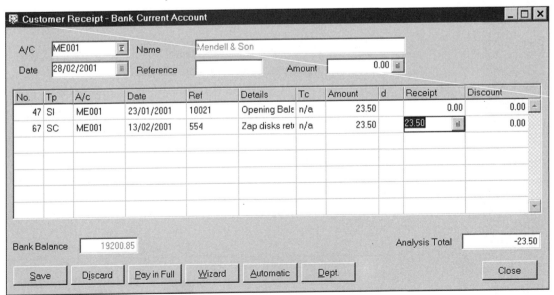

DEALING WITH PAYMENTS THAT ARE TOO HIGH OR TOO LOW

the problem

Sometimes a customer will send an amount which does not tally with the amount that appears on the customer's statement and the amount on the computer records. For example:

■ the customer sends a part payment of an invoice because he or she is short of money, or thinks a credit note is due

■ the customer sends too much money, ignoring a credit note that has been issued

the solution – underpayment

The amount that has been received is allocated against the relevant invoice. The amount that is still owing will show on the computer records.

the solution – overpayment

The amount that has been received is allocated against all the relevant invoices. The extra amount that is received will show as a 'Payment on Account' which will be available to allocate against future invoices.

CHAPTER SUMMARY

■ The bank account is a central account in the operation of any business as so many transactions pass through it.

■ A business can set up not only the bank current account in the computer accounting system, but also a number of other 'money' accounts. These, which include petty cash account and credit card accounts, enable the business to keep track of the processing of money in a variety of forms.

■ Payments received from customers who have bought on credit can be processed through the computer accounting system. The accounting system is adjusted in each case by an increase in the bank current account and a reduction of the customer's account balance in the Sales Ledger.

■ Payments to suppliers from whom the business has bought on credit can also be processed on the computer and remittance advices printed if required. The accounting entries in this case are a decrease in the bank current account and a reduction in the supplier's account balance in the Purchases Ledger.

■ It is essential to check the input of payments from customers and to suppliers by obtaining a printout such as a Day Book from the computer.

KEY TERMS

current account	the 'everyday' bank account which handles routine receipts and payments
cash payments	payments made straightaway
credit payments	payments made at a later date following the issue of an invoice to a customer or by a supplier
remittance advice	a document that tells a business that a payment is being made
BACS	a computer payment system which operates between the banks and their customers (short for Bankers Automated Clearing Services)

STUDENT ACTIVITIES

8.1   What do the icons Payment, Supplier, Receipt and Customer represent on a BANK menu bar?

8.2   Why is it important that a business receives a remittance advice when it receives a payment to the bank account from a customer settling an invoice?

8.3   What entries to the accounting system will be made when a business receives a payment from a credit customer and makes a payment to a supplier?

8.4   What printout from a computer accounting system lists payments made to suppliers on any particular day? Why is it important that a report like this is extracted? What might happen if a business decided not to obtain this printout?

8.5   A point to think about. Previous activities in this book have involved VAT. Why does the Case Study in this chapter not include VAT?

PRONTO SUPPLIES INPUTTING TASK

warning note!
This activity involves you in inputting live data into the computer. This activity is only suitable if you are in a supervised training environment.

Task 1

Set the program date to 28 February 2001. Enter the following customer cheques into BANK (CUSTOMERS). Check your total before saving and print out a Day Books: Customer Receipts (Summary) Report to confirm the accuracy of your input.

John Butler & Associates	£5,500.00
Charisma Design	£2,400.00
Crowmatic Limited	£3,234.00
David Boossey	£3,165.00
French Emporium	£5,553.00
Jo Green Systems	£3,461.20
L Garr & Co	£8,500.00
Mendell & Son	£4,276.50
Prism Trading Limited	£2,586.00
Batch total of payments received	£38,675.70

Task 2

Enter the following cheques Tom is paying to suppliers into the computer. Check your total before saving and print out a Day Books: Supplier Payments (Summary) Report to confirm the accuracy of your input. If your system has the facility, print out remittance advices to accompany the cheques.

Delco PLC	£5,186.00	Cheque 123001
Electron Supplies	£8,500.00	Cheque 123002
MacCity	£4,455.35	Cheque 123003
Synchromart	£7,600.00	Cheque 123004
Tycomp Supplies	£6,160.00	Cheque 123005
Batch total of payments made	£31,901.35	

Task 3

If you have not already allocated your credit notes, check through your customer accounts by opening up the Customer Receipts screen for each one. You may find that some of them have a credit note outstanding and an invoice which has not been completely paid. You should in each case allocate the credit note to the appropriate invoice. Ensure in each case that the correct bank account is selected before you make the adjustment.

Task 4

Repeat the procedure in Task 3 by opening up the Supplier Payments screen for each supplier. You should in each case allocate the credit note to the appropriate invoice.

Task 5

Now print out a Trial Balance for Pronto Supplies as at 28 February 2001 from the FINANCIALS icon and compare it with the Trial Balance on page 243.

What changes can you see in the Bank Account balance and Debtors Control Account and Creditors Control Account? What has happened in the accounting system? Keep your printout with your answer.

Reminder! Have you made a backup?

9 CASH RECEIPTS AND PAYMENTS

chapter introduction

■ The last chapter explained how payments settling invoices are recorded in a computer accounting system. These payments received from customers and made to suppliers settle up 'credit sales' where invoices are issued when the sale is made and payment is made later.

■ A business will also process a substantial number of varied 'cash payments' where the money is transferred at the same time as the transaction. Note that 'cash' does not just mean notes and coins in this context; it means immediate payment.

Example of these payments (and receipts) include:

• money received from sales – over the counter sales

• money spent on purchases – buying stock and material for use in the business

• running expenses paid – wages, power bills, rent

• items bought for permanent use in the business – fixed assets not bought on credit

• loans made to the business

• money (capital) put into the business by the ówner(s)

■ A computer accounting system will record these 'cash' items in a different way from the 'credit' items seen in the last chapter. In a Sage system they are processed through the PAYMENT or RECEIPT icons on the BANK menu bar.

■ The transactions mentioned so far involve payments which are made straight through the bank current account. A business may also use other funds for making payments and receiving money. These are covered in the next chapter.

THE BANK ACCOUNTS

The last chapter started by looking at the different bank accounts that a Sage system will allow a business to set up. Whereas the last chapter concentrated on the use of the Bank Current Account for payments made on credit, this chapter examines the way in which cash payments (immediate payments) are recorded in the Bank Current Account of a computer accounting system.

The BANK screen shown below (the default accounts screen) explains the icons that you will be using in this chapter.

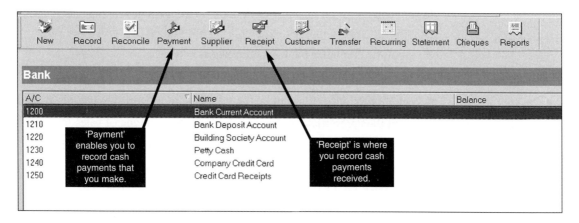

CASH SALES

Cash sales made by a business are usually sales made 'over the counter'.

Cash sales can be made by cash, cheque or debit or credit card – they are not just notes and coins. The important point here is that the business should pay the money into the Bank Current Account as soon as possible – it will be safer in the bank and can be used to meet payments the business may have made.

The input screen for cash sales is reached from the RECEIPT icon on the BANK menu bar. It looks like this:

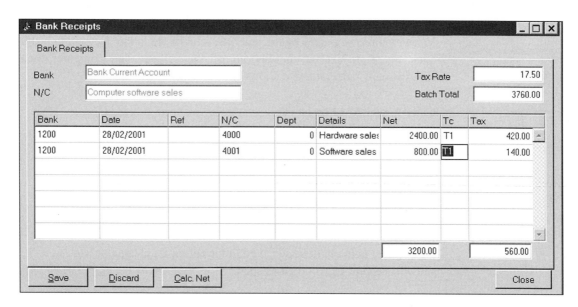

inputting bank receipts

Cash sales paid straight into the bank may be input from the bank paying-in slips recorded in the business cash book or from a sales listing sheet. These receipts are known in Sage as Bank Receipts and are input as follows:

■ input the computer bank account number

■ enter the date (usually the date the money is paid into the bank)

■ enter a reference (this can be the reference number of the paying-in slip)

■ input the appropriate nominal code (N/C) for the type of sales involved

■ enter a description of the payment (eg 'hardware sales') under 'Details'

■ enter the net amount of the sales (ie the sales amount excluding VAT) and then click on T1 if the goods are standard rated for VAT – the computer will then automatically calculate the VAT amount for you and show it in the right-hand column

■ check that the VAT amount shown agrees with your figure and change it on screen if it does not – there may be a rounding difference

■ check the input details and totals and then SAVE

a note on VAT

The rates of VAT (**tax codes**) that you are most likely to come across are:

T1	standard rate (17.5% at the time of writing)
T2	exempt from VAT – eg postage stamps and business rates
T0	zero-rated, ie VAT could be charged but it is zero at the moment – eg books, food and some childrens clothes
T9	transactions not involving VAT

If you are using the Sage screen shown opposite and do not know what the VAT amount is in a sales figure, enter the total figure in the 'Net' column and click on 'Calc.Net' at the bottom of the screen. The computer then automatically calculates and shows the net amount and the VAT.

other cash receipts

You can also enter other cash (= not credit) receipts using the same Bank Receipts screen. Examples include:

■ money invested by the owner(s) of the business – capital

■ loans and grants from outside bodies

■ income from other sources such as rent received or bank interest

This money is likely to be received in the form of a cheque or bank transfer and will need to be recorded as such.

CASH PAYMENTS

Most credit payments made by businesses, as we saw in the last chapter, are to suppliers for goods and services provided and paid for on invoice. But businesses also have to make payments on a day-to-day and cash basis (immediate payment) for a wide variety of running costs such as wages and telephone bills.

These payments are input from the screen reached by clicking on the PAYMENT icon on the BANK menu bar. Study the example shown below. Here a telephone bill and wages have been paid from the Bank Current Account.

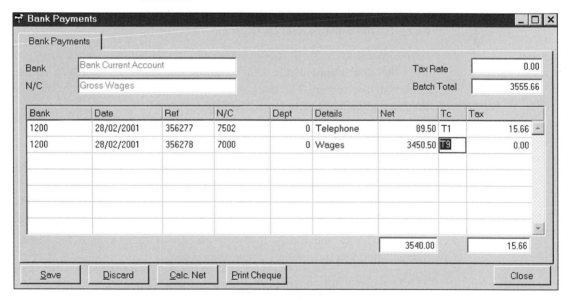

inputting cash payments

Cash payments can be input from the handwritten business **cash book** (if one is used), or from the cheques issued and bills being paid (which should show any VAT element). The procedure for inputting is:

- input the computer bank account number

- enter the date (the date the payment is made)

- enter a reference (normally the cheque number or 'BACS' if the payment is a BACS payment)

- input the appropriate nominal code (N/C) for the type of payment involved

- enter a brief description of the nature of the payment (eg 'Telephone') under 'Details'

■ enter the net amount of the payment (ie the amount excluding VAT) and then click on T1 if the product is standard rated for VAT – the computer will then automatically calculate the VAT amount for you and show it in the right-hand column

■ check that the VAT amount shown agrees with your figure and change it on screen if it does not – there may be a rounding difference

a note on VAT

The VAT rates used here are:

T1   the telephone bill is standard rated

T9   wages do not involve VAT

The code for a zero-rated item would have been T0. The code for a VAT exempt item would have been T2.

If you do not know what the VAT amount is included in a payment figure, enter the total figure in the 'Net' column and click on 'Calc.Net' at the bottom of the screen. The computer will then automatically calculate the VAT and adjust the Net figure accordingly.

checking the input data

You will see that the screen on the previous page shows the Net, Tax and Batch totals. These will automatically update as you enter the transactions. It is important to check your input against the source data for your input.

If you are entering the data as a batch of entries you should add up the three totals (Net, VAT and Batch) manually and check them against the screen figures when you have finished your data entry.

As a final check you should print out a Day Book report (see example below) from Reports in BANK and check the entries against your handwritten records (your cash book, for example).

Day Books: Bank Payments (Summary)

No	Tp	Bank	Date	Refn	Details	Net	Tax	Gross
96	BP	1200	12/02/2001	122992	Cash purchases	15,500.00	2,712.50	18,212.50
97	BP	1200	14/02/2001	122993	Advert	10,200.00	1,785.00	11,985.00
98	BP	1200	15/02/2001	122994	Furniture	5,000.00	875.00	5,875.00
99	BP	1200	16/02/2001	122995	Rent	4,500.00	787.50	5,287.50
100	BP	1200	19/02/2001	122996	Rates	350.00	0.00	350.00
101	BP	1200	23/02/2001	122997	RPower	158.00	27.65	185.65
102	BP	1200	26/02/2001	122998	ZipTelecom	310.00	54.25	364.25
103	BP	1200	26/02/2001	122999	Stationery	340.00	59.50	399.50
104	BP	1200	28/02/2001	123000	Wages	16,780.00	0.00	16,780.00
					Totals:	53,138.00	6,301.40	59,439.40

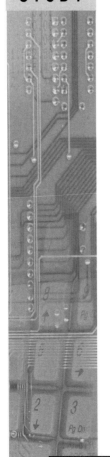

CASE STUDY

PRONTO SUPPLIES LIMITED: CASH RECEIPTS AND PAYMENTS

It is February 28 2001 and Tom has completed and checked his input of customer receipts and supplier payments (see pages 109 to 111).

He now has to input the various cash receipts and payments received and made during the month.

cash receipts

Pronto Supplies Limited paid takings of cash sales into the bank current account three times during the month. The amounts recorded in the cash book are shown below. The reference quoted is the paying-in slip reference.

Date	Details	Net amount (£)	VAT (£)	ref.
9 Feb 2001	Hardware sales	12,500.00	2187.50	10736
9 Feb 2001	Software sales	4,680.00	819.00	10737
16 Feb 2001	Hardware sales	15,840.00	2,772.00	10738
16 Feb 2001	Software sales	3,680.00	644.00	10739
23 Feb 2001	Hardware sales	17,800.00	3,115.00	10740
23 Feb 2001	Software sales	4,800.00	840.00	10741
	Totals	59,300.00	10,377.50	

These sales receipts are entered into the computer accounting system on the RECEIPTS screen reached from the BANK menu bar. Note that the Bank Current Account and the appropriate nominal sales code (N/C) are used each time.

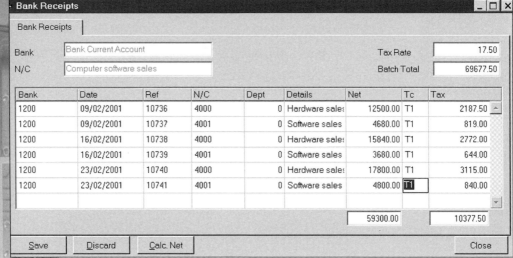

Tom then checks his listing totals against the on-screen totals for accuracy and clicks SAVE. He then prints out a report Day Books: Bank Receipts (Summary) as a paper-based record of the transactions he has processed. This is shown below. He again checks the totals on the report against the totals on his original listing.

Pronto Supplies Limited
Day Books: Bank Receipts (Summary)

Date From:	01/02/2001
DateTo:	28/02/2001
Transaction From:	1
Transaction To:	99999999

No	Tp	Bank	Date	Refn	Details	Net	Tax	Gross
90	BR	1200	09/02/2001	10736	Hardware sales	12,500.00	2,187.50	14,687.50
91	BR	1200	09/02/2001	10737	Software sales	4,680.00	819.00	5,499.00
92	BR	1200	16/02/2001	10738	Hardware sales	15,840.00	2,772.00	18,612.00
93	BR	1200	16/02/2001	10739	Software sales	3,680.00	644.00	4,324.00
94	BR	1200	23/02/2001	10740	Hardware sales	17,800.00	3,115.00	20,915.00
95	BR	1200	23/02/2001	10741	Software sales	4,800.00	840.00	5,640.00
					Totals:	59,300.00	10,377.50	69,677.50

cash payments

Tom sees from the company cash book that Pronto Supplies Limited has made a number of cash payments during the month for a variety of purposes. They are listed below. They include:

- normal day-to-day running expenses paid on a cash basis
- the purchase of furniture for £5,000 (a fixed asset) on 15 February

Date	Details	Net amount (£)	VAT (£)	chq no
12 Feb 2001	Cash purchases	15,500.00	2,712.50	122992
14 Feb 2001	Advertising	10,200.00	1,785.00	122993
15 Feb 2001	Furniture	5,000.00	875.00	122994
16 Feb 2001	Rent	4,500.00	787.50	122995
19 Feb 2001	Rates	350.00	exempt	122996
23 Feb 2001	Electricity	158.00	27.65	122997
26 Feb 2001	Telephone	310.00	54.25	122998
26 Feb 2001	Stationery	340.00	59.50	122999
28 Feb 2001	Wages	16,780.00	no VAT	123000
	Totals	53,138.00	6301.40	

These sales payments are entered into the computer accounting system on the PAYMENTS screen reached from the BANK menu bar. Note that the Bank Current Account and the appropriate nominal code (N/C) is used each time. The reference in each case is the relevant cheque number.

Customers	Suppliers	Nominal	Bank	Products	Invoicing	Financials	Reports	Tasks	sage.com	Help	

Bank Payments

Bank	Bank Current Account					Tax Rate	0.00
N/C	Gross Wages					Batch Total	59439.40

Bank	Date	Ref	N/C	Dept	Details	Net	Tc	Tax
1200	12/02/2001	12292	5000	0	Cash purchases	15500.00	T1	2712.50
1200	14/02/2001	12293	6201	0	Advert	10200.00	T1	1785.00
1200	15/02/2001	12294	0040	0	Furniture	5000.00	T1	875.00
1200	16/02/2001	12295	7100	0	Rent	4500.00	T1	787.50
1200	19/02/2001	12296	7103	0	Rates	350.00		0.00
1200	23/02/2001	12297	7200	0	RPower	158.00	T1	27.65
1200	26/02/2001	12298	7502	0	ZipTelecom	310.00	T1	54.25
1200	26/02/2001	12299	7504	0	Stationery	340.00	T1	59.50
1200	28/02/2001	12300	7000	0	Wages	16780.00	T9	0.00
						53138.00		6301.40

Save	Discard	Calc. Net	Print Cheque		Close

Tom then checks his listing totals against the on-screen totals for accuracy and clicks SAVE. He prints out a report Day Books: Bank Payments (Summary) as a record of the transactions he has processed. This is shown below. He compares the totals on the report against the totals on his original listing as a final check of input accuracy.

Pronto Supplies Limited

Day Books: Bank Payments (Summary)

Date From: 01/02/2001
DateTo: 28/02/2001

Transaction From: 1
Transaction To: 99999999

No	Tp	Bank	Date	Ref#	Details	Net	Tax	Gross
96	BP	1200	12/02/2001	122992	Cash purchases	15,500.00	2,712.50	18,212.50
97	BP	1200	14/02/2001	122993	Advert	10,200.00	1,785.00	11,985.00
98	BP	1200	15/02/2001	122994	Furniture	5,000.00	875.00	5,875.00
99	BP	1200	16/02/2001	122995	Rent	4,500.00	787.50	5,287.50
100	BP	1200	19/02/2001	122996	Rates	350.00	0.00	350.00
101	BP	1200	23/02/2001	122997	RPower	158.00	27.65	185.65
102	BP	1200	26/02/2001	122998	ZipTelecom	310.00	54.25	364.25
103	BP	1200	26/02/2001	122999	Stationery	340.00	59.50	399.50
104	BP	1200	28/02/2001	123000	Wages	16,780.00	0.00	16,780.00
					Totals:	53,138.00	6,301.40	59,439.40

RECEIPTS AND PAYMENTS AND THE ACCOUNTING SYSTEM

It is important to appreciate how the cash receipts and payments in this chapter relate to the accounting system of a business, particularly if you are also studying double-entry book-keeping.

Remember that transactions involve debits and credits and that the debit amount always equals the credit amount. Because of the VAT included in many sales and purchases, these transactions may involve three entries:

- the amount posted to the bank account (the full amount)
- the 'net' amount (the amount before VAT is added on) posted to the sales account or purchases (or expense) account
- any VAT involved in the transaction being posted to Sales or Purchases VAT account

The whole cash payment system is summarised in the linked diagram below. This shows how the money comes into and out of the bank account and illustrates how the double-entry book-keeping works. If you are not studying double-entry, just concentrate on the types of receipts and payments and see how they are input.

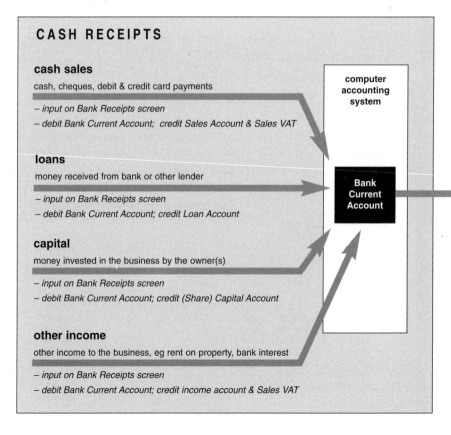

CASH RECEIPTS

cash sales
cash, cheques, debit & credit card payments

– input on Bank Receipts screen
– debit Bank Current Account; credit Sales Account & Sales VAT

loans
money received from bank or other lender

– input on Bank Receipts screen
– debit Bank Current Account; credit Loan Account

capital
money invested in the business by the owner(s)

– input on Bank Receipts screen
– debit Bank Current Account; credit (Share) Capital Account

other income
other income to the business, eg rent on property, bank interest

– input on Bank Receipts screen
– debit Bank Current Account; credit income account & Sales VAT

computer accounting system

Bank Current Account

CASH PAYMENTS

Bank Current Account

cheque payments

payment of running costs and cash purchase of assets

– input on Bank Payments screen

– debit expense or asset Account & Purchases VAT; credit Bank Current Account

CHAPTER SUMMARY

- Cash payments are payments which are immediate, unlike credit payments which are made at a later date.

- Cash payments can be made using cash, cheques, debit and credit cards.

- Businesses receive cash payments from a variety of sources: cash sales, loans, capital introduced by the owner(s) and other income such as rent of property and bank interest.

- A computer accounting program will record cash payments coming in – ie cash receipts – by adding the money to the bank account and by adjusting the appropriate other account (eg sales, loan, capital, income account) and the Sales VAT account (if there is any VAT involved).

- A computer accounting program will record cash payments going out – ie cash payments – by deducting the money from the bank account and by adjusting the appropriate other account (eg expense, asset purchase) and the Purchases VAT account (if there is any VAT involved).

KEY TERMS

cash sales	sales made where payment is immediate
current account	the 'everyday' bank account which handles routine receipts and payments
tax codes	a term used by Sage to refer to the rate of VAT which is applied to transactions; T1 refers to standard rate, T0 to the zero rate, T2 to VAT exempt items and T9 to transactions which do not involve VAT
cash book	the manual record kept by some businesses which records money paid in and out of the bank account

STUDENT
ACTIVITIES

9.1 From which icon on the BANK menu bar will the screen needed for recording a cash sale from a customer be reached? RECEIPT or CUSTOMER?

9.2 From which icon on the BANK menu bar will the screen needed for recording a cash purchase from a supplier be reached? PAYMENT or SUPPLIER?

9.3 Complete the sentences below using the following computer account names:

■ Bank   ■ Purchases   ■ Sales   ■ Purchases VAT   ■ Sales VAT

(a) A business makes a cash sale for £117.50, which is made up of £100 net and £17.50 VAT. The postings to the computer accounts will be:

£117.50 to .... account

£100.00 to .... account

£17.50 to .... account

(b) A business makes a cash purchase for £940, which is made up of £800 net and £140 VAT. The postings to the computer accounts will be:

£140.00 to .... account

£940.00 to .... account

£800.00 to .... account

9.4 Businesses from time-to-time pay into the bank cash payments which are not received from cash sales. Give three examples of this type of cash receipt.

PRONTO SUPPLIES INPUTTING TASK

warning note!
This activity involves you in inputting live data into the computer. This activity is only suitable if you are in a supervised training environment.

Task 1

Set the program date to 28 February 2001. Enter the following bank receipts into the computer. Check your totals before saving and print out a Day Books: Bank Receipts (Summary) Report to confirm the accuracy of your input.

Date	Details	Net amount (£)	VAT (£)	ref.
9 Feb 2001	Hardware sales	12,500.00	2187.50	10736
9 Feb 2001	Software sales	4,680.00	819.00	10737
16 Feb 2001	Hardware sales	15,840.00	2,772.00	10738
16 Feb 2001	Software sales	3,680.00	644.00	10739
23 Feb 2001	Hardware sales	17,800.00	3,115.00	10740
23 Feb 2001	Software sales	4,800.00	840.00	10741
	Totals	59,300.00	10,377.50	

Task 2 (a)

Keep the program date as 28 February 2001.

Enter the following cash payments into the computer. Take care over the nominal accounts that you chose and the VAT Tax codes used. T1 is the standard rate code, T2 is for exempt items and T9 is the code for transactions which do not involve VAT.

Check your totals before saving.

Date	Details	Net amount (£)	VAT (£)	chq no
12 Feb 2001	Material purchases	15,500.00	2,712.50	122992
14 Feb 2001	Advertising	10,200.00	1,785.00	122993
15 Feb 2001	Furniture	5,000.00	875.00	122994
16 Feb 2001	Rent	4,500.00	787.50	122995
19 Feb 2001	Rates	350.00	exempt	122996
23 Feb 2001	Electricity (RPower)	158.00	27.65	122997
26 Feb 2001	Telephone (ZipTelecom)	310.00	54.25	122998
26 Feb 2001	Stationery	340.00	59.50	122999
28 Feb 2001	Wages	16,780.00	no VAT	123000
	Totals	53,138.00	6301.40	

Task 2 (b)

Keep the program date as 28 February 2001.

Tom has won £5,000 on a Premium Bond. He decides to pay the cheque into the business as extra share capital under reference 10742, Code T9. He also visits his local computer dealer on 28 February and spends £4,000 plus VAT on a new colour printer for his office, using cheque number 123001 for the cash purchase. Make the necessary entries into the computer accounts (the nominal accounts used will be Ordinary Shares and Office Equipment).

Now print out a Day Books: Bank Payments (Summary) Report to confirm the accuracy of your input for Task 2.

Task 3

Print out a Trial Balance as at 28 February 2001 to check the accuracy of your input to date. Check with the Trial Balance on page 244.

Reminder! Have you made a backup?

10 BANK ACCOUNTS AND RECURRING ENTRIES

chapter introduction

- The last chapter explained how cash payments made directly in and out of the bank current account are recorded in a computer accounting system. 'Cash payment' here means 'immediate payment'. It can involve both cash, cheques and payments by debit and credit card.

- The computer program also enables a business to set up accounts on the system which record funds of money held by the business. These funds are classified by Sage as 'Bank' accounts, but the money is not held at the bank – it is held by the business and managed by the business. These accounts cover both cash payments and cash receipts.

- The 'Bank' accounts – which allow payments to be made – include:

  - petty cash account – a cash fund held under lock and key in the office, used for making small purchases and payments

  - credit card account – company credit cards issued to employees which enable the employees to pay expenses and for the business to be billed by the credit card company

  The money for these accounts will come from the bank current account and be recorded in Sage by a Bank Transfer.

- If a business – a shop for example – receives cash payments and then holds them on the premises for a length of time before paying them into the bank, it may decide to open a Cash Account to record the takings.

  When the money is eventually paid into the bank, the business will record a Bank Transfer from Cash Account in Sage to show the money being paid into the bank.

- Businesses will from time-to-time need to record regular payments made in and out of the bank current account. Examples include standing orders and direct debits for outgoing payments of insurance premiums and business rates and incoming receipts of rent from tenants.

  In Sage the Recurring Entries facility enables the business to set up the payments so that they can be recorded automatically each month in the accounts on the click of a button.

THE BANK ACCOUNTS IN COMPUTER ACCOUNTING

The bank accounts and all the functions associated with them are found in Sage by clicking on the BANK icon in the main menu bar.

The accounts listed come from the default list in the chart of accounts. The business does not have to adopt all the accounts, but may use some of them if it needs them. It can also set up new accounts within the appropriate account number range by clicking on NEW on the menu bar and using the new account Wizard. A summary of the Sage bank accounts is on page 101.

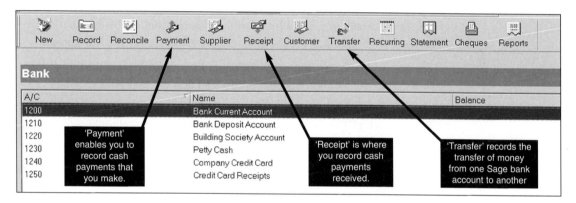

when is a bank account not a bank account?

The first three types of account shown on the above screen are actually maintained at the bank or building society. They are true 'bank' accounts. The last three accounts – petty cash and credit card payment and receipts accounts – are not kept at the bank but within the business. They are the accounts Sage uses to record money funds within the business which originally came from the bank or will be paid into the bank.

transfers between accounts

A TRANSFER facility on the BANK menu bar records movements between the 'bank' accounts. The screen below shows a business paying a company credit card bill with a cheque (no 176423) for £1,267.50. The money comes out of the current account and wipes out all the payments made with the card and recorded on the Company Credit Card Account (see page 135).

Account from	1200		Bank Current Account			
Account to	1240		Company Credit Card			
Ref	176423		Dept.	0	Date	22/11/2001
Details	Visa statement 25/10/2001				Amount	1267.50

OPENING UP A PETTY CASH ACCOUNT

what is a petty cash payment?

Petty cash is a float of cash – notes and coins – kept in an office, normally in a locked tin. It provides employees with the cash to make small purchases for the business. Examples of the type of payments include: stationery, office supplies, bus, rail and taxi fares incurred on behalf of the business, petrol bought for business use and postage stamps.

The petty cash is topped up with cash periodically to a set limit, known as the 'imprest' amount, £100 for example. The amount of the top up will also be the amount that has been spent: for example £80 of the £100 imprest.

The document used is the petty cash voucher (see below). When a payment is made, a petty cash voucher is completed and the appropriate evidence of payment is attached, for example:

■ a till receipt from a shop or a Post Office receipt for stamps

■ a rail or bus ticket or a receipt from a taxi firm

The cash can be paid out (or refunded) when the voucher is completed and authorised.

petty cash voucher		Number *807*	
	date	*12 May 2001*	
description			amount
		£	p
Envelopes		6	*00*
	VAT	1	05
Receipt obtained		7	05
signature	*T Harris*		
authorised	*R Singh*		

petty cash and the accounting system

Petty cash is a fund of money kept in the business in the same way as the bank current account is a fund of money kept in the bank. A 'bank' account will be set up for petty cash which will handle all the transactions:

■ payments of cash into petty cash from the bank current account

■ payments out of petty cash to pay for small expense items

payments into petty cash

The Sage computer system has a default Petty Cash Account which it classes as a bank account, although, of course, the money is not in the bank. The computer sees it as a 'money fund'.

When cash is needed to top up the petty cash to the imprest amount, the business will cash a cheque at the bank and then put the money in the cash tin. The computer program requires the business to input the transaction as a TRANSFER from the BANK menu bar. In the screen below, the business has cashed a £100 cheque at the bank (using cheque 132003) to provide the cash.

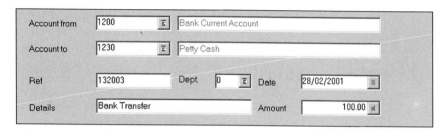

Account from	1200	£	Bank Current Account
Account to	1230	£	Petty Cash
Ref	132003	Dept. 0 £ Date	28/02/2001
Details	Bank Transfer	Amount	100.00

payments out of petty cash

Payments out of Petty Cash Account are handled in exactly the same way on the computer as payments out of Bank Current Account. The PAYMENTS screen is reached through the BANK menu bar. The details are then input from the petty cash vouchers or the petty cash book in which they are recorded.

The screen below shows the input of the petty cash voucher for stationery shown on the opposite page.

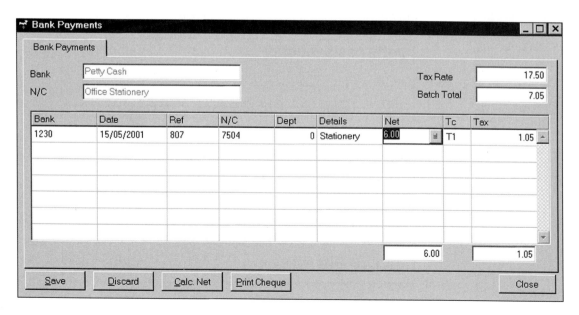

Bank Payments

Bank Payments

Bank	Petty Cash					Tax Rate	17.50
N/C	Office Stationery					Batch Total	7.05

Bank	Date	Ref	N/C	Dept	Details	Net	Tc	Tax
1230	15/05/2001	807	7504	0	Stationery	6.00	T1	1.05
							6.00	1.05

Save | Discard | Calc. Net | Print Cheque | Close

Points to remember are:

- the bank account number used is the Petty Cash Account number
- the reference is the petty cash voucher number
- petty cash vouchers and their receipts will not always show the VAT amount – the VAT and net amount can be calculated on the computer by inputting the full amount under 'Net' and then clicking on 'Calc.Net' at the bottom of the screen (using T1 code to denote standard rate VAT)
- when the details have been checked you should SAVE
- the details can also be checked against a Cash Payments Day Book printout if required (accessed through Reports in BANK)

CASE STUDY

PRONTO SUPPLIES LIMITED: SETTING UP THE PETTY CASH SYSTEM

At the beginning of February Tom Cox set up a petty cash system at Pronto Supplies Limited. The situation at 28 February is as follows:

- Tom notes that he cashed cheque no 122991 for £100 at the bank on 1 February.
- The £100 cash was transferred to the petty cash tin on 1 February.
- The tin contains three vouchers for payments made during the month – these are shown below and on the next page. They are ready for entry in the petty cash book as part of the month-end routine.

Voucher PC101 shows the VAT included in the total (standard rate: T1)

Voucher PC102 does not have any VAT in it (postage stamps are exempt:T2)

Voucher PC103 does not show the VAT included in the total (standard rate: T1) because it was not shown on the original receipt.

petty cash voucher		Number *PC101*	
		date *7 Feb 2001*	
description			amount
		£	p
Stationery		36	00
	VAT	6	30
Receipt obtained		42	30
signature *Nick Vellope*			
authorised *Tom Cox*			

petty cash voucher   Number *PC102*

date   *14 Feb 2001*

description		amount	
		£	p
Postages		*25*	*00*
	VAT		
Receipt obtained		*25*	*00*

signature   *R Patel*

authorised   *Tom Cox*

petty cash voucher   Number *PC103*

date   *20 Feb 2001*

description		amount	
		£	p
Stationery			
	VAT		
Receipt obtained		*18*	*80*

signature   *B Radish*

authorised   *Tom Cox*

the transfer to petty cash

Tom Cox first inputs the £100 transfer from the Bank Current Account to the Petty
Cash Account. The screen is illustrated below. Note the use of the cheque number as
the reference.

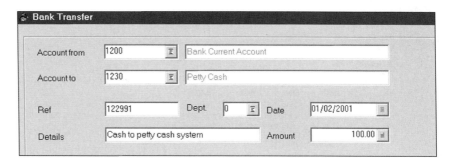

inputting the vouchers

The petty cash payments are entered into the computer accounting system on the PAYMENTS screen reached from the BANK menu bar.

Note that the bank Petty Cash Account number and the appropriate nominal code (N/C) is used each time.

The postages nominal code was taken from the default nominal list.

The reference in each case is the relevant petty cash voucher number.

Postages are VAT exempt. The VAT on the third petty cash voucher was not on the receipt but has been calculated on-screen by inputting the total amount of £18.80 in the 'Net' column and clicking on 'Calc.Net' at the bottom of the screen:

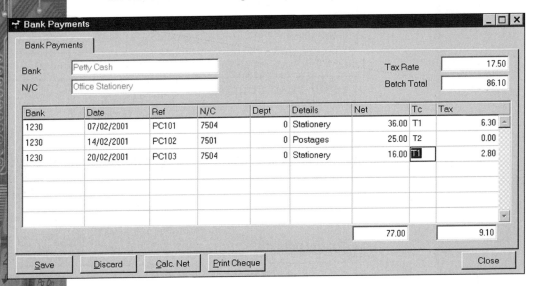

Tom then checks the batch total with the total of the vouchers and when he is happy that all the details are correct he will SAVE. The Day Book report will now show the petty cash payments. Note that the transaction code is 'CP' (second column from the left). This stands for 'Cash Payment'. This distinguishes the petty cash payments from payments by cheque (input through the same screen). These cheque payments have the code 'BP' which stands for 'Bank Payment'.

Pronto Supplies Limited
Day Books: Cash Payments (Summary)

| Date From: | 01/02/2001 | | | | | Bank From: | | |
| DateTo: | 28/02/2001 | | | | | Bank To: | 99999999 | |

Transaction From: 1
Transaction To: 99999999

No	Tp	Bank	Date	Refn	Details	Net	Tax	Gross
107	CP	1230	07/02/2001	PC101	Stationery	36.00	6.30	42.30
108	CP	1230	14/02/2001	PC102	Postages	25.00	0.00	25.00
109	CP	1230	20/02/2001	PC103	Stationery	16.00	2.80	18.80
					Totals:	77.00	9.10	86.10

CREDIT CARD ACCOUNTS

use of company credit cards

Credit cards are often issued by an employer for use by their employees when they are out on business – for example a sales representative who needs to buy petrol for the company car and to take a client out to lunch. All expenses are billed to the company on the credit card statement and are checked by the management to make sure that the expenses are business expenses and that there are no fiddles going on! The employee will be expected to keep all receipts for the accounting system.

company credit card payments in the accounts

The business with a computer accounting system can make use of the credit card account in the BANK function. This will be used to record all payments in Sage using the BANK PAYMENT screen seen earlier in this chapter, but inputting the payments to the Company Credit Card Account.

The credit card payment input screen looks like this:

Bank Payments										_ □ ×

| Bank | Company Credit Card | | | | | | Tax Rate | | | 17.50 |
| N/C | Travelling | | | | | | Batch Total | | | 375.23 |

Bank	Date	Ref	N/C	Dept	Details	Net	Tc	Tax	
1240	06/09/2001	TGarden	7400	2	Travel	85.00		0.00	
1240	12/09/2001	RMendes	8201	2	Subscription	75.00	T1	13.13	
1240	18/09/2001	TGarden	7403	2	Entertainment	126.00	T1	22.05	
1240	20/09/2001	NSingh	7400	2	Petrol	46.00	T1	8.05	
						332.00		43.23	

When the business pays the credit card bill the total amount will be input on the TRANSFER screen in the same way as the petty cash is topped up to the imprest amount (see page 130).

credit card receipt accounts

A business with a computer accounting system can also open up credit card accounts in BANK for credit card receipts. These will record incoming payments from sales where a credit card has been used. These are rather less common as credit card receipts can be posted straight to the Bank Current Account anyway as a cash receipt – a far simpler process.

USING A CASH RECEIPTS ACCOUNT

We have seen so far that cash receipts – for example the cash and cheques takings from a shop – are best paid into the bank current account as soon as possible. This reduces the risk of theft and means that the business has the use of the money earlier rather than later. This money is paid in Sage straight into the Bank Current Account.

There may be a case, however, where a business keeps its cash takings on the premises for some time before paying in. This could happen when a week's takings are paid in the following Monday. The business here could open up a special Cash Receipts Account in BANK to record the money fund kept on the premises. The procedure would be:

■ open up a Cash Receipts Account in BANK as a 'Cash' Account

■ enter the totals of daily takings in RECEIPTS from the BANK menu – the totals could be taken from the various till listings or a summary

■ using TRANSFER from the BANK menu, record the amounts as and when they are paid into the bank current account – the source document is the paying-in slip and the transfer is made from Cash Receipts Account to Bank Current Account

The RECEIPT and TRANSFER screens are shown below and on the next page.

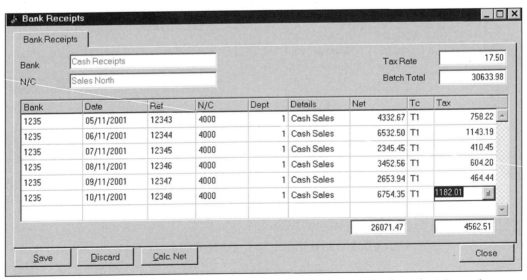

Here the takings for a week's trading (Monday to Saturday) by a shop are recorded on the BANK RECEIPTS screen. The money will be paid in on the following Monday and is held securely on the shop premises.

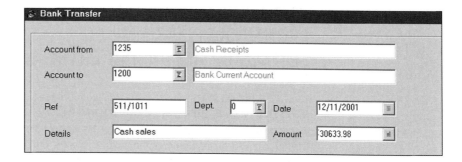

Here the shop takings for the week are being paid into the bank on a paying-in slip on Monday. The amount is transferred from Cash Receipts Account to Bank Current Account. The balance on the Cash Receipts Account should then revert to nil as all the money will have left the premises.

RECURRING PAYMENTS AND RECEIPTS

Recurring entries are payments or transfers which are made monthly or weekly or at other intervals. Businesses, for example

- ■ *receive* recurring payments, for example rent from an office owned
- ■ *make* recurring payments, for example loan repayments, insurance premiums

These payments are often made direct from the bank account of the payer to the bank account of the recipient ('beneficiary') by direct debit or standing order using the computer transfer BACS system.

If a business operates a manual accounting system these payments will be written individually in the cash book each time they are made or received – a laborious and time-consuming process. A business using a computer accounting system such as Sage can automate this procedure.

setting up recurring entries in Sage

The RECURRING ENTRIES routine is reached from the RECURRING icon on the BANK menu bar.

The RECURRING ENTRIES screen shows any existing entries already set up. If there are none, the screen will be blank.

To add a recurring entry, the Add button at the bottom of the screen should be clicked.

Now study the Case Study on the next two pages.

PRONTO SUPPLIES LIMITED:
SETTING UP RECURRING ENTRIES

setting up a recurring payment

Tom has set up a maintenance contract for his Xerax 566 photocopier. He has to pay £19.80 plus VAT every month for the next 12 months and has completed a direct debit form so that the money can be taken directly from Pronto's bank current account.

The RECURRING ENTRIES routine is reached from the RECURRING icon on the BANK menu bar.

The RECURRING ENTRIES screen is blank because there are no existing recurring entries.To add a recurring entry, Tom clicks the Add button at the bottom of the screen and then inputs the details as follows:

Add / Edit Recurring Entry		☒
Trans. Type	Payment ▼	
Bank A/C	1200 ⫶	Bank Current Account
Nominal Code	7701 ⫶	Office Machine Maintenance
Ref	DD	
Details	Zerax 566 maintenance	
Department	0 ▼	
Day to post	15 ☐ Use Program Date	
Last Posted	☐ Suspend Posting	

Net Amount `19.80 ▥` Tax Code `T1 17.50 ▼` VAT `3.47 ▥`

OK   Cancel

Note the following:

- ▓ Tom indicates that the entry is a Payment
- ▓ he inputs the bank account and nominal account to be used (which is already set up on the Chart of Accounts)
- ▓ the reference is 'DD" which stands for Direct Debit
- ▓ the details explain what the payment is
- ▓ the transfer date is the 15th of the month
- ▓ the VAT (tax) code is entered to generate the VAT amount

setting up a recurring receipt

Pronto Supplies receives regular monthly rent payments of £456 (plus VAT) from the tenant of a small office at 10A High Street. The payment is made by standing order to the bank current account.

Tom clicks the Add button at the bottom of the RECURRING ENTRIES and then inputs the details as follows:

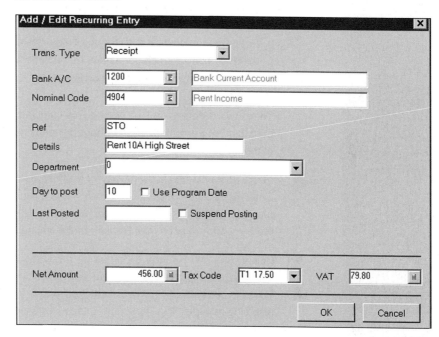

Note the following:

- Tom indicates that the entry is a Receipt

- he inputs the bank account and nominal account to be used (which is already set up on the Chart of Accounts)

- the reference is 'STO' which stands for Standing Order

- the details explain what the payment is

- the transfer date is the 10th of the month

- the VAT (tax) code is entered to generate the VAT amount

Tom returns to the RECURRING ENTRIES screen, which shows the two payments:

Tp	Ref	Details	Amount	Next Posting
BP	DD	Xerax 566 maintenance	23.27	
BR	STO	Rent 10A High Street	535.80	

Tom can choose whether to process all the payments for that month or just the payments up to that date. He will then click on the Process button. The program will only allow him to process a payment once a month.

■ Businesses can set up accounts on a computer accounting program for funds of money held by the business. These accounts are classified as 'bank' accounts, but the money is not held at the bank. The money for these accounts will come from the bank or will be paid into the bank and recorded in Sage by a Bank Transfer.

■ Payment 'Bank' accounts – in addition to the ordinary Bank Current Account include:
- Petty Cash Account – a cash fund held under lock and key in the office, used for making small purchases and payments
- Credit Card Account – records payments by employees on company credit cards

These two accounts will be 'topped up' regularly by a transfer from the bank current account (a cash cheque for petty cash and cheque payment of the credit card bill).

■ 'Bank' accounts for receiving payments may also be set up, for example a Cash Receipts account or a Credit Card account. These record money received from sales and held in the business. When the money is paid into the bank current account a Bank Transfer will be made on the computer.

■ Businesses use Recurring Entries on the computer accounting system to record regular payments made in and out of the bank current account. These include standing orders and direct debits for outgoing payments and incoming receipts. The Recurring Entries facility enables the business to set up the payments so that they can be recorded automatically each month in the accounts on the click of a button.

petty cash	a float of cash kept in the office for making small purchases
petty cash account	an account used to record payments of small cash purchases from the office petty cash fund
petty cash voucher	the document which records and authorises a payment out of petty cash
company credit card account	an account used to record payments made on credit cards issued to employees to cover business expenses
cash receipts account	an account used to record cash receipts made by a business where the money is kept for a time by the business before it is paid into the bank
recurring entry	a bank payment or receipt which occurs on a regular basis and which is automated within the computer accounting program

STUDENT ACTIVITIES

10.1 Which of the following accounts held in the 'Bank' section of the computer is not actually held by the bank of the business?

▪ Petty Cash Account   ▪ Cash Receipts Account   ▪ Bank Current Account

▪ Company Credit Card Account

10.2 What entries to the computer accounts are made when the Petty Cash system is operated? State which screens are used.

(a)   for payments into Petty Cash

(b)   for payments out of Petty Cash

10.3 You are getting some petty cash vouchers ready for input and notice some points which you think might cause problems:

(a)   A petty cash voucher for postage stamps does not have any VAT shown on it.

(b)   A petty cash voucher for stationery does not have any VAT shown on it.

(c)   A petty cash voucher does not have an authorisation signature on it.

Write down what you think should be done in these three situations?

10.4 R R Printers Limited is setting up a company credit card scheme whereby its sales reps can use company credit cards for business expenses.

(a)   How should the credit card scheme be set up in the company's computer accounting system? How would the scheme work?

(b)   What advantages are there for the business and the sales reps in such a scheme?

10.5 If a shop kept the cash and cheques taken from sales on the premises and only paid into the bank at the end of every week, it might set up a Cash Receipts Account on the computer.

(a)   Describe the entries the business would make to the Cash Receipts Account.

(b)   Write down two disadvantages to the business of keeping money on the premises.

10.6 Describe the circumstances in which a business might set up Recurring Entries on the computer.

PRONTO SUPPLIES INPUTTING TASK

warning note!
This activity involves you in inputting live data into the computer. This activity is only suitable if you are in a supervised training environment.

Task 1

Set the program date as 28 February 2001.

On 1 February Tom cashed cheque 122991 for £100 at his bank to set up a petty cash system.

Carry out a bank transfer from Bank Current Account to Petty Cash Account for this amount.

Task 2

Keep the program date as 28 February 2001.

Tom has just authorised two more petty cash vouchers (shown below). Input these together with the three petty cash vouchers on pages 132 to 133 into Bank Payments, taking particular care with the VAT element on each one (postages are VAT exempt and stationery is standard-rated). Print out a Day Books: Cash Payments (Summary) Report to confirm the accuracy of your input of the five vouchers. (Hint: remember to select the Petty Cash Bank account on screen before running the report).

petty cash voucher Number *PC104*

date *28 Feb 2001*

description	amount £	p
Postage stamps	*5*	*00*
VAT		
Receipt obtained	*5*	*00*

signature *R Cook*

authorised *Tom Cox*

petty cash voucher Number *PC105*

date *28 Feb 2001*

description	amount £	p
Stationery		
VAT		
Receipt obtained	*4*	*70*

signature *R Patel*

authorised *Tom Cox*

Task 3

Keep the program date as 28 February 2001.

Create an account for Cash Receipts within BANK using the number 1235. Designate the account a cash account. No bank reconciliation is required at present.

Tom sees that he has three days' of cash takings in the office safe and so decides to enter these in the Cash Receipts Account. Take care over selecting the correct Sales account number.

The details are as follows:

Date	Details	Net amount (£)	VAT (£)	ref.
26 Feb 2001	Hardware sales	5,000.00	875.00	10743
26 Feb 2001	Software sales	480.00	84.00	10743
27 Feb 2001	Hardware sales	1,200.00	210.00	10744
27 Feb 2001	Software sales	890.00	155.75	10744
28 Feb 2001	Hardware sales	600.00	105.00	10745
28 Feb 2001	Software sales	120.00	21.00	10745
	Totals	8,290.00	1,450.75	

Enter these transactions, check the totals, SAVE and print out a Cash Receipts (Detailed) Day Book.

Task 4

Keep the program date as 28 February 2001.

Create Recurring Entries for the two payments in the Case Study on pages 138 to 139.

You will need to ensure that you have the following nominal accounts open:

   7701 Office Machine Maintenance Account   4904   Rent Income Account

The payments are as follows:

1   Direct debit to Zerax Machines for £19.80 plus VAT (T1) for the maintenance of a Xerax 566 photocopier paid on the 15th of the month, starting in February 2001.

2   Standing order from rent income of 10A High Street, received 10th of each month, starting in February 2001. The amount received is £456 plus VAT (T1). (Pronto Supplies is VAT registered).

When the recurring entries have been set up, process them for February.

Note that when you subsequently enter the Sage program you may get a message asking you if you want to process recurring entries. You should select the NO answer (unless of course you do want to!).

Task 5

Keep the program date as 28 February 2001. Print out from FINANCIALS:

(a)   an audit trail (brief version) of all the transactions on the computer so far

(b)   a Trial Balance as at 28 February 2001 (this can be checked against the Trial Balance on page 245)

Check with your tutor that all your input to date is accurate. These reports will be dealt with in the next chapter. Corrections of errors will be dealt with in Chapter 12.

Reminder! Have you made a backup?

chapter introduction

■ One of the major advantages of running a computer accounting system is that it will provide the business manager and administrative staff with a wide range of reports – on demand.

■ These reports are often produced at the end of each month to enable the business to check regularly the accuracy of its records and to ensure that customer and supplier payments are being made on time.

■ The reports that can be produced to help with checking the accuracy of the records include:

• the trial balance – a full list of the Nominal account balances

• the audit trail – a full numbered list of the transactions input on the computer in order of input

■ The reports that can be produced to help with dealing with customers and suppliers include:

• 'aged' analyses – separate lists of customers and suppliers which show what payments are due and when

• activity reports – lists of transactions on individual accounts

• account lists – lists of customers and suppliers with telephone numbers

• label lists – names and addresses of customers and suppliers – suitable for mailing labels

• customer statements – sent to each sales ledger customer, listing transactions and telling the customer the amount that is due

■ The end of the month is also a good time to process recurring entries and other regular account transfers and to tidy up transaction files (deleting items that are not needed any more).

■ The business in the Case Study – Pronto Supplies Limited – has reached the end of February and so will be used in this chapter to illustrate the various reports and routines and their uses.

THE IMPORTANCE OF INFORMATION

information for management

The accounting system of any business – whether hand-written or computer-based – contains important information for management and provides an accurate basis for decision-making. The advantage of using a computer accounting system is that this information is available instantly.

The **trial balance** is a list of the Nominal account balances at a set date – which is often the last day of the month. The figures are set out in balancing debit and credit columns to prove the accuracy of the book-keeping entries. If the column totals are not the same, there is likely to be one or more errors in the double-entry book-keeping – if a manual system is used. Computerised trial balances *should* normally balance.

The trial balance figures show how much money there is in the bank and provides management with details about sales and expense accounts.

information for finance and administrative staff

The computer accounting program also enables finance and administrative staff to extract useful information, for example:

- The **audit trail** is a full list of the transactions input into the computer, presented in order of input. Accounts staff will use the audit trail to check the accuracy of the input and trace any discrepancies and errors.

- The analysis of customer accounts (the **aged debtor analysis**) tells credit control staff which customers need chasing for payment and which debts may need writing off.

- The analysis of supplier accounts (the **aged creditor analysis**) tells accounts staff which bills and invoices need paying and when.

- The computer will also produce **activity reports** on individual customer and supplier accounts; these list all the transactions on each individual account and are useful to bring up on screen when a customer telephones in with a query.

- Computer-produced **account lists** set out the names, account codes and telephone numbers of customers and suppliers. These are useful to sales and accounts staff when contacting customers and suppliers and when coding invoices and credit notes.

- The computer will also produce the names and addresses of customers and suppliers on **labels**, which is useful when doing a promotional mailing or a change of address notification

We will now illustrate these procedures with a continuation of the Case Study.

CASE STUDY

PRONTO SUPPLIES LIMITED: END-OF-MONTH REPORTS

It is 28 February 2001. Tom Cox has completed the input into his computer accounting system. Looking back over the month he can see that he has:

- set up the company details and the Nominal ledger balances as they stood at the beginning of February
- entered customer and supplier records and balances as they stood at the beginning of February
- input customer and supplier invoices and credit notes processed during February
- input payments received from customers and sent to suppliers during February
- input cash receipts and payments for February
- set up a petty cash system and recurring entries for standing orders and direct debits

trial balance

Tom first extracts his Trial Balance as at the end of February. He does this by clicking on TRIAL on the FINANCIALS menu bar. His printout is shown below.

	Pronto Supplies Limited		**Page:** 1
	Period Trial Balance		

To Period: Month 2, February 2001

N/C	Name	Debit	Credit
0020	Plant and Machinery	35,000.00	
0030	Office Equipment	19,760.00	
0040	Furniture and Fixtures	30,000.00	
1100	Debtors Control Account	8,991.00	
1200	Bank Current Account	30,174.98	
1230	Petty Cash	4.20	
1235	Cash Receipts	9,740.75	
2100	Creditors Control Account		11,797.00
2200	Sales Tax Control Account		30,150.75
2201	Purchase Tax Control Account	35,281.02	
2300	Loans		35,000.00
3000	Ordinary Shares		80,000.00
4000	Computer hardware sales		138,980.00
4001	Computer software sales		30,214.00
4002	Computer consultancy		2,640.00
4904	Rent Income		456.00
5000	Materials Purchased	93,362.00	
6201	Advertising	22,600.00	
7000	Gross Wages	33,010.00	
7100	Rent	9,000.00	
7103	General Rates	800.00	
7200	Electricity	308.00	
7501	Postage and Carriage	30.00	
7502	Telephone	585.00	
7504	Office Stationery	571.00	
7701	Office Machine Maintenance	19.80	
	Totals:	329,237.75	329,237.75

The trial balance shows the balances of the Nominal accounts. The debit money column on the left equals the credit money column on the right because in double entry book-keeping debit entries always equal credit entries.

If in a manual accounting system the two columns totals were not the same, there could be one or more errors in the book-keeping entries. In a computer-based system the totals should always be the same because the computer generates equal debits and credits from every entry. If Tom's column totals were not the same it would mean that the computer data had become corrupted, which could be a major problem. Fortunately this is not the case!

audit trail

As a further check (and also to satisfy his accountants) Tom prints out an audit trail which shows each transaction entered into the computer in order of input. This is done from the AUDIT icon on the FINANCIALS menu bar. An extract is shown below.

Pronto Supplies Limited
Audit Trail (Brief)

Page: 2

No	Items	Tp	A/C	Date	Refn	Details	Net	Tax	Gross
45	1	SI	LG001	17/01/2001	10019	Opening Balance	8,500.00	0.00	8,500.00
46	1	SI	JG001	23/01/2001	10020	Opening Balance	3,480.00	0.00	3,480.00
47	1	SI	ME001	23/01/2001	10021	Opening Balance	4,300.00	0.00	4,300.00
48	1	SI	PT001	26/01/2001	10022	Opening Balance	2,586.00	0.00	2,586.00
49	1	PI	DE001	04/01/2001	4563	Opening Balance	5,750.00	0.00	5,750.00
50	1	PI	EL001	05/01/2001	81222	Opening Balance	8,500.00	0.00	8,500.00
51	1	PI	MA001	09/01/2001	9252	Opening Balance	4,500.00	0.00	4,500.00
52	1	PI	SY001	16/01/2001	1094	Opening Balance	7,600.00	0.00	7,600.00
53	1	PI	TY001	17/01/2001	3455	Opening Balance	6,160.00	0.00	6,160.00
54	1	SI	JB001	05/02/2001	10023	1 x 17" Monitor	400.00	70.00	470.00
55	1	SI	CH001	06/02/2001	10024	1 x printer lead	16.00	2.80	18.80
56	1	SI	CR001	06/02/2001	10025	1 x Macroworx	100.00	17.50	117.50
57	1	SI	KD001	08/02/2001	10026	2 hours consultancy	120.00	21.00	141.00
58	1	SC	DB001	06/02/2001	551	Software return	200.00	35.00	235.00
59	1	SC	FE001	06/02/2001	552	Disks returned	40.00	7.00	47.00
60	1	SI	JB001	12/02/2001	10027	2 hours consultancy	120.00	21.00	141.00
61	1	SI	DB001	13/02/2001	10028	1 x EF102 printer	200.00	35.00	235.00
62	1	SI	FE001	14/02/2001	10029	1 x QuorkEdit softwar	400.00	70.00	470.00
63	1	SI	LG001	16/02/2001	10030	2 x Zap drive	180.00	31.50	211.50
64	1	SI	JG001	16/02/2001	10031	1 x Fileperfect softwar	264.00	46.20	310.20
65	1	SI	PT001	16/02/2001	10032	1 x 15" Monitor	320.00	56.00	376.00
66	1	SC	JG001	12/02/2001	553	1 x printer lead faulty	16.00	2.80	18.80
67	1	SC	ME001	13/02/2001	554	Zap disks returned	20.00	3.50	23.50
68	1	PI	DE001	09/02/2001	11365	Desktop computers	3,600.00	630.00	4,230.00
69	1	PI	EL001	09/02/2001	8576	Peripherals	2,000.00	350.00	2,350.00
70	1	PI	MA001	12/02/2001	2947	Powerbooks	2,400.00	420.00	2,820.00
71	1	PI	SY001	16/02/2001	34983	Software	1,280.00	224.00	1,504.00
72	1	PC	DE001	06/02/2001	7223	1 x computer	480.00	84.00	564.00
73	1	PC	MA001	08/02/2001	552	1 x optical mouse	38.00	6.65	44.65
74	1	PI	DE001	14/02/2001	11377	Desktop computers	400.00	70.00	470.00
75	1	PI	EL001	14/02/2001	8603	Laser printer	360.00	63.00	423.00
76	1	SR	JB001	28/02/2001	chq	Sales Receipt	5,500.00	0.00	5,500.00
77	1	SR	CH001	28/02/2001	chq	Sales Receipt	2,400.00	0.00	2,400.00
78	1	SR	CR001	28/02/2001	chq	Sales Receipt	3,234.00	0.00	3,234.00

Every transaction input into the computer (within the time period stipulated) is shown on the audit trail. The columns of the audit trail show, from the left . . .

• the unique number allocated by the computer to the transaction

  • the nature of the transaction, for example SI = sales invoice, PI = purchase invoice

- the account into which the item is entered
- the date of the transaction (not necessarily the date of input!)
- the transaction reference input at the time
- the description of the transaction
- the net amount, any VAT and the gross amount

Tom could choose to print out the detailed audit trail (extract shown below), but only if he needs the level of detail it provides.

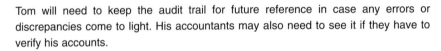

Pronto Supplies Limited
Audit Trail (Detailed)

Page: 5

No	Tp	A/C	N/C	Dp	Details	Date	Refn	Net	Tax	T/C	Pd	Paid	V	B
93	BR	1200				16/02/2001	10739	3,680.00	644.00		Y	4,324.00	-	
		93	4001	0	Software sales			3,680.00	644.00	T1		4,324.00	N	
94	BR	1200				23/02/2001	10740	17,800.00	3,115.00		Y	20,915.00	-	
		94	4000	0	Hardware sales			17,800.00	3,115.00	T1		20,915.00	N	
95	BR	1200				23/02/2001	10741	4,800.00	840.00		Y	5,640.00	-	
		95	4001	0	Software sales			4,800.00	840.00	T1		5,640.00	N	
96	BP	1200				12/02/2001	122992	15,500.00	2,712.50		Y	18,212.50	-	
		96	5000	0	Cash purchases			15,500.00	2,712.50	T1		18,212.50	N	

Tom will need to keep the audit trail for future reference in case any errors or discrepancies come to light. His accountants may also need to see it if they have to verify his accounts.

aged debtors analysis

It is important to Tom that he knows that his customers who buy on credit pay up on time. The credit period is indicated to them on the bottom of each invoice. Tom allows his customers 30 days from the date of the invoice in which to pay.

An Aged Debtors Analysis shows the amount owing by each customer and splits it up according to the length of time it has been outstanding. The Aged Debtors Analysis can be printed from the REPORTS icon on the CUSTOMERS menu bar. (Note that you cannot print from the screen reached through the AGED icon on CUSTOMERS).

Tom's Aged Debtors Analysis as at 28 February 2001 is shown below:

Pronto Supplies Limited
Aged Debtors Analysis (Summary)

Page: 1

Report Date: 28/02/2001
Include future transactions: No
Exclude later payments: No

Customer From:
Customer To: ZZZZZZZZZ

A/C	Name	Crd Limit	Turnover	Balance	Future	Current	Period 1	Period 2	Period 3	Older
CH001	Charisma Design	5,000.00	2,416.00	18.80	0.00	18.80	0.00	0.00	0.00	0.00
CR001	Crowmatic Limited	5,000.00	3,334.00	117.50	0.00	117.50	0.00	0.00	0.00	0.00
DB001	David Boossey	5,000.00	3,400.00	235.00	0.00	235.00	0.00	0.00	0.00	0.00
FE001	French Emporium	10,000.00	5,960.00	470.00	0.00	470.00	0.00	0.00	0.00	0.00
JB001	John Butler & Associates	10,000.00	6,020.00	611.00	0.00	611.00	0.00	0.00	0.00	0.00
JG001	Jo Green Systems	5,000.00	3,728.00	310.20	0.00	310.20	0.00	0.00	0.00	0.00
KD001	Kay Denz	10,000.00	6,620.00	6,641.00	0.00	141.00	6,500.00	0.00	0.00	0.00
LG001	L Garr & Co	15,000.00	8,680.00	211.50	0.00	211.50	0.00	0.00	0.00	0.00
PT001	Prism Trading Limited	5,000.00	2,906.00	376.00	0.00	376.00	0.00	0.00	0.00	0.00
	Totals:		43,064.00	8,991.00	0.00	2,491.00	6,500.00	0.00	0.00	0.00

The columns show (from left to right)

- the customer name and account number
- the credit limit (the maximum amount of credit Tom will allow on the account)
- the turnover (total net sales for each customer in the current financial year)
- the balance (the total balance on the customer's account)
- any transactions dated in future months
- 'current' invoices are invoices less than 30 days old, period 1 is 30 to 59 days, period 2 is 60 to 89 days, and so on

Note that the Report can be dated at any date required. Here it is dated 28 February.

The Report shows the following:

- All the accounts are trading within their credit limits (ie the figure in the 'Balance' column is less than the 'Crd Limit' column) – this is a good sign.
- There is one account – Kay Denz – which has an invoice outstanding for more than 30 days. Tom will need to keep an eye on this account and to chase it up by sending a reminder or telephoning Kay Denz to find out when the payment is coming.
- The total of the Balance column shows that Pronto Supplies Limited is owed a total of £8,991.00 on 28 February. As a further check this figure should be agreed with the balance of Debtors Control Account on the Trial Balance (see page 146).

aged creditors analysis

Tom also needs to check on the amounts that Pronto Supplies Limited owes its Suppliers (creditors) for goods purchased, and to make sure that there are no amounts outstanding for longer than they should be. The Aged Creditors Analysis enables him to do this. It can be printed from REPORTS on the SUPPLIERS menu bar. The layout of the columns works on the same principles as the Aged Debtors Analysis (see above).

Pronto Supplies Limited

Aged Creditors Analysis (Summary)

Page: 1

Report Date:		28/02/2001					Supplier From:			
Include future transactions:		No					Supplier To:	ZZZZZZZZ		
Exclude Later Payments:		No								

A/C	Name	C Limit	Turnover	Balance	Future	Current	Period 1	Period 2	Period 3	Older
DE001	Delco PLC	10,000.00	9,270.00	4,700.00	0.00	4,700.00	0.00	0.00	0.00	0.00
EL001	Electron Supplies	15,000.00	10,860.00	2,773.00	0.00	2,773.00	0.00	0.00	0.00	0.00
MA001	MacCity	10,000.00	6,862.00	2,820.00	0.00	2,820.00	0.00	0.00	0.00	0.00
SY001	Synchromart	15,000.00	8,880.00	1,504.00	0.00	1,504.00	0.00	0.00	0.00	0.00
	Totals:		35,872.00	11,797.00	0.00	11,797.00	0.00	0.00	0.00	0.00

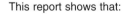

This report shows that:

- Pronto Supplies Limited is up-to-date with payments to suppliers – all amounts due are 'Current', ie there is nothing outstanding for more than 30 days.
- The total owed by Pronto Supplies Limited is £11,797.00 on 28 February. As a further check this figure should be agreed with the balance of Creditors Control Account on the Trial Balance (see page 146).

activity reports

Tom wants to find out about the activity on the account of Kay Denz, the customer who has not paid her invoice on time. The screen version can be seen by clicking on the ACTIVITY icon on the CUSTOMERS menu bar with the appropriate account selected.

If Tom wants to print out this report he will have to select the account on the CUSTOMERS screen and click on the REPORTS icon to select the Customer Activity (Summary) Report. The report shows that the overdue amount was an invoice for £6,500, issued on 10 January 2001 and input into the computer as an Opening Balance. This is the item Tom may decide to chase up.

Pronto Supplies Limited
Customer Activity (Summary)   Page: 1

Date From:	01/01/2001				Customer From:		
Date To:	28/02/2001				Customer To:	ZZZZZZZZ	
Inc b/fwd transaction:	No				Transaction From:	1	
Exc later payment:	No				Transaction To:	99999999	

A/C: KD001   Name: Kay Denz   Contact: Tel: 01908 624945

No	Items	Tp	Date	Refn	Details	Value	O/S	Debit	Credit
43	1	SI	10/01/2001	10017	Opening Balance	6,500.00 *	6,500.00	6,500.00	
57	1	SI	08/02/2001	10026	2 hours consultancy	141.00 *	141.00	141.00	
						6,641.00	6,641.00	6,641.00	0.00

Amount Outstanding   6,641.00
Amount Paid this period   0.00
Credit Limit   10,000.00

other useful reports

Tom has also printed from his computer an alphabetically sorted account list of customers, together with their contact numbers. These are run as a Customer List Report from the REPORTS icon on the CUSTOMERS menu bar.

Pronto Supplies Limited
Customer List

Customer From:
Customer To: ZZZZZZZZ

A/C	Name	Contact Name	Telephone	Fax
CH001	Charisma Design	Lindsay Foster	01908 345287	01908 345983
CR001	Crowmatic Limited	John Crow	01908 674237	01908 674345
DB001	David Boossey		01908 333981	01908 333761
FE001	French Emporium	Henri Fevrier	01621 444342	01621 444976
JB001	John Butler & Associates	John Butler	01908 824342	01908 824295
JG001	Jo Green Systems	Jo Green	01908 234974	01908 234956
KD001	Kay Denz		01908 624945	01908 624945
LG001	L Garr & Co	Ted Nigmer	01621 333691	01621 333982
ME001	Mendell & Son	Felix Mendell	01908 234116	01908 234387
PT001	Prism Trading Limited	Helen Lenz	01908 748083	01908 748423

The same exercise can be carried out from the SUPPLIERS menu bar to produce a list of Suppliers with contact numbers.

The computer will also enable Tom to print out name and address labels for Customers and Suppliers. This could be very useful when marketing products to Customers – sending out a catalogue, for example. The labels can be printed by clicking on the LABELS icon on the CUSTOMERS or SUPPLIERS menu bar and selecting the appropriate label format. The labels shown below are extracted from Tom's Customer details printed as Laser Sales Labels.

Lindsay Foster	John Crow	
Charisma Design	Crowmatic Limited	David Boossey
36 Dingle Road	Unit 12 Severnside Estate	17 Harebell Road
Mereford	Mereford	Mereford Green
MR2 8GF	MR3 6FD	MR6 4NB

customer statements

At the end of each month Tom will print out statements and send them to his Customers. This can be done in Sage from the STATEMENT icon on the CUSTOMER menu bar. A suitable format can then be chosen from the list shown on the screen. The statements set out the transactions on the Customer account and state the amount owing. Statements are important documents because many customers will pay from the monthly statement rather than the invoice.

OTHER MONTH-END ROUTINES

It is important for a business with a computer accounting system to establish an end-of-month routine which will include the production of the reports illustrated in the Case Study.

There are, of course, other month-end routines involving the computer accounting system . . .

checking that all transactions have been input

The business must check that all the necessary transactions – sales and purchases transactions, payments made and received – have been input into the computer before extracting the reports.

recurring entries

Recurring entries – standing orders and direct debits – are often processed monthly, and it should become part of the month-end routine to ensure that this is done. Sage helps by displaying a warning message on the screen when you open the program up, letting you know if there are outstanding recurring entries.

advanced month-end entries

Sage also allows you to process other monthly entries which fall outside the scope of this book. The month-end procedure is reached from TOOLS on the main menu bar. For your information these include:

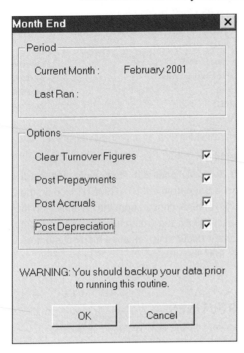

- **depreciation** – regular reductions in the value of assets which are entered in the accounts each month

- **prepayments** – payments made in advance of the time period to which they relate; for example, an annual insurance premium paid in January can be spread out over twelve months

- **accruals** – payments made after the time period to which they relate; for example, a telephone bill for call charges paid at the end of a quarter can be estimated and spread over the previous three months

clearing turnover figures from the audit trail

The audit trail is a list of all your transactions set out in order of input. If you are running a large business this list can grow very long and cumbersome. A long list will slow down the computer when you are carrying out operations such as running reports. Sage allows you, as part of the month-end routine, to clear out transactions that you are unlikely to need to refer to. The month-end procedure is reached from TOOLS on the main menu bar. These transactions include common items such as

- sales invoices which have been issued to customers and paid
- purchase invoices which have been received from suppliers and paid

If you are faced with clearing the turnover figures it is critical that you **first of all**

- print out an up-to-date audit trail
- back up your data and keep a secure copy

As far as small businesses such as Pronto Supplies are concerned, clearing the turnover figures is best left to the end of the financial year (December 31 in the case of Pronto Supplies). This is for two reasons:

- there are relatively few transactions anyway
- the full audit trail is a useful check on activity when you are in a training situation

**CHAPTER
SUMMARY**

- A computer accounting system has the advantage that it can provide a wide range of useful printed reports quickly and accurately. These are useful both for the management of the business and also for accounts assistants.

- Reports can be produced to help with checking the accuracy of the records. These are often produced at the end of each month and include:
  - the trial balance – a full list of the Nominal account balances
  - the audit trail – a numbered list of transactions set out in order of input on the computer

- Reports can be produced to help with day-to-day dealings with customers and suppliers. Month-end reports include:
  - 'aged' analyses – separate lists of customers and suppliers which show when payments are due and hence if any payments are overdue
  - activity reports – lists of transactions on individual accounts which need to be looked into

  Other day-to-day useful printouts include:
  - account lists – lists of customers and suppliers with telephone numbers
  - label lists – names and addresses of customers and suppliers – suitable for mailing labels

- The end-of-month is the time to process recurring entries and other regular account transfers. It can also be the opportunity to tidy up the audit trail and remove transaction records that are no longer needed.

**KEY
TERMS**

trial balance	a list of Nominal account balances set out in debit and credit columns, the totals of which should be the same
audit trail	a numbered list of transactions on the computer produced in order of input
aged debtor analysis	a list of Customer (debtor) balances which are split up according to the length of time they have been outstanding
aged creditor analysis	a list of Supplier (creditor) balances which are split up according to the length of time they have been outstanding
activity report	a list of transactions on individual Customer and Supplier accounts
recurring entry	a bank payment or receipt which occurs on a regular basis – often monthly – and which is automated within the computer accounting program

STUDENT
ACTIVITIES

11.1   What is the purpose of a trial balance in a manual accounting system?

11.2   Why should the debit and credit columns in a trial balance add up to the same total when a computer accounting system is used?

11.3   What else does a trial balance tell the owner of a business?

11.4   An audit trail is a numbered list of transactions input into a computer accounting system. How is it set out – in date order or in order of input?

11.5   A computer accounting system normally has the facility to remove from the audit trail transactions that are no longer needed – paid invoices, for example. Why should a business want to remove transactions from the audit trail?

11.6   What are the two security procedures that should always be carried out before removing items from an audit trail?

11.7   What is the main purpose of

(a)   an Aged Debtors Analysis?

(b)   an Aged Creditors Analysis?

11.8   The Aged Debtors Analysis of Pronto Supplies Limited as at 28 February 2001 is shown below. Pronto Supplies allows customers to pay up to 30 days from the date of the invoice.

	Pronto Supplies Limited									Page:	1
	Aged Debtors Analysis (Summary)										

Report Date:	28/02/2001						Customer From:				
Include future transactions:	No						Customer To:		ZZZZZZZZ		
Exclude later payments:	No										

A/C	Name	Crd Limit	Turnover	Balance	Future	Current	Period 1	Period 2	Period 3	Older
CH001	Charisma Design	5,000.00	2,416.00	18.80	0.00	18.80	0.00	0.00	0.00	0.00
CR001	Crowmatic Limited	5,000.00	3,334.00	117.50	0.00	117.50	0.00	0.00	0.00	0.00
DB001	David Boossey	5,000.00	3,400.00	235.00	0.00	235.00	0.00	0.00	0.00	0.00
FE001	French Emporium	10,000.00	5,960.00	470.00	0.00	470.00	0.00	0.00	0.00	0.00
JB001	John Butler & Associates	10,000.00	6,020.00	611.00	0.00	611.00	0.00	0.00	0.00	0.00
JG001	Jo Green Systems	5,000.00	3,728.00	310.20	0.00	310.20	0.00	0.00	0.00	0.00
KD001	Kay Denz	10,000.00	6,620.00	6,641.00	0.00	141.00	6,500.00	0.00	0.00	0.00
LG001	L Garr & Co	15,000.00	8,680.00	211.50	0.00	211.50	0.00	0.00	0.00	0.00
PT001	Prism Trading Limited	5,000.00	2,906.00	376.00	0.00	376.00	0.00	0.00	0.00	0.00
	Totals:		43,064.00	8,991.00	0.00	2,491.00	6,500.00	0.00	0.00	0.00

(a)   Are there any customers who might give the manager of the business cause for concern? Why? What other report could the manager print out to give him more information?

(b)   What is the total amount owed by the customers of Pronto Supplies Limited?

(c)   Against which figure in the Trial Balance should this total in (b) be checked?

11.9   The Trial Balance of Pronto Supplies Limited as at 28 February 2001 is shown below. Study the figures and answer the questions that follow.

Pronto Supplies Limited   Page: 1
Period Trial Balance

To Period: Month 2, February 2001

N/C	Name	Debit	Credit
0020	Plant and Machinery	35,000.00	
0030	Office Equipment	19,760.00	
0040	Furniture and Fixtures	30,000.00	
1100	Debtors Control Account	8,991.00	
1200	Bank Current Account	30,174.98	
1230	Petty Cash	4.20	
1235	Cash Receipts	9,740.75	
2100	Creditors Control Account		11,797.00
2200	Sales Tax Control Account		30,150.75
2201	Purchase Tax Control Account	35,281.02	
2300	Loans		35,000.00
3000	Ordinary Shares		80,000.00
4000	Computer hardware sales		138,980.00
4001	Computer software sales		30,214.00
4002	Computer consultancy		2,640.00
4904	Rent Income		456.00
5000	Materials Purchased	93,362.00	
6201	Advertising	22,600.00	
7000	Gross Wages	33,010.00	
7100	Rent	9,000.00	
7103	General Rates	800.00	
7200	Electricity	308.00	
7501	Postage and Carriage	30.00	
7502	Telephone	585.00	
7504	Office Stationery	571.00	
7701	Office Machine Maintenance	19.80	
	Totals:	**329,237.75**	**329,237.75**

(a)   How much money has the company got in the bank?

(b)   How much money has the company got on the premises?

(c)   What is the company's total sales income (excluding rent) for the period up to 28 February?

(d)   Compare this trial balance with the trial balance at the beginning of the month (see page 73) and comment on changes to two debit balances and changes to two credit balances. Explain what has happened in each case.

11.10   The Administration Supervisor of Pronto Supplies asks for:

(a)   a list of customers together with their contact telephone numbers

(b)   a set of labels for sending seasonal greetings cards to the company's suppliers

Print out the two reports the supervisor needs.

Optional task: Export the relevant reports from the Sage system (either by e-mail or by saving in an appropriate format) and transfer the data into a word-processing program (the list) and a database program (the labels file). See Chapter 1 for explanations of this procedure.

11.11   Print a selection of Customer statements for Pronto Supplies Limited as at the end of February 2001. You will need to select a suitable format from the list produced through the STATEMENT icon on the CUSTOMERS menu bar. Note: your tutor may suggest that you print out only one or two statements in order to save on the consumables bill!

■ When you are operating a computer accounting program it is inevitable that errors will be made. These might be your own input errors or they might be errors on the part of a customer or a supplier. Whatever the source of the error might be, it will have to be put right.

■ The sort of errors that might occur include:
  • an incorrect description
  • an incorrect price of goods on a sales invoice
  • the wrong VAT rate applied
  • the wrong account used

■ The CORRECTIONS function contained in Sage will enable you to change most details on invoices, credit notes and payments. It is most commonly used for internal corrections – before any documents are sent out of the business.

■ The JOURNAL function contained in Sage is used for transferring amounts from one nominal account to another. One of its uses is therefore for correcting mistakes where the wrong nominal account number has been used. A knowledge of the use of debits and credits is needed for the JOURNAL.

■ If a significant mistake – for example a wrong amount – is discovered after an invoice has been sent out, the invoice will normally be cancelled by a credit note and a new invoice issued in its place. An invoice or credit note can also be cancelled if it has been input on the computer but has not yet been sent out.

■ If data on the computer has become corrupted or is in such a mess that it needs to be input again, Sage provides a REBUILD function which will set up all or part of the accounts again ready for the re-input of data. This is a very drastic measure.

■ The computer also allows you to make adjustments to the records, for example:
  • you need to 'write off' a customer account because you consider you will never get the money – the customer may have become a bankrupt, for example
  • you need to refund a customer because he or she has paid too much
  • you need to cancel a cheque you have written or you have received a cheque which has 'bounced' (been returned by the customer's bank)

THE CORRECTIONS FUNCTION

You will be able to correct most input errors within Sage using the CORRECTIONS function which is part of MAINTENANCE reached through the FILE icon on the main menu bar.

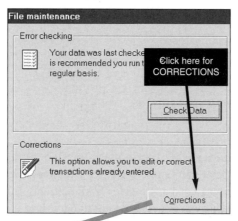

This leads to a screen which lists all the transactions which have passed through the computer accounting system and are available for correction.

You highlight the transaction which needs correcting (see screen below) and click on Edit to bring up the screen shown at the bottom of the page.

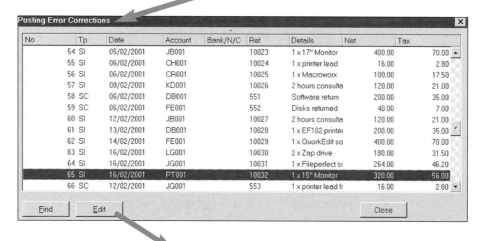

There are three tabs on this screen. The first tab shows the details of (in this case) the sales invoice; the second tab sets out the amount and the third tab any subdivisions (splits) of the amount - for example an invoice with three items on it.

The possible corrections include:

■ the account to which the invoice is posted

■ the product description

■ the amount charged

■ the VAT rate and VAT amount

JOURNAL ENTRIES

Journal entries enable you to make transfers from one nominal account to another. Journal entries are used, for example, when you are completing a VAT return and need to transfer VAT amounts from one VAT account to another. It is also useful if you want to put things right when you have input an entry to the wrong account.

journals and double entry

You need to be confident about **double-entry** book-keeping and using debits and credits when doing journal entries. You will have to decide which accounts have debit entries and which accounts have credit entries. The rule is that for every transaction there are balancing debit and credit entries:

debits	=	money paid into the bank
		purchases and expenses
		an increase in an asset
credits	=	payments out of the bank
		sales and income
		an increase in a liability

If you are still in any doubt about debits and credits, use CORRECTIONS wherever possible to adjust account entries. If you want to learn about double-entry, read Chapter 14 (pages 186 to 200).

example

Suppose you were inputting a batch of Bank Payments which included a number of bills that had to be paid. You have written out a cheque for £94 to RPower for a gas bill, but when inputting it you thought it was for electricity and so posted it to electricity (nominal account 7200) instead of gas (7201).

the solution

You could either use CORRECTIONS, but as you are a double-entry expert you choose to correct your mistake using a journal entry. You bring up the screen by clicking on the JOURNALS icon on the NOMINAL menu bar:

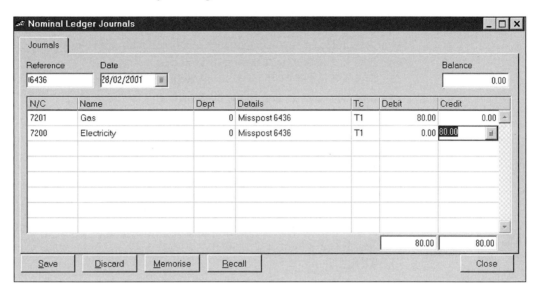

The procedure is:

- enter your reference (this could be the transaction number you can find by opening up the FINANCIALS screen and locating the transaction)
- enter the nominal code of the account to which you are going to post the debit; here it is Gas Account because you are recording an expense
- enter the reason for the transaction – here you are adjusting a mispost
- enter the VAT tax code input on the original (wrong) entry
- enter the net amount in the debit column (ie the amount before VAT has been added on) – here the net amount is £80 and VAT (assumed here at standard rate) is £14 and the total is £94; note that neither the VAT nor the total appear on the screen because you are not adjusting the VAT; *only the net amount* has gone to the wrong account

then on the next line . . .

- enter the nominal code of the account to which you are going to post the credit; here it is Electricity Account because you are effectively refunding the amount to the account – it is an income item and so a credit
- enter the remaining data as you did for the debit, but enter the net amount in the right-hand credit column
- make sure the Balance box reads zero – meaning that the debit equals the credit – and SAVE

CORRECTION BY DOCUMENT

Documents such as invoices have to be checked carefully before they are despatched because once they have been sent out by the business they cannot be changed. They must instead be replaced.

For example, an invoice sent to a customer with a wrong price used, or a mistake in calculation, a wrong discount, or a wrong VAT code, will need to be refunded in full by the issue of a credit note. A second and correct invoice will then have to be sent to the customer.

The net effect of all this on the accounting system and the input into a computer accounting system is that the final amount owing by the customer will be correct.

If, on the other hand, a problem is discovered with an invoice or credit note *before* it has been sent out, it can be deleted through the 'Details' tab in CORRECTIONS and a replacement document issued and input.

REBUILD

The REBUILD function is exactly what it says it is. Sage provides the facility to reconstruct selections of data files. This could happen for one of two reasons:

■ the data is corrupted – something has gone wrong with the computer and the data cannot be used because the program will not work properly

■ the data is dummy data – for example in a training situation where new 'companies' are set up each time a new set of exercises is started and the old data has to be deleted

REBUILD can be reached from MAINTENANCE through the FILE icon on the main menu bar:

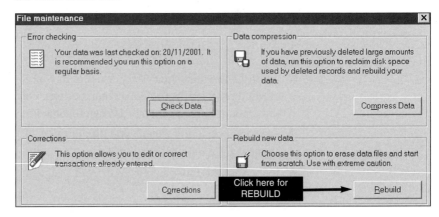

THE CORRECTIONS FUNCTION

You will be able to correct most input errors within Sage using the CORRECTIONS function which is part of MAINTENANCE reached through the FILE icon on the main menu bar.

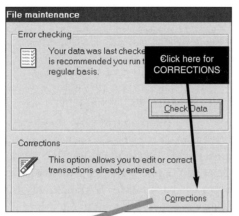

This leads to a screen which lists all the transactions which have passed through the computer accounting system and are available for correction.

You highlight the transaction which needs correcting (see screen below) and click on Edit to bring up the screen shown at the bottom of the page.

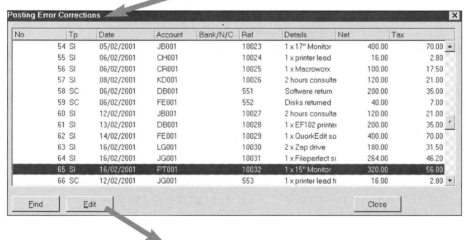

No		Tp	Date	Account	Bank/N/C	Ref	Details	Net	Tax
54	SI	05/02/2001	JB001		10023	1 x 17" Monitor	400.00	70.00
55	SI	06/02/2001	CH001		10024	1 x printer lead	16.00	2.80
56	SI	06/02/2001	CR001		10025	1 x Macroworx	100.00	17.50
57	SI	08/02/2001	KD001		10026	2 hours consulta	120.00	21.00
58	SC	06/02/2001	DB001		551	Software return	200.00	35.00
59	SC	06/02/2001	FE001		552	Disks returned	40.00	7.00
60	SI	12/02/2001	JB001		10027	2 hours consulta	120.00	21.00
61	SI	13/02/2001	DB001		10028	1 x EF102 printei	200.00	35.00
62	SI	14/02/2001	FE001		10029	1 x QuorkEdit so	400.00	70.00
63	SI	16/02/2001	LG001		10030	2 x Zap drive	180.00	31.50
64	SI	16/02/2001	JG001		10031	1 x Fileperfect sc	264.00	46.20
65	SI	16/02/2001	PT001		10032	1 x 15" Monitor	320.00	56.00
66	SC	12/02/2001	JG001		553	1 x printer lead fc	16.00	2.80

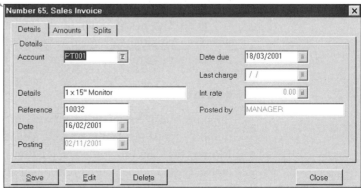

There are three tabs on this screen. The first tab shows the details of (in this case) the sales invoice; the second tab sets out the amount and the third tab any subdivisions (splits) of the amount - for example an invoice with three items on it.

The possible corrections include:

- the account to which the invoice is posted
- the product description
- the amount charged
- the VAT rate and VAT amount

JOURNAL ENTRIES

Journal entries enable you to make transfers from one nominal account to another. Journal entries are used, for example, when you are completing a VAT return and need to transfer VAT amounts from one VAT account to another. It is also useful if you want to put things right when you have input an entry to the wrong account.

journals and double entry

You need to be confident about **double-entry** book-keeping and using debits and credits when doing journal entries. You will have to decide which accounts have debit entries and which accounts have credit entries. The rule is that for every transaction there are balancing debit and credit entries:

debits	=	money paid into the bank
		purchases and expenses
		an increase in an asset
credits	=	payments out of the bank
		sales and income
		an increase in a liability

If you are still in any doubt about debits and credits, use CORRECTIONS wherever possible to adjust account entries. If you want to learn about double-entry, read Chapter 14 (pages 186 to 200).

example

Suppose you were inputting a batch of Bank Payments which included a number of bills that had to be paid. You have written out a cheque for £94 to RPower for a gas bill, but when inputting it you thought it was for electricity and so posted it to electricity (nominal account 7200) instead of gas (7201).

the solution

You could either use CORRECTIONS, but as you are a double-entry expert you choose to correct your mistake using a journal entry. You bring up the screen by clicking on the JOURNALS icon on the NOMINAL menu bar:

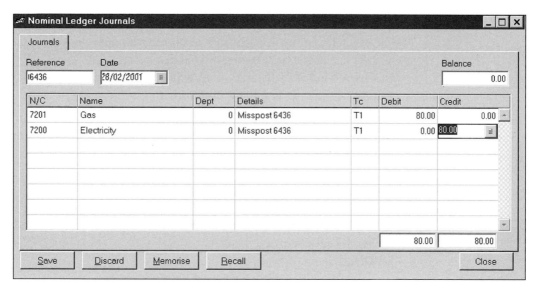

The procedure is:

■ enter your reference (this could be the transaction number you can find by opening up the FINANCIALS screen and locating the transaction)

■ enter the nominal code of the account to which you are going to post the debit; here it is Gas Account because you are recording an expense

■ enter the reason for the transaction – here you are adjusting a mispost

■ enter the VAT tax code input on the original (wrong) entry

■ enter the net amount in the debit column (ie the amount before VAT has been added on) – here the net amount is £80 and VAT (assumed here at standard rate) is £14 and the total is £94; note that neither the VAT nor the total appear on the screen because you are not adjusting the VAT; *only the net amount* has gone to the wrong account

then on the next line . . .

■ enter the nominal code of the account to which you are going to post the credit; here it is Electricity Account because you are effectively refunding the amount to the account – it is an income item and so a credit

■ enter the remaining data as you did for the debit, but enter the net amount in the right-hand credit column

■ make sure the Balance box reads zero – meaning that the debit equals the credit – and SAVE

CORRECTION BY DOCUMENT

Documents such as invoices have to be checked carefully before they are despatched because once they have been sent out by the business they cannot be changed. They must instead be replaced.

For example, an invoice sent to a customer with a wrong price used, or a mistake in calculation, a wrong discount, or a wrong VAT code, will need to be refunded in full by the issue of a credit note. A second and correct invoice will then have to be sent to the customer.

The net effect of all this on the accounting system and the input into a computer accounting system is that the final amount owing by the customer will be correct.

If, on the other hand, a problem is discovered with an invoice or credit note *before* it has been sent out, it can be deleted through the 'Details' tab in CORRECTIONS and a replacement document issued and input.

REBUILD

The REBUILD function is exactly what it says it is. Sage provides the facility to reconstruct selections of data files. This could happen for one of two reasons:

- the data is corrupted – something has gone wrong with the computer and the data cannot be used because the program will not work properly
- the data is dummy data – for example in a training situation where new 'companies' are set up each time a new set of exercises is started and the old data has to be deleted

REBUILD can be reached from MAINTENANCE through the FILE icon on the main menu bar:

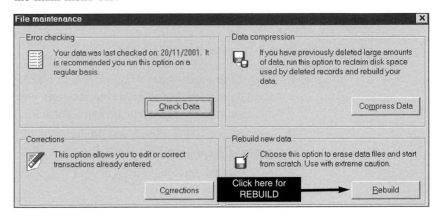

The screen looks like this . . .

You will need to deselect, ie remove the ticks from the data files that you want to reconstruct.

Rebuilding the nominal accounts will also involve reconstructing the chart of accounts (see page 67). You will be asked which chart of accounts you want – including the default layout.

As you can see, REBUILD is a drastic remedy to be used only when all else fails.

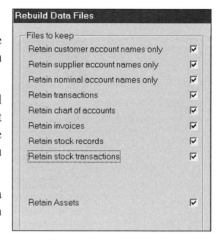

ADJUSTMENTS TO THE ACCOUNTS

A business may from time-to-time need to make adjustments to the data which has already been input into the computer accounting system. Situations where this happens include:

- A credit customer is going or has gone 'bust' (bankrupt) and cannot pay invoices – the account will need to be 'written off' as a bad debt

- A credit customer has paid too much and a refund payment has to be made (by cheque or BACS)

- a cheque paid to the business by a credit customer has 'bounced' – it has been returned by the bank after it has been paid in and the money is taken off the account of the business by the bank

- a cheque issued by the business needs to be cancelled – it may have been lost in the post or it may have been stopped

We will look at each of the procedures in turn.

write offs

All businesses from time-to-time will encounter bad debts. A **bad debt** is a credit customer who does not pay. It may be that the customer has gone 'bust' or that the cost of continuing to send statements, reminders and demands is too high in relation to the amount owing. A business will decide in these circumstances to **write off** the debt in the accounts. This involves:

- debiting 'Bad Debts Account' set up in NOMINAL

- crediting the customer with the amount due – wiping it off the account

In Sage this transfer is carried out from the WRITE OFF, REFUNDS AND RETURNS Wizard, which is reached through TOOLS on the main menu bar.

The Wizard (Sales ledger option) gives a choice of account adjustments . . .

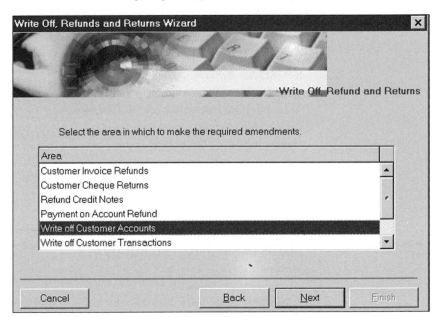

Then a choice of Sales ledger customers . . .

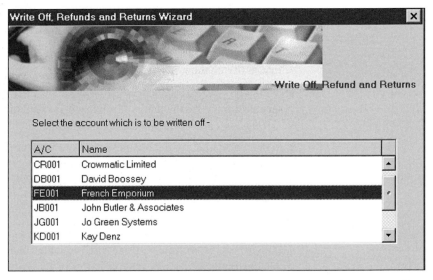

Screens then follow which allow the business to select the outstanding invoices to write off (all of them as the whole account is being written off) and then to date and confirm the details.

After this procedure the customer account will show as a nil balance and a corresponding Bad Debts account in NOMINAL will show the write off amount as an expense to the business. Eventually a write off – like any expense – will reduce the business profits.

customer refunds

A business may sometimes be asked by a credit customer to send a refund cheque. This could happen when a customer, who has been sold goods on credit and has paid for them, has then decided (with the agreement of the business) to return them. The business will have to refund the money.

The computer accounting entries in Sage will again be made through TOOLS and the WRITE OFF, REFUNDS AND RETURNS Wizard. If payment has already been made, as in the above example, the 'Payment on Account' option will be chosen as the refund amount will appear with this description on the account. The accounting entries here are:

■ adjusting the customer's account with the cheque amount (a debit)

■ deducting the cheque amount from the Bank Current Account (a credit)

adjusting for a 'bounced' cheque

Opening the post in the morning to find a letter from the bank with a 'bounced' cheque enclosed is bad news for a business. A **bounced cheque** is a cheque which has been received by a business and paid in but returned by the cheque issuer's bank because there is not enough money on the account to pay the cheque.

The appropriate computer accounting entries in Sage will be made through TOOLS and the WRITE OFF, REFUNDS AND RETURNS Wizard under 'Customer Cheque Returns'. The cheque screen is shown below.

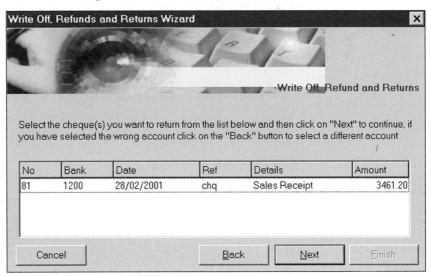

The accounting entries created by this process for this are:

■ *increasing* the customer's account with the amount of the cheque (a debit)

■ deducting the amount from the Bank Current Account (a credit)

cancelling a cheque

A business may wish to delete from the accounting records a cheque that it has issued. For example, the cheque may have been lost in the post or it may be cancelled before it leaves the business. In these circumstances a new cheque will be issued and input into the computer accounting system.

The appropriate computer accounting entries in Sage will be made using the WRITE OFF, REFUNDS AND RETURNS Wizard (Purchase Ledger) under 'Supplier Cheque Returns'. The screens appear as follows:

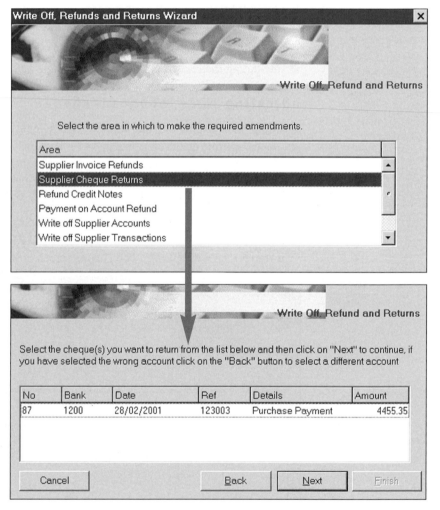

The accounting entries created by this process for this are:

■ adding the amount back to the Bank Current Account because the cheque is cancelled (a debit)

■ increasing the supplier's account balance with the amount of the cheque (a credit)

CASE STUDY

PRONTO SUPPLIES LIMITED: CORRECTIONS AND ADJUSTMENTS

It is 28 February 2001. Tom is still finalising his accounts. He encounters a number of situations which require him to carry out corrections and adjustments straightaway.

incorrect invoice description

Tom has an email from Prism Trading Limited. The text reads:

> We have just noticed that Sales Invoice 10032 for £376.00 has the product description '1 x 15" monitor'. What we ordered and what was supplied was 1 x 14" flatscreen. The amount was correct and so no action needs to be taken. You may wish to amend your records.
> Regards. Accounts, Prism Trading Limited.

Tom identifies the invoice from the audit trail he has printed out. It is transaction 65. Tom goes into CORRECTIONS from FILE MAINTENANCE and selects transaction 65. He then amends the product description on the Details tab and Saves.

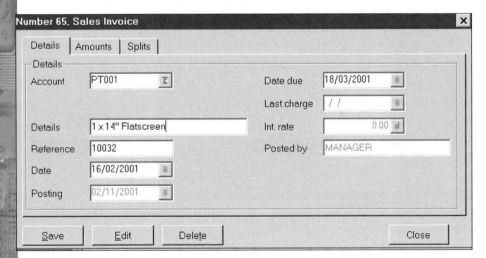

incorrect account postings

Tom has a note from an accounts assistant.

> Cash Sales: 9 February 2001
>
> Cash Sales for computer hardware paid into the bank on 9 February contained a cheque for £2,350 that was from sales of computer software (£2,000 plus £350 VAT). There is no problem with the bank as all the money is held on the current account, but there is a problem with our nominal account postings. The figures are:

Amounts that were posted

ref	details	nominal	net £	VAT £	gross £
90	Hardware Sales	A/c 4000	12,500.00	2,187.50	14,687.50
91	Software Sales	A/c 4001	4,680.00	819.00	5,499.00

Amounts that should have been posted

ref	details	nominal	net £	VAT £	gross £
90	Hardware Sales	A/c 4000	10,500.00	1,837.50	12,337.50
91	Software Sales	A/c 4001	6,680.00	1,169.00	7,849.00

Please can you arrange for the necessary correcting entries to be made.

Tom goes into CORRECTIONS from MAINTENANCE and selects transactions 90 and 91. He then edits the amounts on the Details tab and Saves.

The amendments to Transactions 90 and 91 are shown below:

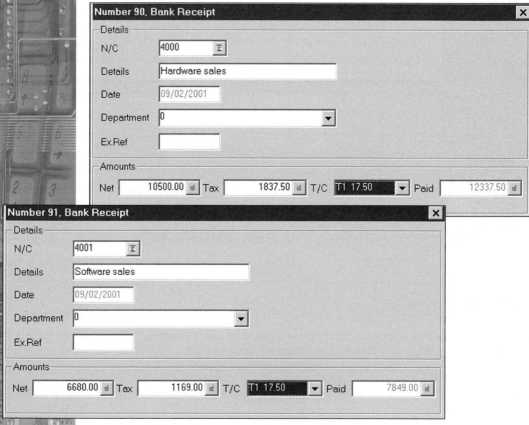

journal entries

On checking the paperwork relating to the accounts for the month Tom spots that a bill from RPower has been paid but the expense has been posted by mistake to Electricity Account instead of Gas account. The bill was for £158 plus VAT.

Tom decides to carry out journal entries to switch the expense from one account to the other. In double-entry book-keeping terms this means:

    debit   Gas Account (code 7201) £158 – recording an expense

    credit   Electricity Account (code 7200) £158 – recording a refund

Tom accesses the Journal through the JOURNALS icon on the NOMINAL menu bar. The journal screen after input appears as follows:

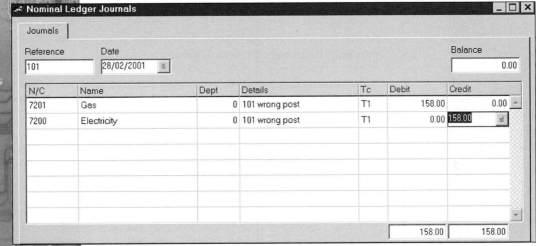

Note that:

- no VAT is involved here because it is only the net amount (amount before VAT is added on) that has gone to the wrong account

- the reference used is the audit trail number of the original transaction

- the Balance box shows as zero because the debit entry equals the credit entry – as you would expect (the Balance is the difference between the entries)

cancelling a supplier's cheque

On checking his Purchases Ledger documentation Tom realises that he has made out (but not yet posted) a cheque to Tycomp Supplies for £6,160, but that the goods supplied were faulty. He has got a note on file to suspend payment until the problem has been resolved. He therefore decides to cancel the cheque and await further developments. He does this through TOOLS, using the WRITE OFF, REFUNDS AND RETURNS Wizard (selecting Purchases Ledger and Supplier Cheque Returns).

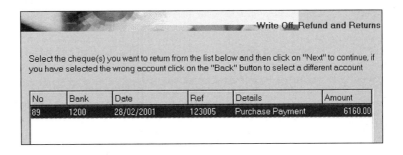

CHAPTER SUMMARY

■ Errors inevitably occur when processing accounts on the computer. Errors can involve incorrect descriptions, incorrect prices, wrong VAT codes and wrong accounts used.

■ Most errors within Sage can be corrected using the CORRECTIONS routine within MAINTENANCE. This will enable corrections to be made to invoices, credit notes and payments.

■ Adjustments to Nominal accounts can also be carried out by transfers through the JOURNALS function within Sage. This process requires a knowledge of double-entry book-keeping.

■ Once financial documents such as invoices and credit notes have been sent out they can normally only be corrected by document – for example an invoice overcharge adjusted by a credit note.

■ If computer files become corrupted beyond repair the Sage REBUILD function can be used to reconstruct the ledgers. This may result in data being lost in the process. REBUILD is also used in a training context.

■ The computer accounting records may also be adjusted for situations such as account write-offs, refunds to customers, 'bounced' customer cheques and cheques to suppliers that need to be cancelled.

KEY TERMS

journal	the part of the accounting system which enables you to make transfers from one nominal account to another
double-entry	the system of book-keeping which involves each transaction having two entries made – a debit and a credit; computer accounting programs (which are largely single entry systems) deal with the double entry automatically
write off	the removal of a Customer (or Supplier) account from the accounting records
bad debt	a debt that is never likely to be paid and so will need to be written off
bounced cheque	a cheque that has been paid into a bank account but has been returned by the bank because the issuer of the cheque does not have the money in the bank to pay the cheque

STUDENT ACTIVITIES

12.1 What method of adjustment in a computer accounting program would you use if . . .

(a) One of your supplier's cheques which you have paid in is returned to you marked 'refer to drawer' – ie it 'bounces'.

(b) You discover that a payment for advertising has been input in error to the stationery account.

(c) You need to make a refund to a customer because they have purchased goods on credit, paid for all of them and then returned some of them.

(d) You find you have input an invoice with the wrong amount and Saved it, but you have not yet sent out the invoice to the customer.

(e) You have input an invoice with the wrong products and wrong amount and have Saved it. You have sent out the invoice to the customer who rings you up to say that the wrong goods have arrived.

PRONTO SUPPLIES INPUTTING TASK

important note!
Before attempting these tasks, ensure that your Trial Balance and Audit Trail printed out at the end of the last chapter have been checked and approved by your Tutor.
Ensure the program date is set at 28 February 2001.

Task 1
Correct invoice 10032 (transaction 56) in the Case Study on page 165 using CORRECTIONS.

Task 2
Correct the Cash Sales postings (90 and 91) in the Case Study on page 166 using CORRECTIONS.

Task 3
Carry out the Journal entries for the RPower misspost in the Case Study on page 167.

Task 4
Cancel the cheque to Tycomp Supplies for £6,160 in the Case Study on page 167, using the WRITE OFF, REFUNDS AND RETURNS Wizard through TOOLS.

Task 5
When you have completed your corrections, print out an Audit Trail and a Trial Balance. Check the figures on the Trial Balance with the figures on page 246. Then explain the changes in the Trial Balance to:

(a) Bank Current Account

(b) Computer Hardware Sales Account and Computer Software Sales Account

(c) Electricity Account

SALES INVOICING –
FURTHER ASPECTS

chapter introduction

- In Chapter 6 – 'Selling to customers on credit' – we looked at the way in which Customers are invoiced for goods and services sold. The method of invoicing used was the 'batch' method in which the invoices are produced independently (eg typed out) and the details then entered onto the computer screen. This is the method to be used when first setting up a computer accounting system when you have existing invoices which need to be input onto the system.

- In this chapter we illustrate the way in which invoices are printed out by the business using the computer invoicing function and the way in which the details are then updated on the Customer's account.

- If the business is selling goods rather than services, producing invoices in this way usually involves setting up stock codes, known in Sage as 'product codes', which are entered on the invoice screen to produce the appropriate price and product description automatically.

- If the business is selling services rather than goods, Sage provides a facility known as a 'service invoice' which does not require the setting up of product codes, and so is simpler to operate.

- Processing invoices may also involve the use of discounts. There are two main types of discount:

  - trade discount, a percentage reduction in the price of goods and services allowed to established customers

  - cash discount (also known as settlement discount),a percentage reduction in the price of goods and services allowed to customers who pay the invoice early (for example within seven days, rather than the usual thirty days)

- We will again look at the business in the Case Study – Pronto Supplies Limited – and see how it deals with printing service invoices and how it deals with Customer discounts.

METHODS OF INVOICING IN SAGE

There are two main methods of producing sales invoices in Sage:

- **batch invoice production** – the business produces invoices manually (ie not with the computer) and then inputs the details of each invoice on the computer screen to enter the transaction into the computer

- **computer-produced invoices** – the business uses an invoicing function available in Sage programs to input the details into the computer and to record and print out each invoice

So far in this book we have concentrated on the method of batched invoice production because of its simplicity and because not all training centres are geared up to print computer accounting stationery. In this chapter, however, we cater for those who are able to print out invoices, and those who may have to do so for certain examination courses.

THE INVOICING FUNCTION IN SAGE

The invoicing function in Sage is reached by clicking on INVOICING in the main menu bar. This brings up the INVOICING menu bar:

The most important icons here are:

Product   this enables you to process invoices for products – ie physical stock items (goods) that a business sells, eg cars, telephones, paper clips

Credit   this enables you to process sales credit notes to set against product invoices

Service   this enables you to produce invoices for services that a business provides, eg a hotel room for the night, a session of computer consultancy

SrvCredit   this enables you to process credit notes to set against service invoices

Print   this enables you to print invoices and credit notes

Update   this enables you to update the ledgers, ie to post the entries to the computer accounting records after the input has been checked

PRODUCT INVOICES

Setting up product invoicing in a Sage system is normally a complex procedure because product invoicing requires a **product code**. This is a reference code made up of numbers and/or letters which is specific to each stock item sold.

The business will have to set up product codes in the PRODUCTS function for every item sold. This will involve setting up a reference code, a price, product details, product quantities, and so on. Once in operation the PRODUCTS function can record details of all stock held and automatically adjust the recorded stock level each time a product invoice is issued. Setting up the PRODUCTS function is a time-consuming operation which requires much planning and forethought. It is therefore beyond the scope of this book (and most computer accounting examinations).

The product invoice screen (shown at the bottom of the page) is reached by clicking on PRODUCT on the INVOICING menu bar.

invoicing without product codes – a short cut

Sage does, however, have a short cut to overcome the problem of setting up product codes. If you click on the Product Code box on the invoice screen you can access a drop down menu which allows you to choose option S1 (goods with VAT) or S2 (goods without VAT). You can then input through a screen reached from the Description box (see below) details of products that you sell without having to set up product codes or the PRODUCT function.

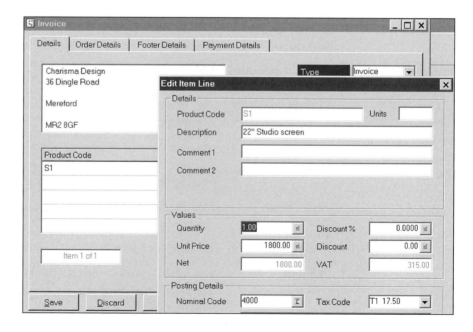

processing the product invoice

There are a number of distinct stages in processing and printing product invoices:

1 Enter the details of the invoice on screen

On the first tab – 'Details' – the invoice number and date are normally set automatically, although they can be over-ridden. The order number and account reference need to be input. The product code also needs to be entered; if S1 or S2 are used, the details and price will also need to be input through the separate screen. If a PRODUCTS function has been set up the product code will automatically generate the details and price.

The details of the order and payment terms also need to be checked on the other tabs and amended as required.

2 Save the invoice when you have checked the details on screen

The invoice should be Saved once it has been correctly entered. It is now ready for printing.

3 Print the invoice

Invoices are normally better printed in batches rather than one by one, which would be very time consuming. Invoices for printing should be selected on the opening INVOICING screen. When the PRINT icon has been clicked you should choose the format in which you want the invoice printed and then set the print run going. Invoices in SAGE are normally preprinted with all the headings and boxes in place; the printer just puts in the figures and details. You are likely to need help when setting up invoice printing for the first time – it can be extremely time-consuming!

4 Updating the ledgers

When the invoices have been printed they should be carefully checked:

- against the appropriate purchase orders to make sure that the details are correct and that no orders have been missed
- to make sure that they have not been 'chewed up' in the printer

When you are satisfied that the invoices are correct they should be selected on the INVOICING screen and updated to the Sales Ledger. This means that the amount of the invoice will be added to the account of the Customer and appropriate entries made to Sales and Sales VAT Account.

5 Printing a report

The final stage in invoice processing is the printing of a report, either the ledger update report which is automatically generated when the update takes place, or a Day Book Customer Invoices (Summary) report for the appropriate transactions from REPORTS on the CUSTOMERS menu bar.

SERVICE INVOICES

Service invoices are issued for services provided by a business and not for goods sold. The advantage of service invoices is that they do not require product codes.

Service invoices may be accessed from the SERVICE icon on the INVOICING menu bar. The input screen looks like this:

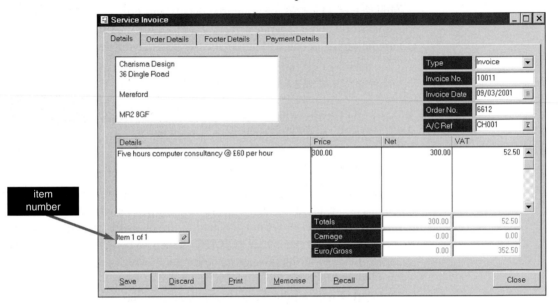

The procedure is much the same as with the Product Invoice (see previous page for the steps to be taken) except that the details and price have to be entered manually, because no product code is entered. Note the following:

Details   You can enter as much text as you like in this box.

Price   You enter the net amount here, ie the amount before VAT is added on and before discounts are calculated (see later in this chapter for an explanation of discounts)

VAT   This is automatically calculated, based on the tax code entered. The tax code can be checked if you click on the Item number box (see above).

Nominal code   The Nominal account code to which the invoice is posted (eg Computer Consultancy Account) can also be checked and amended on the Item number box screen. Look at the illustration of this screen on the next page.

The item number screen appears as follows:

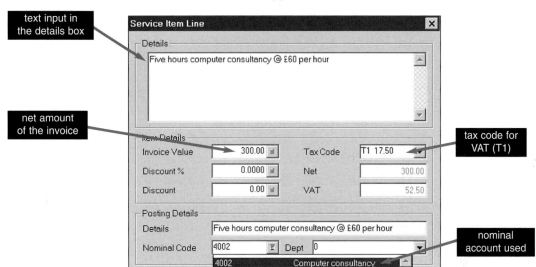

text input in
the details box

net amount
of the invoice

tax code for
VAT (T1)

nominal
account used

'memorising' service invoices

If you repeatedly invoice the same service at the same price you can save the details as a 'skeleton' invoice by clicking on the Memorise button at the bottom of the service invoice screen and providing a file name and description. If you need to bring up these same details again for another invoice, click the Recall button and select the file you need.

printing and updating – service invoices

The procedure for printing service invoices and **updating** the ledgers is exactly the same as for a product invoice, as explained on page 173. It is advisable also to print out a report for all invoices produced, either by updating the ledgers in INVOICING or as a Day Book Customer Invoices (Summary) from CUSTOMERS.

CREDIT NOTE PRODUCTION

Exactly the same procedure is followed for processing and printing Product and Service credit notes. These are accessed from the Credit and SrvCredit icons respectively on the INVOICING menu bar.

The Case Study which follows shows how Pronto Supplies Limited decides to process and print its invoices on the computer, starting with service invoices for computer consultancy work carried out by Tom Cox.

PRONTO SUPPLIES LIMITED:
SERVICE INVOICE PRINTING

During February Tom Cox had placed an advert in the local paper for 'Pronto' computer consultancy services. This was a sideline for Tom's business. Tom had seen that small businesses – particularly start-ups – needed help in setting up computer systems for wordprocessing, databases, spreadsheets and Computer accounting. Tom decided to charge £60 per hour for this service, in view of his qualifications and experience.

It is now 9 March 2001. Tom has already done work for three clients and has decided to invoice them using the Service Invoice function in Sage. He has worked out how to print out the invoices on the office printer and has designed his own stationery to take one of the Sage standard A4 layouts.

setting up the Customer Accounts

The details of the three new customers (with designated account codes) are as follows:

MP001	**M Patel**
	16 Wildwood Street
	Mereford
	MR1 2PT

Contact name: M Patel
Telephone 01908 356745, Fax 01908 356777
Email MPatel@goblin.com
Credit limit £2,000
Computer consultancy work to 9 March; 3 hours @ £60 per hour
Order ref C01

PD001	**Petal Design Company**
	17 Marcus Close
	Mereford
	MR3 1TF

Contact name: Fallon McVeigh
Telephone 01908 640317, Fax 01908 640466
Email mail@petaldesign.co.uk
www.petaldesign.co.uk
Credit limit £2,000
Computer consultancy work to 9 March; 5 hours @ £60 per hour
Order ref C02

EA001   **121 Escort Agency**
2B Verey Close
Stourminster
ST1 9TF

Contact name: Astrid Bergman
Telephone 01603 625150, Fax 01603 625625,
Email mail@121escortagency.co.uk
www.121escortagency.co.uk
Credit limit £2,000
Computer consultancy work to 9 March; 7 hours @ £60 per hour
Order ref C03

Tom first sets up these customers in CUSTOMERS using the RECORD button and the Customer defaults already established. Tom realises he will have to be careful about the Nominal Code (default 4000 - computer hardware sales) when processing the service invoices which are for Computer Consultancy (account 4002). The other defaults already set include:

Payment due days   30 days

Terms of payment   Payment 30 days of invoice

VAT rate   Standard rate of 17.5% (this is Tax Code T1)

Tom does not allow discounts on Computer Consultancy at this stage. He ticks the Terms Agreed box on the Credit Control tab for each customer.

The initial input screen for the third customer is shown below.

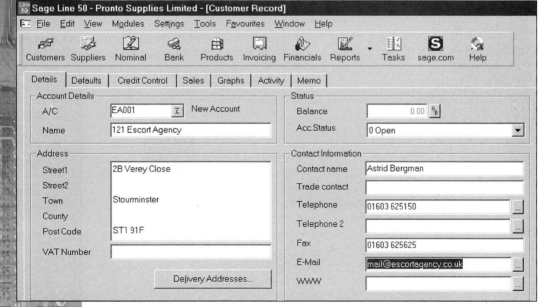

entering the service invoices

Tom has three service invoices to input on 9 March 2001. He selects the INVOICING menu and clicks on SERVICE.

He has to set up the invoice number on the first invoice screen. The last invoice he issued was 10032 so he edits the number from 1 (the default) to 10033.

He then inputs the order reference and account reference and types in the text of the service provided in the Details box.

The amount he is charging (before VAT) is entered in the Price box and the computer then calculates the VAT amount and invoice total.

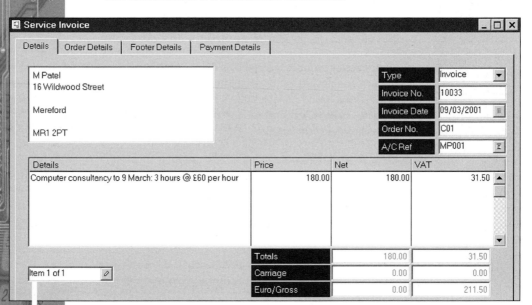

Tom now has to make sure that the invoice is posted to Computer Consultancy Account and so clicks on the Item number box to bring up the necessary screen. He then changes account 4000 (the default) to account 4002 (see the screen below).

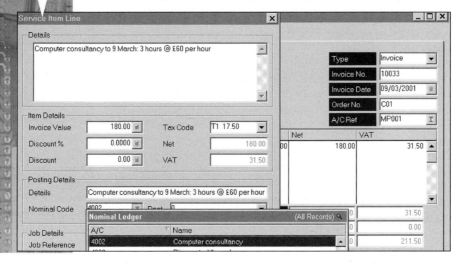

saving and updating

After processing each of the three invoices and Saving them, Tom then selects them on the INVOICES opening screen and clicks on the PRINT icon and selects the invoice layout on screen he has set up for his stationery.

Tom then prints the invoices and checks them. When he is happy that they are all correct he selects the three invoices on the INVOICES opening screen and clicks the Update icon on the INVOICES menu bar. This then posts the invoices in the accounting records (Ledgers) as follows:

- £900 to Nominal Account 4002 Computer consultancy – the net Sales
- £157.50 to Nominal Account 2200 Sales Tax Control Account – the VAT
- The three invoices (totalling £1,057.50) to the three Customer Accounts and at the same time to Debtors Control Account

printing a report

Tom should check the computer input against his input details by printing a report. This should ideally be the Update Report which is generated and can be printed when the Ledgers are updated. This shows all the details of the transactions, including the Nominal account to which each invoice is posted:

Pronto Supplies Limited   **Page:** 1

Update Ledgers

Inv	Tp	Tran	Date	A/C	N/C	Stock Code	Details	Qty	Net	Tax	Gross
10033	SI	129	09/03/2001	MP001	4002		Computer consultancy to 9 March: 3 h		180.00	31.50	211.50
							Invoice Total:		180.00	31.50	211.50
10034	SI	130	09/03/2001	PD001	4002		Computer consultancy to 9 March 200		300.00	52.50	352.50
							Invoice Total:		300.00	52.50	352.50
10035	SI	131	09/03/2001	EA001	4002		Computer consultancy to 9 March 200		420.00	73.50	493.50
							Invoice Total:		420.00	73.50	493.50
							Grand Total for Invoices:		900.00	157.50	1,057.50
							Grand Total for All:		900.00	157.50	1,057.50

Tom could alternatively print out a Day Books: Customer Invoices (Summary) from REPORTS on the CUSTOMERS menu bar, but this does not show so much detail.

Pronto Supplies Limited   **Page:** 1

Day Books: Customer Invoices (Summary)

Date From:	09/03/2001		Customer From:	
Date To:	09/03/2001		Customer To:	ZZZZZZZZ

Transaction From:	1
Transaction To:	99999999

Tran No.	Item s	Tp	Date	A/C Ref	Inv Ref	Details	Net Amount	Tax Amount	Gross Amount
129	1	SI	09/03/2001	MP001	10033	Computer consultancy to 9 March: 3 hou	180.00	31.50	211.50
130	1	SI	09/03/2001	PD001	10034	Computer consultancy to 9 March 2001:	300.00	52.50	352.50
131	1	SI	09/03/2001	EA001	10035	Computer consultancy to 9 March 2001:	420.00	73.50	493.50
						Totals:	900.00	157.50	1,057.50

DISCOUNTS ON INVOICES

A **discount** is a reduction in the selling price of goods or services. If a discount is given by the seller to the buyer, the discount will be shown on the invoice. There are two main types of discount given by sellers:

- **Trade discount** is a percentage reduction in the price of goods and services allowed to well-known Customers.

  For example, a supplier may give Customers an overall 20% discount. A sale of goods with a list price of £100 would therefore cost

  £100 less £20 (20% trade discount) = £80

- **Cash discount** (also known as settlement discount) is a percentage reduction in the price of goods and services allowed to Customers who pay the invoice early, for example within seven days, rather than the usual thirty days. (Remember that 'cash' means immediate payment).

  For example, a supplier may allow a 2.5% cash discount if a Customer pays up within seven days rather than the usual agreed credit period of 30 days. If the original invoice was for £100, the Customer could pay within seven days

  £100 less £2.50 (2.5% cash discount) = £97.50

Remember, however, that VAT will normally have to be added on to these amounts.

VAT and discount

The normal practice on an invoice is for VAT to be calculated on the sales amount *after* the discount has been deducted.

In the examples given the total amount charged will be (assuming 17.5% standard rate VAT):

- **Trade discount**

  £80 (ie £100 minus £20) + VAT of £14 = total of £94

- **Cash discount**

  £97.50 (ie £100 minus £2.50) + VAT of £17.06 = total of £114.56

  The important thing to remember with VAT on cash discount is that the VAT is always calculated on the amount after the discount has been deducted, even if the cash discount is not taken. It may seem odd and illogical but the printed invoice will always show the *pre-discount total* as the net total (ie the higher amount) but will then add on the VAT calculated on the amount *after the discount has been deducted!*

discounts and computer accounting

One of the advantages of using a computer accounting package such as Sage is that the program calculates discount automatically and accurately. There are a number of ways in which to input the discount details: using Customer Defaults, amending the Customer Record and editing the invoice itself.

customer defaults

It is possible to set up discount rates on the computer which will apply to all Customer accounts unless the user specifies otherwise. This is carried out through CUSTOMER DEFAULTS under SETTINGS. The screen is shown below. Note that this covers both cash discount (known as 'Sett.Discount), and trade discount. This would be useful if the business sold goods in a trade where there was a common trade discount rate.

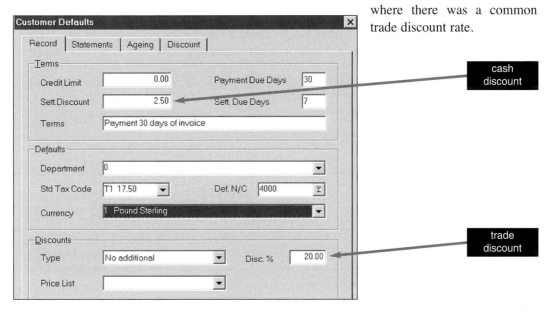

customer record

The default rates on the above screen (default) rates could be over-ridden by amending the RECORD in CUSTOMERS. The Defaults tab will enable the user to set up the trade discount:

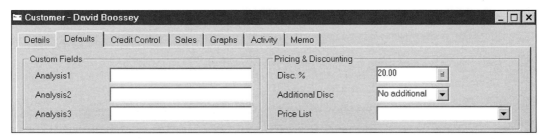

The Credit Control tab in the Customer Record will enable the user to set up the cash (settlement) discount:

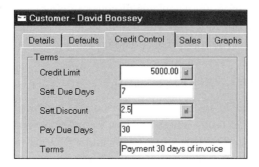

customer invoice

The cash discount can be amended on the invoice footer tab as required (see below) and the trade discount can be amended on the Edit Item screen.

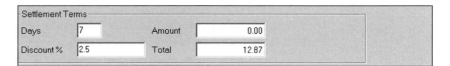

PRONTO SUPPLIES LIMITED: APPLYING DISCOUNTS

It is 9 March 2001. Tom Cox has now been trading for over two months and has been approached by some of his customers asking for **trade discount**. After some negotiation he has agreed to give 10% trade discount to five customers:

JB001	John Butler & Associates
CR001	Crowmatic Ltd
FE001	French Emporium
LG001	L Garr & Co
JG001	Jo Green Systems

Tom carries out this procedure by amending the Customer Record in each case, as shown below.

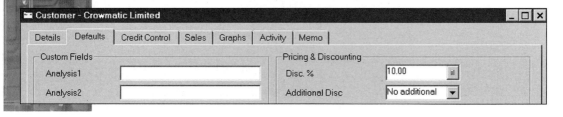

A week later Tom receives an email about **cash discounts** from 121 Escort Agency. The text reads as follows:

> Hello Tom
>
> Thanks for your recent invoice for computer work done for us. We will settle it by the end of the month.
>
> As we have a good bank balance these days, is there any possibility of you giving us a cash discount on future invoices of say 5% for settlement within seven days?
>
> Thanks
>
> Astrid

Tom replies:

> Hello Astrid
>
> We will be happy to give you a cash discount on future invoices. The highest we can go to at the moment is 3% for settlement within 7 days. Is this OK?
>
> Tom

Astrid replies:

> Hello Tom
>
> 3% cash settlement discount would be fine. Many thanks.
>
> Regards
>
> Astrid

Tom then amends the RECORD of 121 Escort Agency in CUSTOMERS as follows:

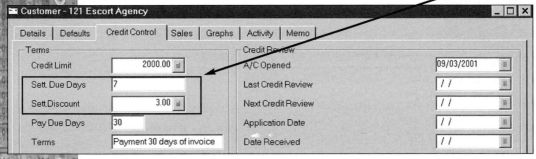

■ Sage provides two ways of processing sales invoices. The first method is batch entry, where the invoice is produced independently of the computer and the details are input afterwards. The second method is the invoicing function in Sage which enables the details to be input and an invoice to be printed from the computer.

■ There are two main types of invoice which can be produced in Sage:
  • a product invoice which is used for invoicing actual goods
  • a service invoice which is used for invoicing services provided

  Invoicing using product invoices normally involves the setting up of the products facility within Sage which provides the product codes needed by the computer. Service invoices do not need product codes.

■ Processing an invoice involves a number of stages:
  • the input of the invoice details
  • saving and printing the invoice
  • updating the ledgers
  • printing a report in order to check the accuracy of the input

■ The issue of credit notes follows the same principles as the issue of invoices.

■ Processing invoices may also involve the use of discounts. There are two main types of discount: trade discount and cash discount.

product code	a reference code made up of letters and/or numbers which is specific to each stock item sold
product invoice	an invoice used for invoicing actual goods
service invoice	an invoice used for invoicing a service provided
ledger update	posting the details of invoices issued to the computer accounting records
trade discount	a percentage reduction in the price of goods and services allowed to established customers
cash discount	a percentage reduction in the price of goods and services allowed to customers who pay an invoice early (also known as settlement discount)

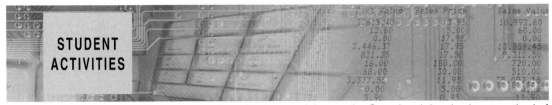

13.1 Describe the circumstances in which a business might use the Sage batch invoice input method of invoice production.

13.2 Explain what is meant, with an example, by 'updating the ledger' after processing and printing an invoice on the computer.

13.3 Describe the full range of checking procedures (including the update) that should be carried out when processing and printing an invoice on the computer.

13.4 In what way does a service invoice differ from a product invoice in Sage?

13.5 Explain the difference between trade discount and cash (settlement) discount.

13.6 A stationery wholesaler issues invoices for the goods it sells and gives a 25% trade discount to established customers. Assuming it charges VAT at the standard rate, what would the final invoice total be for goods where the net total (ie total before discount and VAT) is (a) £400 (b) £640.50?

13.7 An advertising agency issues invoices for the services it provides and gives a 2.5% cash discount to customers for settlement within seven days. Assuming it charges VAT at the standard rate, what would the final invoice total be for goods where the net total (ie total before discount and VAT) is (a) £4,000.00 (b) £840.00

Assume in both cases that the customer takes advantage of the cash discount.

PRONTO SUPPLIES INPUTTING TASKS

Before attempting these tasks, ensure the program date is set at 9 March 2001. Also check that the Customer Defaults are set correctly, as on page 52, with the VAT set as T1.

Task 1

Input the three new Customer accounts from the Case Study details (pages 176 to 177) in CUSTOMERS, remembering to use default N/C 4000, and ticking the Terms Agreed box on the Credit Control tab.

Task 2

Process the service invoices for the work done for the three new clients (see page 178). Remember to use Nominal code 4002 and to check the input carefully before Saving. Print the invoices and when you are happy with them, update the ledgers and print out an Update Ledgers Report to confirm the batch totals.

Task 3

Apply the discounts to the appropriate Customer Records, as in the Case Study (see pages 182 to 183).

Task 4 *(check with Trial Balance on page 247 when you have finished this Task)*

Fallon from Petal Design Company telephones on 14 March to say that Tom has only done (order ref. CO2) 4 hours consultancy and not 5 as invoiced. Change the program date to 14 March and process and print a service Credit Note 555 to make the adjustment. Remember to post the credit to Nominal Account 4002.

Reminder! Have you made a backup?

14 DOUBLE-ENTRY BOOK-KEEPING AND MANUAL SYSTEMS

chapter introduction

■ Earlier chapters in this book have shown how computer accounting involves the use of 'accounts' and 'ledgers' maintained on computer files. It is easy to accept these terms at face value when you are sitting in front of a computer – but they make much more sense once you know how they work in a manual accounting system.

■ The basis of many manual accounting systems is a set of double-entry accounts grouped into separate ledgers – eg sales ledger, purchases ledger. Each time a transaction is recorded, it is entered twice in the accounts, once as a debit and once as a credit.

■ The basis of computer accounting is the input of a financial transaction as a single entry on the screen. The computer then processes that entry to two separate accounts (or three accounts if VAT is involved). In other words, the computer does the double-entry for you.

■ The problem with manual double-entry book-keeping is knowing which entry is the debit and which is the credit. This is best understood when it is seen as part of the 'dual aspect' of double-entry book-keeping, which sets down the principles of which entry is which. These principles are sometimes needed in computer accounting, for example when you are processing a journal entry or a nominal opening balance. You then have to decide whether an amount should be entered as a debit or as a credit. If you understand the principles of manual double-entry book-keeping you are at a great advantage.

■ Remember that double-entry book-keeping is only one part of the accounting process, whether a manual or a computerised accounting system is used. The first step is the financial transaction and the document it generates, the second is the listing and summarising of financial transactions and the third is the entry of this data in the accounts. The final stage is the summary of the accounts in the Trial Balance and the production of reports such as the Profit & Loss Statement and the Balance Sheet from the double-entry records. We will start off in this chapter by looking at this overall accounting system.

THE ACCOUNTING SYSTEM

The overall accounting system as it relates to both manual and computer accounting is a simple series of stages which starts off with financial transactions such as as sales and purchases and concludes with information used by management such as aged debtor summaries and profit and loss statements. The stages can be summarised as follows:

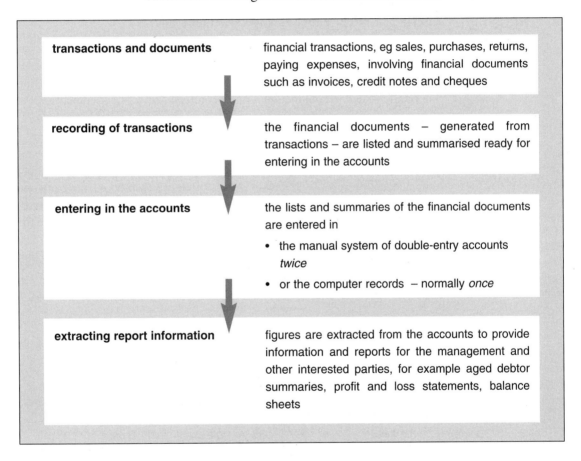

transactions and documents	financial transactions, eg sales, purchases, returns, paying expenses, involving financial documents such as invoices, credit notes and cheques
recording of transactions	the financial documents – generated from transactions – are listed and summarised ready for entering in the accounts
entering in the accounts	the lists and summaries of the financial documents are entered in • the manual system of double-entry accounts *twice* • or the computer records – normally *once*
extracting report information	figures are extracted from the accounts to provide information and reports for the management and other interested parties, for example aged debtor summaries, profit and loss statements, balance sheets

stage 1 – transactions and documents

Financial transactions involve financial documents. You will already be familiar with many of these.

sale and purchase of goods and services – the invoice

When a business buys or sells goods or a service the seller prepares an invoice which sets out the amount owing, the date on which it should be paid and the details of the goods sold or the service provided.

refunds – the credit note

If the buyer returns goods which are bought on credit or has a problem with a service supplied on credit, the seller will issue a credit note which is sent to the buyer, reducing the amount of money owed.

small cash payments – the petty cash voucher

If the business operates a petty cash system for making small cash payments, the payments will be recorded and authorised using petty cash vouchers.

paying-in slips, cheques and remittance advices

Businesses need to pay money into the bank current account, and draw out cash and make payments. Money can be paid in on paying-in slips or electronically. Payments made using cheques and BACS transfers are normally issued in conjunction with a remittance advice, a document sent to the person receiving the money, explaining what the payment represents.

stage 2 – recording transactions

Businesses need to list and summarise these documents ready for entry into the accounting records. Manual systems often use cash books for bank and cash transactions and 'day books' for listing sales, purchases and returns. Each day book will normally be totalled each day a listing is made, hence the name 'day book'. Computer systems often use the **batch** system which is a listing of the items with an overall total to check against the computer input. It is common to find batches for sales, purchases, returns, cheques received, cheques issued.

stage 3 – entering transactions in the accounts

When the financial documents have been suitably listed in a day book or batch they are then entered in the accounts of the business. The format of a manual double-entry account with a debit entry might look like this:

Debit				**Computer Account**			**Credit**
Date	Details	Folio	£ p	Date	Details	Folio	£ p
01 02 02 ↑ date of the trans-action	Bank ↑ name of the account in which the other entry is made	CB007 ↑ page or reference number of the other account	450.00 ↑ amount of the trans-action	↑ date of the trans-action	↑ name of the account in which the other entry is made	↑ page or reference number of the other account	↑ amount of the trans-action

The double-entry system used by many manual systems involves two entries for each amount or total (or three entries if VAT is involved). This form of account and the way it works is explained in more detail on page 191.

A computer system, as you know, needs only one entry to be made for each transaction, but will require the account code of the other entry when that single entry is made.

Most accounting systems use the **ledger** system to organise the accounts. The word 'ledger' means 'book' but is used freely by both manual and computer systems to represent a section of the accounts kept on paper or on the computer. The ledgers can be summarised as follows:

■ sales ledger — the accounts of customers who have bought on credit (also known as debtors), referred to in computer accounting as CUSTOMERS

■ purchases ledger — the accounts of suppliers who have sold to the business on credit, referred to in computer accounting as SUPPLIERS

■ cash book ledger — the cash and bank accounts of the business – referred to in computer accounting as BANK

■ main 'general' ledger — all the other accounts – expenses, income, assets (items owned) and liabilities (items owed), also referred to in computer accounting as NOMINAL

stage 4 – extracting report information

Financial data in the accounts is only useful when it can be extracted and used by the management of the business or presented to outsiders such as shareholders. The advantage of computer accounting systems is that reports can be generated automatically from a menu. You may encounter a number of different reports in your studies:

■ **trial balance** — a list of the balances of the accounts in two separate columns, which will show whether or not the book-keeping has been accurate

■ **account history** — a list of the transactions on a particular account which may need investigation, eg an expense account or the account of a customer

■ **aged debtors analysis** — a listing of the balances of credit customers, setting out what they owe, when they need to pay and if any payments are overdue

■ **aged creditors analysis** — a listing of the balances of suppliers, setting out when payments need to be made

■ **financial statements** — these include the **profit and loss statement**, which states what profit/loss has been made and the **balance sheet** which sets out what a business owns and owes and how it is financed

Now study the diagram below which summarises the various stages in a manual and a computerised accounting system. The workings of double-entry used in a manual system are explained on the next page.

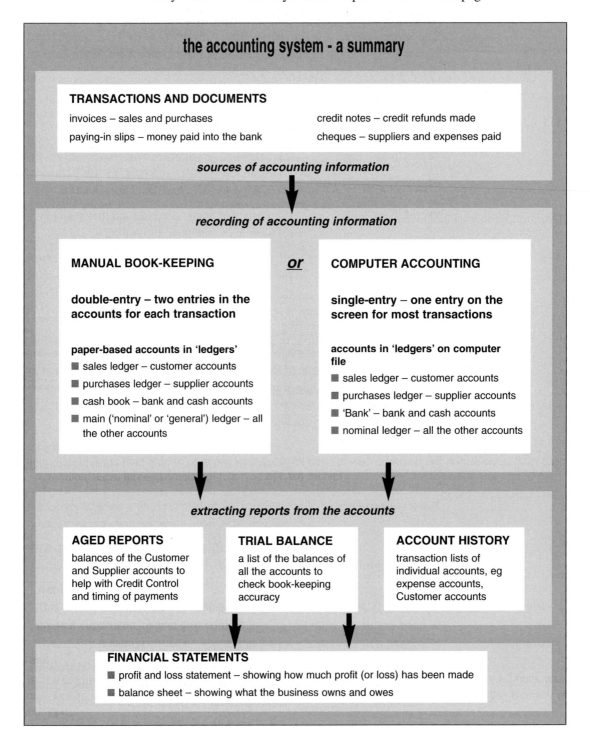

the accounting system - a summary

TRANSACTIONS AND DOCUMENTS

invoices – sales and purchases

paying-in slips – money paid into the bank

credit notes – credit refunds made

cheques – suppliers and expenses paid

sources of accounting information

recording of accounting information

MANUAL BOOK-KEEPING

or

COMPUTER ACCOUNTING

double-entry – two entries in the accounts for each transaction

single-entry – one entry on the screen for most transactions

paper-based accounts in 'ledgers'

- sales ledger – customer accounts
- purchases ledger – supplier accounts
- cash book – bank and cash accounts
- main ('nominal' or 'general') ledger – all the other accounts

accounts in 'ledgers' on computer file

- sales ledger – customer accounts
- purchases ledger – supplier accounts
- 'Bank' – bank and cash accounts
- nominal ledger – all the other accounts

extracting reports from the accounts

AGED REPORTS

balances of the Customer and Supplier accounts to help with Credit Control and timing of payments

TRIAL BALANCE

a list of the balances of all the accounts to check book-keeping accuracy

ACCOUNT HISTORY

transaction lists of individual accounts, eg expense accounts, Customer accounts

FINANCIAL STATEMENTS

- profit and loss statement – showing how much profit (or loss) has been made
- balance sheet – showing what the business owns and owes

DOUBLE-ENTRY ACCOUNTS

Double-entry book-keeping in a manual accounting system involves entries being made in accounts for each transaction – debit entries (on the left-hand side of the account) and credit entries (on the right-hand side of the account). If a transaction does not involve VAT there will be two entries: an equal debit and credit. If VAT is involved there will be three entries, but the debit(s) must always equal the credit(s).

The questions faced by anyone operating the system are:

■ deciding which two (or three) accounts should be used for each transaction, and more critically ...

■ deciding which entry is the debit and which is the credit

There are simple rules which guide you here, but, as with learning to drive a car, the early stages require both thought and concentration!

We will first look at the layout of a typical double-entry account. The illustration here shows an account for computer equipment purchased.

Debit				Computer Account			Credit
Date	**Details**	**Folio**	**£ p**	**Date**	**Details**	**Folio**	**£ p**
01 02 02	Bank	CB007	450.00				
date of the trans-action	name of the account in which the other entry is made	page or reference number of the other account	amount of the trans-action				

Note the following:

■ the name of the account – Computer Account – is written at the top

■ the account is divided into two identical halves, separated by a central double vertical line: the left-hand side is called the 'debit' side ('debit' is abbreviated to 'Dr'), the right-hand side is called the 'credit' (or 'Cr') side

   A note for UK drivers! –   **Dr**ive on the left   **Cr**ash on the right

■ the date, details and amount of the transaction are entered in the columns:

   - in the 'details' column is entered the name of the other account involved in the book-keeping transaction – here it is the Bank Account

   - the 'folio' column is used as a cross-referencing system to the other entry of the double-entry book-keeping transaction – here CB007 stands for page 7 in the Cash Book where the Bank Account entry is made

In a manual book-keeping system each account would occupy a whole page or more, but in textbooks to save space it is usual to simplify the format and put several accounts on a page. The Computer Account set out in this way is shown at the bottom of this page.

You will see that the Folio column has gone and the column divisions have also disappeared. It is all much simpler, with just a single vertical line dividing the debit and credit sides.

The problem remains: if you are given a transaction to enter, how do you decide which is the debit entry and which is the credit entry?

dual aspect theory of double-entry

The principle of double-entry book-keeping is that every business transaction has a dual aspect: one account gains value (the debit), the other gives value (the credit). The Computer Account shows a gain in value for the business (the debit), ie the new computer, while the Bank Account will give value as the purchase price is paid (the credit).

practical aspects of double-entry

If this sounds too theoretical, look at the *practical* aspects of the system. For each double-entry transaction (ignoring any VAT for the sake of simplicity):

■ one account is debited (entry on the left of the account)

■ another account is credited (entry on the right of the account)

The *practical* rules for debits and credits are:

debit entry	**credit entry**
■ money paid into the bank	■ money paid out of the bank
■ purchases made, expenses paid	■ an income item is received
■ an asset (item owned) is acquired or increased	■ a liability (item owed) is incurred or increased

Look at the example below and read the text in the grey boxes:

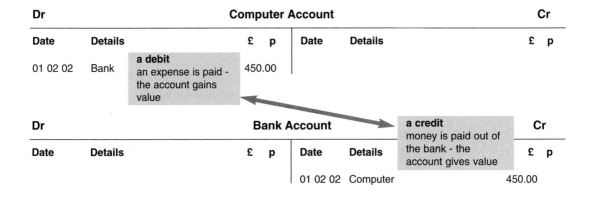

CASE STUDY

HARRY PORTER LIMITED: DOUBLE-ENTRY TRANSACTIONS

Harry Porter runs a magic and jokes shop. During the first week of September 2002 he has five transactions to enter in his double-entry accounts:

2 Sep 2002	Sale of goods for £12,000 cheque received.
3 Sep 2002	Payment of wages of £1,200 by cheque.
4 Sep 2002	Purchase of goods for £3,000, paid for by cheque.
5 Sep 2002	Received loan of £5,000 from D B Dore, and paid cheque into bank.
6 Sep 2002	Purchase of computer costing £4,000, paid for by cheque.

Again, for the sake of simplicity we have ignored any Sales or Purchases VAT.

If you look at these five transactions for Harry Porter Limited, you will see that they all involve the bank account. One invariable rule for the bank account is that money received is recorded on the left-hand (debit) side, and money paid out is recorded on the right-hand (credit) side. By applying this rule, you can say that for a bank account:

Money in is a debit (on the left); money out is a credit (on the right)

Using this rule, the bank account for Harry Porter Limited, after entering the five transactions, appears as follows:

Dr			Bank Account				Cr
Date	Details	£ p		Date	Details		£ p
2002		**money in**		2002		**money out**	
02 Sep	Sales	12,000.00		03 Sep	Wages		1,200.00
05 Sep	D B Dore Loan	5,000.00		04 Sep	Purchases		3,000.00
				06 Sep	Computer		4,000.00

It is now a simple step to work out onto which side, debit or credit, the entries are recorded in the other accounts involved. If you bear in mind that money received is a debit (left hand side) and money paid out is a credit (right hand side), by looking at any double-entry transaction which involves the bank account you should:

- identify on which side of the bank account, debit (money in) or credit (money out), the item is recorded
- record the other double-entry item on the other side of the appropriate account

We are now in a position to set out the other accounts involved in the five transactions entered in the bank account. Note that in each case the description in the account is 'Bank'.

transaction

2 September 2002: sale of goods for £12,000, cheque received

double-entry

Debit Bank Account (money in); Credit Sales Account (an income item)

Dr				Sales Account					Cr
Date	**Details**		**£**	**p**	**Date**	**Details**		**£**	**p**
2002					2002				
					02 Sep	Bank		12,000.00	

transaction

3 September 2002: payment of wages £1,200 by cheque

double-entry

Debit Wages Account (an expense); Credit Bank Account (money paid out)

Dr				Wages Account					Cr
Date	**Details**		**£**	**p**	**Date**	**Details**		**£**	**p**
2002					2002				
03 Sep	Bank		1,200.00						

transaction

4 September 2002: purchase of goods for £3,000, paid for by cheque

double-entry

Debit Purchases Account (an expense); Credit Bank Account (money paid out)

Dr				Purchases Account					Cr
Date	**Details**		**£**	**p**	**Date**	**Details**		**£**	**p**
2002					2002				
04 Sep	Bank		3,000.00						

transaction

5 September 2002: received loan from D B Dore, £5,000, and paid cheque into bank

double-entry

Debit Bank Account (money in); Credit D B Dore Loan Account (a liability)

Dr				D B Dore Loan Account					Cr
Date	**Details**		**£**	**p**	**Date**	**Details**		**£**	**p**
2002					2002				
					05 Sep	Bank		5,000.00	

transaction

6 September 2002: purchase of computer costing £4,000, paid for by cheque

double-entry

Debit Computer Account (asset acquired); Credit Bank Account (money paid out)

Dr				Computer Account			Cr	
Date	**Details**	**£**	**p**	**Date**	**Details**		**£**	**p**
2002				2002				
06 Sep	Bank	4,000.00						

Note that the acquisition of a computer is the purchase of an item which will be retained in the business. It is therefore a fixed asset and will be recorded in a separate account, and not in Purchases Account, which is used solely for recording the purchase of goods which the business is going to sell – ie magic and joke products.

DOUBLE-ENTRY FOR CREDIT SALES AND CREDIT PURCHASES

So far in this chapter we have examined the treatment of double-entry transactions involving the bank account, and have used the bank account as a guide to working out which entry is a debit and which is a credit. In business many entries will involve the bank account, because cash and cheques are a common method of payment.

There will, however, be some transactions which do not involve the bank account. Purchases and sales on credit (ie where payment is made later) are the most common, and the double-entry rules for these follow the same logic: the book-keeper, on entering a credit purchase or credit sale, records the item in the sales account or purchases account as normal, but then records the second entry in the relevant account in the name of either the customer or the supplier, instead of in the bank account, because no money has yet changed hands. The entries (again ignoring any VAT) are therefore:

- credit sale
  - Debit   Customer's Account
  - Credit   Sales Account

- credit purchase
  - Credit   Supplier's Account
  - Debit   Purchases Account

Let us now take an example of a credit sale made by Harry Porter Limited, and payment received after thirty days. On 10 September 2002 Harry Porter Limited sells goods invoiced at £5,000 on credit to Owl Promotions. The ledger entries are: debit Owl Promotions' Account; credit Sales Account.

Dr   **Sales Account**   **Cr**

Date	Details	£	p	Date	Details	£	p
2002				2002			
				10 Sep	Owl Promotions	5,000.00	

Dr   **Owl Promotions**   **Cr**

Date	Details	£	p	Date	Details	£	p
2002				2002			
10 Sep	Sales	5,000.00					

On 10 October, thirty days after this sale has been made, Harry Porter Limited receives a cheque for £5,000 from Owl Promotions in settlement of the amount due; the cheque is paid into the bank. Harry Porter Limited's book-keeper will:

■ debit Bank Account £5,000 (money received)

■ credit the account of Owl Promotions £5,000

The accounts will appear as set out below. Note the existing entry from 10 September on the account of Owl Promotions.

Dr   **Bank Account**   **Cr**

Date	Details	£	p	Date	Details	£	p
2002				2002			
10 Oct	Owl Promotions	5,000.00					

Dr   **Owl Promotions**   **Cr**

Date	Details	£	p	Date	Details	£	p
2002				2002			
10 Sep	Sales	5,000.00		10 Oct	Bank	5,000.00	

double-entry and credit purchases

Credit purchases made by a business are recorded in a similar way. If Harry Porter Limited purchases £2,500 of goods from H A Gridd Supplies on 12 September, and is given 30 days in which to pay, the entries in the books will be:

■ debit Purchases Account £2,500

■ credit H A Gridd Supplies' Account £2,500

Dr   **Purchases Account**   **Cr**

Date	Details	£	p	Date	Details	£	p
2002				2002			
12 Sep	H A Gridd Supplies	2,500.00					

Dr   **H A Gridd Supplies**   **Cr**

Date	Details	£	p	Date	Details	£	p
2002				2002			
				12 Sep	Purchases	2,500.00	

Settlement of the invoice by Harry Porter Limited in thirty days' time will be recorded by the book-keeper with the following entries:

- debit H A Gridd Supplies Account £2,500

- credit Bank Account £2,500 (money paid out)

Dr   **H A Gridd Supplies**   **Cr**

Date	Details	£	p	Date	Details	£	p
2002				2002			
12 Oct	Bank	2,500.00		12 Sep	Purchases	2,500.00	

Dr   **Bank Account**   **Cr**

Date	Details	£	p	Date	Details	£	p
2002				2002			
				12 Oct	H A Gridd Supplies	2,500.00	

balancing off accounts

You will probably have noticed that in the above examples, the accounts of the customer (Owl Promotions) and the supplier (H A Gridd Supplies) have finished up with the same amounts on each side. In these cases, nothing is owing to Harry Porter Limited, or is owed by Harry Porter Limited.

In practice, as the business trades, there will be many entries on both sides of customer and supplier accounts. It is a useful exercise to balance off each account periodically, to see how much in total each customer owes, and how much is owed to each supplier of the business. This balancing off procedure is also applied to other accounts in the books of the business. A computer accounting system will, of course, do this balancing automatically.

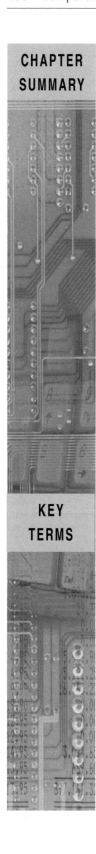

■ The accounting system of a business involves a number of stages:
- financial transactions and the documents they generate
- recording and listing of transactions ready for entering in the accounts
- entering the data into the accounts of the business – either manual accounts or a computer accounting system
- extracting report information from the accounts

■ Double-entry book-keeping transactions involve two entries, a credit and a debit. Debits are recorded on the left-hand side of an account, credits on the right-hand side.

■ The dual aspect theory of double-entry accounting states that one account gains value (the debit entry) while the other gives value (the credit entry).

■ In practical terms, debit entries include:
- money paid into the bank
- an expense incurred or a purchase made
- an acquisition of an asset or an increase in that asset
- money owing by customers (debtors)

■ In practical terms, credit entries include:
- money paid out of the bank
- income received
- a liability incurred or increased
- money owed to suppliers (creditors)

batch	a group of items totalled together for input into an accounting system
ledger	a section of the accounts of a business
trial balance	a list of the balances of accounts compiled to check the accuracy of the book-keeping
account history	a list of the transactions on a particular account
aged debtors analysis	a list of credit customers showing what they owe and if payment is overdue
aged creditors analysis	a list of suppliers showing what they are owed and when payment is due
profit and loss statement	a financial statement showing the amount of profit or loss made by a business
balance sheet	a financial statement showing what a business owns and owes and how it is financed

You are a trainee accountant in the firm of Arthur Andrews & Co. Your job is to assist with the accounts of start-up businesses, a number of which have no double-entry records. You are to carry out the following tasks.

14.1 Will Abbott has kept his bank account up-to-date, but has not got around to the other double-entry items. Rule out the other accounts for him, and make the appropriate entries.

Dr			Bank Account			Cr
20-1		£	20-1			£
1 Feb	Sales	5,000	1 Feb	Purchases		3,500
2 Feb	Sales	7,500	2 Feb	Wages		2,510
3 Feb	Bank Loan	12,500	3 Feb	Van purchase		12,500
5 Feb	Sales	9,300	3 Feb	Purchases		5,000
			4 Feb	Rent paid		780

14.2 Sarah Banks has opened up a health food shop 'Just Nuts', but has not yet started to write up the books. As she is inexperienced she asks you to set up an accounting system for her.

She provides you with the following list of transactions for the first week's trading, starting on Monday 8 June 20-1. You are to enter up the double-entry accounts for her.

Monday

Paid £ 5,000 cheque as capital into the bank; purchases of £4,000, paid by cheque.

Paid £750 sales into the bank; paid week's rent £75 by cheque.

Tuesday

Paid £500 sales into the bank; made purchases of £425 by cheque.

Wednesday

Paid £420 sales into the bank; bought computer £890 by cheque.

Thursday

Paid £550 sales into the bank; made purchases £510 by cheque.

Friday

Paid £925 sales into the bank; paid assistant's wages £75 by cheque.

14.3 Anu Sharma has made a mess of recording entries in the bank account. You are to set out the bank account as it should appear, rule up the other double-entry accounts and make the appropriate entries.

Dr			Bank Account			Cr
20-1		£	20-1			£
1 Jan	Purchases	1,000	2 Jan	Sales		5,000
5 Jan	Wages	2,700	3 Jan	Sales		7,000
5 Jan	Rent paid	150	4 Jan	Bank Loan		5,500
8 Jan	Rates paid	6,210	9 Jan	Machine purchased		4,000
9 Jan	Sales	5,205	10 Jan	Sales		9,520
10 Jan	Purchases	6,750	12 Jan	Wages		2,850
11 Jan	Car purchase	5,500	12 Jan	Rent paid		150

14.4 Sam McRae is a lazy individual and has not entered up his double-entry accounts. He has listed all his transactions, and mentions that all cheques are paid into the bank account on the day of receipt. You are to draw up the accounts for Sam McRae and make the necessary entries.

20-1	
1 March	Received £5,000 cheque as loan from brother
2 March	Bought goods £200; paid by cheque
3 March	Bought goods £1,200 on credit from H Lomax
4 March	Sold goods £800; cheque received
5 March	Sold goods £1,200 on credit to V Firth
6 March	Paid rent £955 by cheque
9 March	Bought cash register £1,200 on credit from Broadheath Business Supplies
10 March	Paid wages £780 by cheque
11 March	Bought goods on credit £5,920 from W Gould
12 March	V Firth pays for goods £1,200 by cheque
15 March	Bought goods £1,650 on credit from H Lomax
16 March	Made payment £750 by cheque to H Lomax

extended exercises

EXTENDED EXERCISE 1
PRONTO SUPPLIES LIMITED

introduction to activities

This exercise continues the Pronto Supplies Limited Case Study through to the end of March, developing the computer accounting techniques covered in the earlier chapters of this book. The activities carried out are:

1   Tidying up loose ends relating to the bank accounts left from February: topping up the petty cash to the imprest amount and transferring receipts recorded in Cash Receipts account to the Bank Current Account.

2   Opening up new customer accounts as the business expands and issuing invoices to those customers

3   Opening up new supplier accounts as the business expands and recording invoices received from those suppliers

4   Processing sales invoices and credit notes. This will also involve dealing with discounts and making corrections where they are needed

5   Processing purchase invoices and credit notes. This will also involve dealing with making corrections where they are needed.

6   Processing payments received – including payments from credit customers and cash payments paid straight into the bank.

7   Processing payments made:
     - to suppliers
     - through Petty Cash Account
     - for running expenses
     - for assets to be used in the business
     - for recurring payments through the bank current account.

8   Printing month-end reports and extracting information from the computer accounting records for use in the business.

9   Dealing with security aspects – formulating a back up policy, setting up and changing passwords and access rights, preparing for possible hardware and software failure.

ACTIVITY 1 – INITIAL BANK TRANSACTIONS

---

a note on Recurring Entries
During the course of this Activity you may see a message when you open up the program asking you if you want to process Recurring Entries. The answer to this should always be NO unless, of course, you are carrying out Activity 7, Task 7 which involves Recurring Entries.

introduction

During the month of February Pronto Supplies made a number of payments through the Petty Cash Account. These payments had depleted the Petty Cash fund from its imprest amount of £100 to a balance of £4.20. Tom cashes a cheque at the bank on 1 March to bring the Petty Cash fund back up to £100.

During February Tom decided to set up a Cash Receipts Account to record cash takings (ie cash and cheques) received from sales over a period of three days. This money was kept on the premises before being paid into the bank on 1 March. The balance on Cash Receipts Account on 1 March was £9,740.75.

In this Activity we go back to the beginning of March to deal with the Petty Cash cheque and the Cash Receipts Account.

When you have finished each Task, remember to backup your data as appropriate.

task 1

Ensure the program date is set to 1 March 2001.

Calculate the amount needed to 'top up' the Petty Cash to the imprest amount of £100.

Process a Bank transfer to record the cheque cashed to 'top up' the Petty Cash. The transfer is from Bank Current Account 1200 to Petty Cash Account 1230.

The date of the transfer is 1 March 2001 and the cheque number is 123006.

task 2

Process a Bank transfer to record the payment into the bank of the cash receipts held on the premises and recorded in Cash Receipts Account. The transfer is from Cash Receipts Account 1235 to Bank Current Account 1200.

The date of the transfer is 1 March 2001 and the reference number is 10743/5.

ACTIVITY 2 – NEW CUSTOMER ACCOUNTS AND INVOICES

introduction

During the month of March Pronto Supplies expands its business substantially and sells products to eight new credit customers. Tom needs to set up these new records in CUSTOMERS in Sage and also to input the sales invoices issued as a batch.

task 1

■   Set the program date to 9 March 2001.

■   Check that the Customer Defaults in SETTINGS are:

Payment due days	30 days
Terms of payment	Payment 30 days of invoice
VAT rate	Standard rate of 17.5% (this is Tax Code T1)
Default nominal code	4000 (this is the hardware sales account, which accounts for most of Pronto's sales to its customers)

Note: there is no default credit limit setting in the Customer Defaults.

■   Open up the following eight new accounts in CUSTOMERS in RECORD. Remember to tick the Terms Agreed box in the Credit Control tab after you have input the credit limit. As these are new customers no discounts will be allowed at this stage.

WS001   **Wendy Sawyer**
16 High Street
Mereford
MR1 2JF
Contact name: Wendy Sawyer
Telephone 01908 876352, Fax 01908 876355, Email wsawyer@quickmail.com
Credit limit £5,000

RB001   **R Brown & Co**
34 Tolleydene Road
Mereford
MR3 9VF
Contact name: Robert Brown
Telephone 01908 345777, Fax 01908 345952, Email rbrown@goblin.com
Credit limit £5,000

LA001 **Landsman Ltd**
Unit 16 Severnside Estate
Mereford
MR3 6FD
Contact name: Tom Grundy
Telephone 01908 674714, Fax 01908 674720, Email mail@landsman.co.uk
www.landsman.co.uk
Credit limit £10,000

JS001 **John Shaw & Associates**
16 Butler Street
Mereford
MR3 8KP
Contact name: John Shaw
Telephone 01908 824176, Fax 01908 824197, Email mail@jshawassociates.co.uk
www.jshawassociates.co.uk
Credit limit £10,000

DF001 **Donn Fishing Tackle**
17 Pitmaster Road
Mereford
MR2 5HP
Contact name: John Donn
Telephone 01908 763129, Fax 01908 763135, Email jdonn@goblin.com
Credit limit £5,000

HC001 **Henwick Consultancy**
16 Hallow Mansions
Grimstoke
MR6 8SZ
Contact name: Ted Hughes
Telephone 01908 674034, Fax 01908 674045, Email ehughes@henwickconsultancy.co.uk
www.henwickconsultancy.co.uk
Credit limit £5,000

DP001 **D Patel**
17 Shaw Street
Mereford
MR4 6KS
Contact name: D Patel

Telephone 01908 824111, Fax 01908 824116, Email dpatel@goblin.com

Credit limit £5,000

PM001 **Paradise Music**

55 Elysium Road

Norton

MR5 9GF

Contact name: Ben Britton

Telephone 01908 352876, Fax 01908 352866, Email bbritton@paradisemusic.co.uk

www.paradisemusic.co.uk

Credit limit £5,000

task 2

Print out a list of customer details from the Customer Address List Report in CUSTOMERS and check your input against the printout. Make corrections to the records if you need to.

task 3

Process the invoices issued to these new customers in a batch dated 9 March 2001. The tax code in each case is T1. Remember to use the correct nominal code for computer hardware sales (4000) and computer software sales (4001).The details of the invoices are as follows:

account	invoice	date	net (£)	VAT (£)	details of sale
WS001	10036	09 03 01	2,000.00	350.00	22" flat screen
RB001	10037	09 03 01	2,200.00	385.00	Z33 desktop computer
LA001	10038	09 03 01	6,200.00	1,085.00	R67 server (hardware)
JS001	10039	09 03 01	5,500.00	962.50	Z32 computer
DF001	10040	09 03 01	2,400.00	420.00	Z34 computer
HC001	10041	09 03 01	3,400.00	595.00	Z30 computer and screen
DP001	10042	09 03 01	400.00	70.00	Pageworx software
PM001	10043	09 03 01	850.00	148.75	Photoshack software
Totals			22,950.00	4,016.25	

task 4

Print out a Day Books: Customer Invoices (Summary) report for 9 March 2001 from CUSTOMERS to check the accuracy of your input. Note that this will also show the three Service Invoices input earlier.

ACTIVITY 3 – NEW SUPPLIER ACCOUNTS AND INVOICES

introduction

During March Pronto Supplies also starts buying products from four new suppliers. It will need to set up records for them in SUPPLIERS in Sage and to input the purchase invoices as a batch.

task 1

■ Set the program date to 9 March 2001.

■ Check that the Supplier Defaults in SETTINGS are:

VAT rate	Standard rate of 17.5% (this is Tax Code T1)
Default nominal code	5000

■ Open up the following four new accounts in SUPPLIERS, using RECORD. The credit limit and payment terms agreed should be input on the Credit Control tab and the Terms Agreed box should be ticked.

CW001 **Compwarehouse PLC**
Compwarehouse House
Romily Drive
Ramshurst
RA1 9JH
Contact name: Jo Fenz
Telephone 01344 298102, Fax 01344 298455, Email sales@compwarehouse.co.uk
www.compwarehouse.co.uk
Credit limit £20,000, payment period 30 days.

NE001 **Newton Supplies**
Apple House
Norwich
NR2 9GH
Contact name: Isaac Smith
Telephone 01865 748991, Fax 01865 749002, Email sales@newtonsupplies.co.uk
www.newtonsupplies.co.uk
Credit limit £15,000, payment period 30 days.
Invoice 9822 issued 05 03 01, £9,987.50

DV001   **DVDWorld**

Vision House

Ramford

RM3 8PF

Contact name: Di Scott

Telephone 01809 765241, Fax 01809 765256, Email sales@dvdworld.co.uk

www.dvdworld.co.uk

Credit limit £10,000, payment period 30 days.

LV001   **Laura Varndean Software Supplies**

Unit 12 Avontree Estate

Bath

BA2 3BL

Contact name: Laura Varndean

Telephone 01225 428998, Fax 01225 428645, Email sales@lvarndean.co.uk

www.lvarndean.co.uk

Credit limit £20,000, payment period 30 days.

task 2

Print out a list of supplier details from the Supplier Addresses report in SUPPLIERS and check your input against the printout. Make corrections to the records if you need to.

task 3

Process the invoices received from these new suppliers in a batch. The tax code in each case is T1 and the nominal code 5000. The details of the invoices are as follows:

account	invoice	date	net (£)	VAT (£)	details of purchase
CW001	8298	07 03 01	11,200.00	1,960.00	Desktop computers
NE001	9822	05 03 01	8,500.00	1,487.50	Desktop computers
DV001	8759	06 03 01	4,500.00	787.50	DVD drives
LV001	1066	05 03 01	15,200.00	2,660.00	Software
Totals			39,400.00	6,895.00	

task 4

Print out a Day Books: Supplier Invoices (Summary) report for 5 - 7 March 2001 from SUPPLIERS to check the accuracy of your input.

ACTIVITY 4 – PROCESSING SALES INVOICES AND CREDIT NOTES

introduction

At the end of the third week in March (Friday 16 March) Tom realises that he will have to input batches of sales invoices and credit notes sent. He has also been requested by some customers to allow discounts.

task 1

■ Set the program date to 16 March 2001.

■ Input the following sales invoices as a batch in CUSTOMERS. Remember that the nominal code for hardware sales is 4000 and the nominal code for software sales is 4001.

account	invoice	date	net (£)	VAT (£)	details of sale
WS001	10044	12 03 01	80.00	14.00	Zap disc drive
RB001	10045	12 03 01	400.00	70.00	Pageworx software
LA001	10046	13 03 01	20.00	3.50	Printer lead
JS001	10047	13 03 01	2,400.00	420.00	Z34 computer
DF001	10048	14 03 01	600.00	105.00	Quorkdesign software
HC001	10049	15 03 01	500.00	87.50	TG30 Scanner
DP001	10050	15 03 01	2,400.00	420.00	Z34 computer
PM001	10051	16 03 01	240.00	42.00	L209 inkjet printer
Totals			6,640.00	1,162.00	

task 2

Print out a Day Books: Customer Invoices (Summary) report for 12 - 16 March 2001 from CUSTOMERS to check the accuracy of your input.

task 3

Tom has had to issue two credit notes on 16 March . . .

Wendy Sawyer has telephoned to say that she thought she was due a 10% discount on invoice 10036 issued on 9 March (see page 206). Tom agrees to issue a credit note (number 556).

Ben Britton of Paradise Music emails to say that the Photoshack software supplied (invoice 10043 – see page 206) was incorrect. It should have been Photopage software. Tom agrees to issue a credit note (number 557) for the full invoice amount and will resupply when Photopage is in stock.

■ Ensure the program date is 16 March 2001.

■ Input the two credit notes as a batch, taking care over the VAT element and the nominal codes for hardware and software.

■ Adjust Wendy Sawyer's account so that it allows a 10% trade discount in future.

task 4

Print out a Day Books: Customer Credits (Summary) report for 16 March 2001 from CUSTOMERS to check the accuracy of your input.

ACTIVITY 5 – PROCESSING SUPPLIER INVOICES AND CREDIT NOTES

introduction

At the end of the third week in March (Friday 16 March) Tom realises that he will also have to input batches of purchase invoices and credit notes received. He also needs to make a correction to one of the transactions.

task 1

■ Set the program date to 16 March 2001.

■ Process the invoices received from these new suppliers in a batch in SUPPLIERS. The tax code in each case is T1 and the nominal code 5000. The details of the invoices are as follows:

account	invoice	date	net (£)	VAT (£)	details of purchase
CW001	8307	12 03 01	4,000.00	700.00	Desktop computers
NE001	9839	14 03 01	3,200.00	560.00	Peripherals
DV001	8793	12 03 01	3,800.00	665.00	Disk drives
LV001	1087	13 03 01	1,160.00	203.00	Software
Totals			12,160.00	2,128.00	

task 2

Print out a Day Books: Supplier Invoices (Summary) report for 12 -14 March 2001 from SUPPLIERS to check the accuracy of your input.

task 3

One of the computers supplied by Compwarehouse on invoice 8298 dated 4 March (see page 208) has been found to be faulty. Tom has received a credit note dated 9 March, ref 1701, for £2,350 (this includes VAT).

Input this credit note on the Credits entry screen in SUPPLIERS.

task 4

Print out a Day Books: Supplier Credits (Summary) report for 9 March 2001 from SUPPLIERS to check the accuracy of your input.

task 5

On checking through the paperwork Tom notes that the description input for invoice 9822 for £9,987.50 from Newton Supplies, code NE001 (see page 208) was 'Desktop computers' whereas it should have been 'Peripherals'.

You are to correct this input description using CORRECTIONS in MAINTENANCE, reached from FILE.

ACTIVITY 6 – PROCESSING PAYMENTS RECEIVED

introduction

It is 30 March and Tom is catching up with his input into the computer accounting system ready for the month-end. Part of this input includes payments received from customers (a batch of cheques he is about to pay into the bank) and also cash receipts which he has already paid into the bank during the course of the month.

task 1

■   Set the program date to 30 March 2001.

■   Tom has made a listing of the cheques recently received from his credit customers. You are to input the following into the Customers screen in BANK. Tom has listed the cheques with their account reference codes for ease of input. The reference is the paying-in slip number.

code	cheque amount (£)	date received	reference
CH001	18.80	26 03 2001	10750
CR001	117.50	26 03 2001	10750
DB001	235.00	27 03 2001	10750
FE001	470.00	27 03 2001	10750
JB001	611.00	28 03 2001	10750
JG001	310.20	28 03 2001	10750
LG001	211.50	26 03 2001	10750
PT001	376.00	29 03 2001	10750
Total	2,350.00		

task 2

Print out a Day Books: Customer Receipts (Summary) report for 26-30 March 2001 from BANK to check the accuracy of your input.

task 3

Tom was advised by the bank at the beginning of the month to pay his cash takings (his takings of cash and cheques over the counter) direct into the bank at the end of each week using the bank night safe facility. This means that instead of keeping the money on the premises over the weekend the takings are totalled up and a paying-in slip prepared late on Saturday. The money and the paying-in slip are then put in a bank-supplied wallet and placed in a locked safe in the wall of the bank each Saturday evening.

Tom therefore has decided to input these cash takings as BANK RECEIPTS in BANK as this seemed an easier and more logical way of dealing with his cash receipts.

The cash receipts are listed on the next page. Tom has decided to deal with the cash receipts for the current week in the next month's input, as they have not yet been lodged with the bank.

date	reference	description	net (£)	VAT (£)
03 03 2001	10746	Hardware sales	5,680.00	994.00
03 03 2001	10746	Software sales	1,250.00	218.75
10 03 2001	10747	Hardware sales	7,840.00	1,372.00
10 03 2001	10747	Software sales	2,370.00	414.75
17 03 2001	10748	Hardware sales	8,400.00	1,470.00
17 03 2001	10748	Software sales	970.00	169.75
24 03 2001	10749	Hardware sales	9,285.00	1,624.88
24 03 2001	10749	Software sales	499.00	87.33
		Totals	36,294.00	6,351.46
		Batch total (gross)		42,645.46

task 4

Print out a Day Books: Bank Receipts (Detailed) report for 3 - 24 March 2001 from BANK to check the accuracy of your input.

ACTIVITY 7 – MAKING PAYMENTS

introduction

It is 30 March. Tom is inputting the payments made during the month. These include payment to suppliers for invoices due, payment for petty cash items and running expenses of the business, and for recurring entries involving standing orders and direct debits.

task 1

■ Set the program date to 30 March 2001.

■ Input the following payments (dated 30 March) through Suppliers in BANK. Tom is happy that they should be paid (the earlier problem with the Tycomp cheque has been resolved).

code	supplier	amount due (£)	cheque number
DE001	Delco PLC	4700.00	123007
EL001	Electron Supplies	2773.00	123008
MA001	MacCity	2820.00	123009
SY001	Synchromart	1504.00	123010
TY001	Tycomp Supplies	6160.00	123011
		17,957.00	

task 2

Print out a Day Books: Supplier Payments (Summary) report for 30 March 2001 from BANK to check the accuracy of your input.

task 3

Tom has a number of petty cash vouchers to process for the month. You are to input the following transactions. The bank account is Petty Cash Account 1230. Petrol expenses should be charged to account 7300 ('Fuel and Oil'). Note that Postages are VAT exempt and should be given a T2 tax code. All other items are standard rated (T1).

voucher	date	description	amount (£)	
PC106	06 03 2001	Postages	15.20	
PC107	14 03 2001	Postages	16.50	
PC108	20 03 2001	Stationery	21.15	(including VAT)
PC109	27 03 2001	Postages	16.00	
PC110	28 03 2001	Petrol	21.76	(including VAT)

task 4

Print out a Day Books: Cash Payments (Summary) report for 6 - 30 March 2001 from BANK to check the accuracy of your input. Remember to select Petty Cash Account first.

task 5

Input the following running cost payments through Payment in BANK.

You will have to work out the nominal codes first. You can work them out from the trial balance shown on the next page.

The cheque number should be used as the reference.

The tax code is T1 except where indicated otherwise.

date	cheque	details	net (£)	VAT(£)
06 03 2001	123012	Stationery	250.00	43.75
09 03 2001	123013	Materials purchased	5,600.00	980.00
09 03 2001	123014	Wages	4,205.00	T9
14 03 2001	123015	Adverts	2,170.00	379.75
15 03 2001	123016	Office equipment	6,590.00	1,153.25
16 03 2001	123017	Materials purchased	5,100.00	892.50
16 03 2001	123018	Wages	4,190.00	T9
20 03 2001	123019	Electricity	165.00	28.88
23 03 2001	123020	Materials purchased	7,850.00	1,373.75
23 03 2001	123021	Wages	4,070.00	T9
27 03 2001	123022	Rent	4,500.00	787.50
28 03 2001	123023	Rates	350.00	T2
29 03 2001	123024	Telephone	426.00	74.55
30 03 2001	123025	Materials purchased	6,370.00	1,114.75
30 03 2001	123026	Wages	4,230.00	T9
		Totals	56,066.00	6,828.68

task 6

Print out a Day Books: Bank Payments (Summary) report for 6 - 30 March 2001 from BANK to check the accuracy of your input.

task 7

Process the recurring entries in BANK for March. They should appear as follows:

1   A direct debit payment (DD) for Zerax566 Maintenance, £23.27 gross on 15 March.

2   A standing order receipt (SO) from office rental (10A High Street), £585.80 gross on 10 March.

task 8

Print out a Trial Balance as at the end of March from FINANCIALS to provide a final check of the accuracy of your input. It should be identical to the one on the next page.

Pronto Supplies Limited
Period Trial Balance

Page:

To Period: Month 3, March 2001

N/C	Name	Debit	Credit
0020	Plant and Machinery	35,000.00	
0030	Office Equipment	26,350.00	
0040	Furniture and Fixtures	30,000.00	
1100	Debtors Control Account	41,162.50	
1200	Bank Current Account	10,636.24	
1230	Petty Cash	9.39	
2100	Creditors Control Account		58,233.00
2200	Sales Tax Control Account		41,723.51
2201	Purchase Tax Control Account	50,792.56	
2300	Loans		35,000.00
3000	Ordinary Shares		80,000.00
4000	Computer hardware sales		195,325.00
4001	Computer software sales		38,703.00
4002	Computer consultancy		3,480.00
4904	Rent Income		912.00
5000	Materials Purchased	167,842.00	
6201	Advertising	24,770.00	
7000	Gross Wages	49,705.00	
7100	Rent	13,500.00	
7103	General Rates	1,150.00	
7200	Electricity	315.00	
7201	Gas	158.00	
7300	Fuel and Oil	18.52	
7501	Postage and Carriage	77.70	
7502	Telephone	1,011.00	
7504	Office Stationery	839.00	
7701	Office Machine Maintenance	39.60	
	Totals:	453,376.51	453,376.51

Trial balance of Pronto Supplies Limited as at 30 March 2001

ACTIVITY 8 – DEALING WITH THE MONTH END PROCEDURES

introduction

It is 30 March and the month-end. Tom is extracting reports and printouts from Sage. These provide him with information and help him to make decisions – all part of the process of managing his business.

Before any reports can be extracted the program date should be set to 30 March 2001.

task 1

If you have not already done so in the last Activity, print out a Trial Balance for Pronto Supplies Limited as at 30 March 2001 and check the figures against the Trial Balance on the previous page.

The trial balance helps to tell Tom how the business is getting on. Answer the following:

(a)   How much cash will he need to top up the petty cash to £100?

(b)   What are his sales figures for the three months of year so far (ie the total of the three sales accounts)?

(c)   How much does Pronto Supplies owe its suppliers?

task 2

Print out an audit trail for the month of March. What can this Report be used for?

task 3

Print out an Aged Debtors Analysis (eg Aged Debtors Analysis [Summary] Fixed from REPORTS in CUSTOMERS). Identify any account which might give cause for concern. Run a Customer Activity Report on that account and send it with a Memorandum to Tom Cox (use your own name), outlining the problem and recommending a suitable course of action.

task 4

Run a Customer Address List from REPORTS in CUSTOMERS. Either email it (if you are online) for the attention of Jim Cox, Sales Manager, or export it to a word processor file so that the details can subsequently be sent in a letter to Jim Cox.

ACTIVITY 9 – DEALING WITH COMPUTER SECURITY

introduction

Security of computer equipment, computer programs and data is essential in a well-run business. Tom has been so busy setting up and running Pronto Supplies Ltd that he has had too little time for setting up the necessary security systems which safeguard the integrity of computer hardware and software.

task 1

Tom is normally a laid back sort of person, but today he looks worried. He has heard from a friend who has just had her business premises ransacked by thieves. All her computers have gone, so too has all her data – the back up discs she had were kept in a drawer near the computer and they have disappeared.

Outline to Tom the security precautions he should take with regard to his computer hardware and software and data.

task 2

Tom is also worried that Jade, a new member of his accounts staff is rather nosey because she keeps looking at parts of the computer accounting system which do not concern her. You explain to Tom how he can set up access rights in Sage to protect valuable and confidential data.

Make the appropriate entries in Sage to enable Tom to have access to all data and Jade to have access to Customers and Suppliers only.

task 3

Tom finds out a week later that Jade has written down her password and left it on her desk because, as she says, "I keep forgetting it!"

Describe the action Tom should take.

exercise introduction

This is a 'standalone' extended exercise which puts into practice all the computer accounting skills you will have developed while working through this book.

It features a sole trader business run by Jo Lane who has set up a translation bureau 'Interlingo' which sells language books and tapes as a sideline. Jo has been operating for a month using a manual book-keeping system and has then decided to set up the accounting records in a Sage system in the second month.

The activities to be covered are:

1   Setting up the business in Sage.

2   Setting up customers and supplier records and inputting opening balances.

3   Setting up the Nominal Ledger in Sage and inputting opening balances from the Trial Balance produced at the end of the first month of trading.

4   Processing and printing service sales invoices and credit notes.

5   Processing purchase invoices and credit notes.

6   Processing payments received – including payments from credit customers and cash payments from small translation jobs, and books and tapes over the counter.

7   Processing payments made to suppliers and for running expenses.

8   Setting up a Petty Cash Account and processing Petty Cash Payments.

9   Setting up recurring payments through the bank current account.

10   Printing month-end reports and extracting information from the computer accounting records for use in the business.

11   Dealing with security aspects – formulating a back up policy, setting up passwords and access rights.

ACTIVITY 1 – SETTING UP THE BUSINESS IN SAGE

introduction

Interlingo Translation Services is a sole trader business run by Jo Lane, a linguist who has worked as a translator with the European Commission in Brussels and has now settled back in her home town of Mereford. The business is very much a 'one person' business. Jo rents a small office in the town and does everything herself.

Interlingo Translation Services provides translation services and also sells books and tapes.

translation services

Larger clients, for example importers and exporters who need documents translated into English and sales literature translated into foreign languages are supplied by Jo on credit terms (ie they are invoiced and pay later).

Small local 'private' translating jobs which come about from local adverts are normally paid for on a cash basis (ie cash or cheque) and are not invoiced.

language books and tapes

Jo has found that selling language books and tapes is a useful sideline. They are all sold for cash, but are bought on credit from the publishers.

the accounting system

Interlingo Translation Services was set up on 2 July 2001. The business is registered for VAT and after a month of using a manual accounting system Jo has decided to transfer her accounts to Sage Line 50 software and sign up for a year's telephone technical support. Her main problem, common to so many sole traders, is that of time – finding time to process her accounts and to see how she is getting on in financial terms.

Jo has chosen Sage Line 50 because it will enable her to:

• process and print the invoices issued to business customers who are supplied on credit

• record the cash sales of books and tapes and small translation jobs

• pay the publishers of the books and tapes on the due date

• keep a record of money received and paid out

• print out reports which will tell her who has not paid on time

• print out reports which will tell her what she is spending

In short Jo hopes that Sage will help her save time (and money) in running her accounting system.

backups

Remember to backup your data after each inputting Task, just as Jo would.

task 1

Ensure that the computer is set up correctly. A Sage Rebuild may be necessary.

The financial year should be set to start on 1 July 2001. This can be done in SETTINGS or as part of the Rebuild process.

task 2

Set up the details of the business in Sage. Company Preferences in SETTINGS can be used if you are not using the ActiveSetup Wizard.

■ Adopt the 'General Business: Standard Accounts' as the chart of accounts to be used.

■ Enter the address details:

Interlingo Translation Services
14 Privet Road
Mereford
MR5 1HP

Tel: 01908 335876

Fax: 01908 335899

Email: mail@interlingo.co.uk

www.interlingo.co.uk

VAT Reg: 416 1385 51

■ Ensure that the non-VAT code in Parameters in Company Preferences (SETTINGS) is set at T9. Also check that the VAT Cash Accounting box and the Access Rights box are blank.

■ Set the program date to 1 August 2001 (SETTINGS).

ACTIVITY 2 – SETTING UP THE CUSTOMER AND SUPPLIER RECORDS

introduction

Interlingo Translation sells on credit to five businesses that use its translation services on a regular basis. Jo will have to set up the details of these customers on the computer.

The business also buys its books and tapes from two wholesale suppliers. These will also have to be input onto the computer.

task 1

The CUSTOMER defaults (reached through SETTINGS) should be set up as follows:

Payment due days	30 days
Terms	Payment 30 days of invoice
VAT rate	17.5% standard rate (code T1)
Default nominal code	4000

task 2

Input the details and opening balance for each of the five customers through RECORD in CUSTOMERS. The opening balance in each case is the total of the invoice already issued and is a gross amount. You do not need to deal with VAT at this stage. Do not post these invoices as a separate batch!

The credit limits and 'Terms Agreed' will also need to be entered (in the Credit Control tab).

Account name	**RS Export Agency**
Account reference	RR001
Address	46 High Street
	Mereford
	MR1 9FD
Contact name	Raspal Singh

Telephone 01908 564187, Fax 01908 564911
Email rsingh@zipnet.co.uk

Credit limit £1,000

Invoice reference 10010 for £850.00 issued on 06 07 01

Account name	**Playgames PLC**
Account reference	PL001
Address	Consul House
	Viney Street
	Mereford
	MR2 6PL
Contact name	Jacquie Mills

Telephone 01908 749724, Fax 01908 749355
Email mail@playgames.com
www.playgames.com

Credit limit £1,000

Invoice reference 10011 for £795.00 issued on 12 07 01

Account name	**Rotherway Limited**
Account reference	RT001
Address	78 Sparkhouse Street
	Millway
	MY5 8HG
Contact name	Darsha Patel

Telephone 01987 875241, Fax 01987 875241
Email mail@rotherway.co.uk
www.rotherway.co.uk

Credit limit £2,000

Invoice reference 10012 for £1,210.00 issued on 17 07 01

Account name	**Hill & Dale & Co, Solicitors**
Account reference	HD001
Address	17 Berkeley Chambers
	Penrose Street
	Mereford
	MR2 6GF
Contact name	Helen Lexington

Telephone 01908 875432, Fax 01908 875444
Email hlex@hilldale.co.uk

Credit limit £1,000

Invoice reference 10013 for £345.00 issued on 19 07 01

Account name	**Schafeld Ltd**
Account reference	SC001
Address	86 Tanners Lane Millway MY7 5VB
Contact name	Hans Rautmann

Telephone 01987 619086, Fax 01987 619097
Email hrautmann@schafeld.com
www.schafeld.com
Credit limit £1,000

Invoice reference 10014 for £800.00 issued on 20 07 01

task 3

Print out a Day Books: Customer Invoices (Summary) Report to check the accuracy of your input. The batch total should be £4,000.

task 4

The SUPPLIER defaults (reached through SETTINGS) should be set up as follows:

VAT rate	17.5% standard rate (code T1)
Default nominal code	5000

task 5

Input the details and opening balance for the two suppliers of books and tapes through RECORD in SUPPLIERS. The credit limits and payment terms agreed will also need to be entered on the Credit Control screen. The 'Terms Agreed' box will also need to be ticked.

Account name	**TDI Wholesalers**
Account reference	TD001
Address	Markway Estate Nottingham NG1 7GH
Contact name	Ron Beasley

Telephone 0115 295992, Fax 0115 295976, Email sales@tdi.co.uk
www.tdi.co.uk

Credit limit granted £5,000, payment terms 30 days of invoice date

Invoice reference 2347 for £780.00 issued on 05 07 01.

TDI Wholesalers supply Jo with language tapes, which are standard-rated for VAT.

Account name	**Bardners Books**
Account reference	BB001
Address	Purbeck House
	College Street
	Cambridge
	CB3 8HP
Contact name	Sarah Rooney

Telephone 01223 400652, Fax 01223 400648
Email sales@bardners.co.uk
www.bardners.co.uk

Credit limit granted £2,000, payment terms 30 days of invoice date

Invoice reference 9422 for £420.00 issued on 06 07 01.

Bardners Books supply Jo with language books, which are zero-rated for VAT. This supplier account may therefore be set up with a default tax code of T0.

task 6

Print out a Day Books: Supplier Invoices (Summary) Report to check the accuracy of your input. The batch total should be £1,200.

task 7

Print out a Trial Balance Report from FINANCIALS to check the total of the Debtors Control Account (the total of the Customer invoices) and the Creditors Control Account (the total of the Supplier invoices). The report should appear as follows:

Interlingo Translation Services

Period Trial Balance

Page:

To Period: Month 1, July 2001

N/C	Name	Debit	Credit
1100	Debtors Control Account	4,000.00	
2100	Creditors Control Account		1,200.00
9998	Suspense Account		2,800.00
	Totals:	4,000.00	4,000.00

ACTIVITY 3 – SETTING UP THE NOMINAL LEDGER

introduction

Interlingo Translations has been set up in Sage with a default Chart of Accounts (nominal accounts list) which can be used as a structure for the nominal account balances which were outstanding at the end of July.

Jo has already set up a Trial Balance on a spreadsheet. The figures are shown below. The right-hand column shows the Nominal Account number which Jo has allocated to each account from the list of Nominal Accounts. The grey backgrounds show where the default account name needs changing.

	Dr £	Cr £	Account
Office computers	5000		0020
Office equipment	2500		0030
Furniture and fixtures	3000		0040
Debtors control account	4000		1100
Bank current account	7085		1200
Creditors control account		1200	2100
Sales tax control account		814	2200
Purchase tax control account	623		2201
Loans		5000	2300
Capital		15000	3000
Translation services income		3660	4000
Sales of language books		456	4100
Sales of language tapes		950	4101
Purchases of books	300		5000
Purchases of tapes	750		5001
Advertising	550		6201
Drawings	2000		7000
Rent	250		7100
General rates	129		7103
Electricity	61		7200
Postage & Carriage	86		7501
Telephone	275		7502
Office Stationery	471		7504
	27,080	27,080	

task 1

Ensure the program date is set at 1 August 2001.

Select the accounts that you wish to enter in the records from the NOMINAL opening screen. Use the account numbers in the right-hand column. Do not worry if the account names are different - they will be amended in Task 3. But do not select the Debtors Control Account or the Creditors Control Account as they should already show their balances.

Select RECORD from NOMINAL and enter the balance of each account from the Trial Balance, using the 31 August date. You may need to click on the Balance field or the O/B button to bring up the balance entry screen. Ensure that the amount is recorded in the correct debit or credit box.

task 2

Print out a Trial Balance as at 1 August 2001 from FINANCIALS.

task 3

Now change the account names that need changing (see the accounts with grey backgrounds on page 225) in RECORD in NOMINAL. Print out a further Trial Balance to check your corrections. The print out should appear as shown below. Check your input against this Report.

Interlingo Translation Services   **Page:**

Period Trial Balance

To Period: Month 2, August 2001

N/C	Name	Debit	Credit
0020	Office computers	5,000.00	
0030	Office Equipment	2,500.00	
0040	Furniture and Fixtures	3,000.00	
1100	Debtors Control Account	4,000.00	
1200	Bank Current Account	7,085.00	
2100	Creditors Control Account		1,200.00
2200	Sales Tax Control Account		814.00
2201	Purchase Tax Control Account	623.00	
2300	Loans		5,000.00
3000	Capital		15,000.00
4000	Translation services income		3,660.00
4100	Sales of language books		456.00
4101	Sales of language tapes		950.00
5000	Purchases of books	300.00	
5001	Purchases of tapes	750.00	
6201	Advertising	550.00	
7000	Drawings	2,000.00	
7100	Rent	250.00	
7103	General Rates	129.00	
7200	Electricity	61.00	
7501	Postage and Carriage	86.00	
7502	Telephone	275.00	
7504	Office Stationery	471.00	
	Totals:	**27,080.00**	**27,080.00**

ACTIVITY 4 – ISSUING INVOICES AND CREDIT NOTES FOR TRANSLATIONS

introduction

It is 31 August and Jo is issuing invoices for the work done. She is using the 'Service Invoice' facility in Sage for this. Her standard rate of charge is £20 plus VAT per hour. A major customer has asked for discount and Jo has agreed to allow 10% on invoices to that customer. She issues a Credit Note on this account to allow for discount on an invoice which had already been issued.

task 1

Set the program date to 31 August 2001.

Input and print out the following invoices under the Service Invoice facility. (Note: if your system does not allow you to do this, use the Batch Invoice entry system).

invoice	account	date	net(£)	VAT(£)	description
10015	HD001	10 08 2001	520.00	91.00	Translation of sales contracts (26 hours)
10016	PL001	16 08 2001	120.00	21.00	Translation of sales literature (6 hours)
10017	RR001	20 08 2001	100.00	17.50	Translation of shipping docs (5 hours)
10018	RT001	20 08 2001	320.00	56.00	Translation of sales contracts (16 hours)
10019	SC001	22 08 2001	160.00	28.00	Translation of sales contracts (8 hours)

task 2

Hill & Dale & Co, who have passed substantial work your way, have written formally to ask for a 10% discount, backdated to the beginning of the month. They also ask if they can be allowed 2.5% cash discount for settlement of invoices within seven days and an increase in credit limit to £3,000.

Process and print out the following Service Credit Note to Hill & Dale & Co:

ref	account	date	net(£)	VAT(£)	description
501	HD001	31 08 2001	52.00	9.10	Refund of 10% discount, invoice 10015

Amend Hill & Dale & Co's account record allowing 10% trade discount and 2.5% cash discount for settlement within seven days. Increase the credit limit to £3,000

task 3

Input and print out the following invoice for Hill & Dale & Co under the Service Invoice facility.

(Note: if your system does not allow you to do this, use the Batch Invoice entry system, but ensure that any adjustments for discount are made first).

The final invoice total should be £1,264.28.

invoice	account	date	description
10020	HD001	31 08 2001	Translation of Contract Tender (60 hours, total £1,200).

task 4

Check your input against the printed documents and when you are happy with your accuracy, update the ledgers for the credit note and invoices and print out an update report.

Note: if you are using the Batch Invoice entry method, print out the appropriate Day Books for Customer Invoices and Credit Notes.

The Update report should look like this:

Interlingo Translation Services
Update Ledgers

Inv	Tp	Tran	Date	A/C	N/C	Stock Code	Details	Qty	Net	Tax	Gross
501	SC	59	30/08/2001	HD001	4000		Refund of 10% discount, invoice 1001		-52.00	-9.10	-61.10
							Credit Total:		-52.00	-9.10	-61.10
10015	SI	60	10/08/2001	HD001	4000		Translation of sales contracts (26 hour		520.00	91.00	611.00
							Invoice Total:		520.00	91.00	611.00
10016	SI	61	16/08/2001	PL001	4000		Translation of sales literature (6 hours		120.00	21.00	141.00
							Invoice Total:		120.00	21.00	141.00
10017	SI	62	20/08/2001	RR001	4000		Translation of shipping docs (5 hours)		100.00	17.50	117.50
							Invoice Total:		100.00	17.50	117.50
10018	SI	63	20/08/2001	RT001	4000		Translation of sales contracts (16 hour		320.00	56.00	376.00
							Invoice Total:		320.00	56.00	376.00
10019	SI	64	22/08/2001	SC001	4000		Translation of sales contracts (8 hours		160.00	28.00	188.00
							Invoice Total:		160.00	28.00	188.00
10020	SI	65	31/08/2001	HD001	4000		Translation of contract tender (60 hou		1,080.00	184.28	1,264.28
							Invoice Total:		1,080.00	184.28	1,264.28
							Grand Total for Invoices:		2,300.00	397.78	2,697.78
							Grand Total for All:		2,248.00	388.68	2,636.68

ACTIVITY 5 – PROCESSING PURCHASE INVOICES AND CREDIT NOTES

When you have completed this Activity you may check your input against the Trial Balance printed on page 248.

introduction

Jo's purchases on credit are her supplies of language tapes and books. During August she received two invoices in total. They are shown below and on the next page.

task 1

Set the program date at 31 August 2001.

Input the two invoices below and on the next page as a batch into Invoices in SUPPLIERS.

Note that the Nominal code for tapes is 5001 and for books is 5000.

task 2

Print out a Day Books: Supplier Invoices (Summary) to check your input.

INVOICE

TDI Wholesalers

Markway Estate, Nottingham, NG1 7GH
Tel 0115 295992 Fax 0115 295976 www.TDI.co.uk

invoice to		invoice no	2561
Interlingo Translation Services 14 Privet Road Mereford MR5 1HP		account	3023
		your reference	984
		date/tax point	15 08 01

product code	description	quantity	price	unit	total	VAT	total
2421	Beginners French tapes	100	5.00	set	500.00	87.50	587.50
2634	Advanced Italian tapes	50	6.00	set	300.00	52.50	352.50
					goods total		800.00
					VAT		140.00
					TOTAL		940.00

INVOICE

BARDNERS BOOKS

Purbeck House, College Street, Cambridge CB3 8HP
Tel 01223 400652 Fax 01223 400648 www.Bardners.co.uk

invoice to

Interlingo Translation Services	invoice no **11231**
14 Privet Road	account **IL9987**
Mereford	your reference **985**
MR5 1HP	date/tax point **20 08 01**

product code	description	quantity	price	unit	total	VAT zero-rate	total
G778	German First Course	60	4.95	each	297.00	00.00	297.00
2634	French Second Course	45	5.95	each	267.75	00.00	267.75
					goods total		564.75
					VAT		00.00
					TOTAL		564.75

task 3

Jo discovers that ten of the sets of Beginners French tapes are faulty. She sends them back and asks for a credit note. This arrives on 31 August. Input the document (see below) into Credit Notes in SUPPLIERS (Nominal Code 5001) and print out a Day Books: Suppliers Credits (Summary).

credit note from TDI Wholesalers (extract)

Interlingo Translation Services	credit note no 1919
14 Privet Road	account 3023
Mereford	your reference 984
MR5 1HP	date/tax point 28 08 01

product code	description	quantity	price	unit	total	VAT	total
2421	Beginners French tapes	10	5.00	set	50.00	8.75	58.75
					goods total		50.00
					VAT		8.75
					TOTAL		58.75

REASON FOR CREDIT
Faulty tapes returned

ACTIVITY 6 – PROCESSING PAYMENTS RECEIVED

introduction

Jo has received payments from a number of different sources during August:

- payments from customers who have bought on credit during July
- cash payments for small translation jobs
- cash payments for books and tapes

They all have to be logged into the computer accounting system.

task 1

Ensure the program date is set at 31 August 2001.

Input in BANK (Customers) the following payments received during August and paid into the bank current account on the dates indicated. The reference number is the paying-in slip number.

account	date	customer	amount (£)	reference
HD001	10 08 2001	Hill & Dale & Co	345.00	100110
PL001	17 08 2001	Playgames PLC	795.00	100112
RR001	24 08 2001	RS Export Agency	850.00	100114
RT001	31 08 2001	Rotherway Limited	1,210.00	100116
SC001	31 08 2001	Schafeld Ltd	800.00	100116
		Total	4,000.00	

task 2

Print out a Day Books: Customer Receipts (Summary) report for the month from BANK to check the accuracy of your input.

task 3

Jo has also paid the takings from cash sales (ie from small translation jobs, books and tapes) into the bank current account each week. She has totalled up each week's takings from these three sources and paid them in on one paying-in slip each Friday (the reference is shown in the right-hand column). The manual records she has kept show the cash receipts as follows:

date paid in	description	net (£)	VAT (£)	gross (£)	reference
10 08 2001	Translations	96.00	16.80	112.80	100111
	Tapes	240.00	42.00	282.00	
	Books	160.00	T0 code	160.00	
	Paying-in slip total			554.80	

date paid in	description	net (£)	VAT (£)	gross (£)	reference
17 08 2001	Translations	116.00	20.30	136.30	100113
	Tapes	180.00	31.50	211.50	
	Books	107.00	T0 code	107.00	
	Paying-in slip total			454.80	
24 08 2001	Translations	104.00	18.20	122.20	100115
	Tapes	220.00	38.50	258.50	
	Books	84.00	T0 code	84.00	
	Paying-in slip total			464.70	
31 08 2001	Translations	82.00	14.35	96.35	100117
	Tapes	190.00	33.25	223.25	
	Books	113.00	T0 code	113.00	
	Paying-in slip total			432.60	
BATCH TOTALS		1,692.00	214.90	1,906.90	

Input each of these cash receipts in BANK as BANK RECEIPTS. Remember to use the correct Nominal Codes for each type of sale: 4000 for translations, 4100 for books, 4101 for tapes. The reference in the right-hand column is the paying-in slip reference and should be used for each line of input.

task 4

Print out a Day Books: Bank Receipts (Detailed) report for the month from BANK to check the accuracy of your input.

ACTIVITY 7 - PAYING SUPPLIERS AND EXPENSES

introduction

During August Jo has had to pay her suppliers (of books and tapes) who have invoiced her in July on 30 days terms. She has also had to pay a number of expenses.

task 1

Input in BANK (Suppliers) these two outstanding items which were paid on 6 August:

TDI Wholesalers	Invoice 2347	£780.00	Due 05 08 2001	Cheque 120006
Bardners Books	Invoice 9422	£420.00	Due 06 08 2001	Cheque 120007

If possible, print out remittance advices from the computer to accompany the cheques.

task 2

Print out a Day Books: Supplier Payments (Summary) report for 6 August from BANK to check the accuracy of your input.

task 3

Input the following expense payments through Payment in BANK.

In most cases you will need to work out the nominal codes from the Trial Balance on page 226.

The cheque number should be used as the reference.

The tax code is T1 unless indicated otherwise.

date	cheque	details	net(£)	VAT(£)
07 08 2001	120009	Office furniture	140.00	24.50
08 08 2001	120010	Advertising	600.00	105.00
15 08 2001	120011	Rent	250.00	43.75
17 08 2001	120012	Stationery	126.00	22.05
20 08 2001	120013	Rates	129.00	T2
22 08 2001	120014	Telephone	186.00	32.55
24 08 2001	120015	Electricity	84.00	14.70
30 08 2001	120016	Postages	45.60	T2
31 08 2001	120017	Drawings	2,000.00	T9
31 08 2001	120018	Wages (account 7005)	240.00	T9
		Totals	3,800.60	242.55
				4,043.15

task 4

Print out a Day Books: Bank Payments (Summary) report for 7 - 31 August from BANK to check the accuracy of your input.

ACTIVITY 8 - SETTING UP A PETTY CASH SYSTEM

When you have completed this Activity you may check your input against the Trial Balance printed on page 249.

introduction

Jo finds that her temporary office assistant, Ella, often needs to make small payments in cash for items such as postage stamps and items of stationery for the office. She therefore decides to set up a petty cash system and cashes a cheque for £80 on 6 August to provide the funds.

task 1

Set the program date to 31 August 2001.

Process a Transfer in BANK for the £80 cheque (No. 120008) cashed on 6 August 2001. The accounts involved are Bank Current Account 1200 and Petty Cash Account 1230.

task 2

Input into BANK (Payments) Petty Cash Account the transactions represented by the four petty cash vouchers shown below.

Note that on one of them you will have to calculate the VAT on screen.

Postages are VAT exempt (Tax code T2)

task 3

Print out a Day Books: Cash Payments (Summary) report from BANK to check the accuracy of your input. Remember to select Petty Cash Account on the Bank opening screen first.

petty cash voucher		Number *0001*	
		date	*7 Aug 2001*
description			amount
		£	p
Office stationery		*16*	*00*
		16	*00*
	VAT	*2*	*80*
VAT receipt obtained		*18*	*80*
signature	*Ella Smith*		
authorised	*Jo Lane*		

petty cash voucher

Number *0002*

date *7 Aug 2001*

description		amount	
		£	p
Postages		24	00
		24	00
	VAT		
		24	00

signature *Ella Smith*

authorised *Jo Lane*

---

petty cash voucher

Number *0003*

date *15 Aug 2001*

description		amount	
		£	p
Office stationery			
	VAT		
Receipt obtained		23	50

signature *Ella Smith*

authorised *Jo Lane*

note that the receipt in this case does not show the VAT charged

---

petty cash voucher

Number *0004*

date *22 Aug 2001*

description		amount	
		£	p
Postages		12	00
		12	00
	VAT		
		12	00

signature *Ella Smith*

authorised *Jo Lane*

ACTIVITY 9 – SETTING UP RECURRING PAYMENTS IN BANK

introduction

Jo has set up monthly standing order and direct debit payments through the bank current account. She can process these in Sage by setting up Recurring Payments in RECURRING in BANK. Click on the ADD button at the bottom of the screen to bring up the necessary window.

task 1

Set up a Recurring Payment for the following:

Bank Account	1200
Payment type	Direct Debit
Payee	Suresafe Insurance (insurance premium)
Nominal code	7104
Tax code	T2
Amount	£98.50 per month
Due date	10th monthly

task 2

Set up a Recurring Payment for the following:

Bank Account	1200
Payment type	Standing order
Payee	Albion Bank (bank standing charge)
Nominal code	7901
Tax code	T2
Amount	£15.00 per month
Due date	25th monthly

task 3

Set the program date to 31 August 2001 and process the Recurring Payments for August in BANK.

task 4

Print out a trial balance of the business as at 31 August 2001. It should agree with the Trial balance shown on the next page.

Interlingo Translation Services
Period Trial Balance

To Period: Month 2, August 2001

N/C	Name	Debit	Credit
0020	Office computers	5,000.00	
0030	Office Equipment	2,500.00	
0040	Furniture and Fixtures	3,140.00	
1100	Debtors Control Account	2,636.68	
1200	Bank Current Account	7,555.25	
1230	Petty Cash	1.70	
2100	Creditors Control Account		1,446.00
2200	Sales Tax Control Account		1,417.58
2201	Purchase Tax Control Account	1,003.10	
2300	Loans		5,000.00
3000	Capital		15,000.00
4000	Translation services income		6,306.00
4100	Sales of language books		920.00
4101	Sales of language tapes		1,780.00
5000	Purchases of books	864.75	
5001	Purchases of tapes	1,500.00	
6201	Advertising	1,150.00	
7000	Drawings	4,000.00	
7005	Wages - Casual	240.00	
7100	Rent	500.00	
7103	General Rates	258.00	
7104	Premises Insurance	98.50	
7200	Electricity	145.00	
7501	Postage and Carriage	167.60	
7502	Telephone	461.00	
7504	Office Stationery	633.00	
7901	Bank Charges	15.00	
	Totals:	31,869.58	31,869.58

Trial balance of Interlingo Translation Services as at 31 August 2001

ACTIVITY 10 – END-OF-MONTH PROCEDURES

introduction

At the end of August Jo is ready to print out her end-of-month reports.

task 1

Print out the following reports and write a brief explanation of their function and how they can help Jo in running the business:

■ the month-end Trial Balance

■ customer statements of account from CUSTOMERS

■ an aged debtor analysis from Reports in CUSTOMERS

■ a brief audit trail from FINANCIALS

task 2

Jo remembers that she had negotiations over discounts with her account customer Hill & Dale & Co earlier in the month. Obtain a Customer Activity report and examine the Customer Record. Describe what has happened on the account and explain to Jo what the discount position is on this account.

task 3

Print out a Supplier Activity report for TDI Wholesalers and examine the Customer Record. Describe what has happened on the account during the month and suggest to Jo what she could do about discounts on this account.

task 4

Jim Draxman, a friend of Jo, who is helping her with her marketing, asks her for a list of the names and addresses of her customers as soon as possible, either by email or by fax.

Produce a suitable list, either from Labels or from a Customer Address List Report (both accessible in CUSTOMERS) and send the data electronically, either by email or by fax.

ACTIVITY 11 – DEALING WITH SECURITY

introduction

At the end of August Jo is concerned that the security of her computer and the data kept on it is not as watertight as it could be. She takes measures to improve the safety of her machines and data.

task 1

Jo finds that her temporary assistant, Ella, has been looking at the computer accounting files which relate to business expenditure and to Wages and Drawings in particular. Ella normally only deals with Customer files.

How can Jo prevent this happening in the future?

task 2

Jo sometimes gets in a muddle over her backup disks for her computer accounting program and has on one occasion had to reinput data.

Recommend to Jo a back up system for computer disks which will prevent this happening in the future.

task 3

Jo has been talking to her solicitor customers Hill & Dale & Co. They have said in passing that they "presume she is complying with the terms of the Data Protection Act". She says that she is.

Describe the main purpose of this Act.

TRIAL BALANCE CHECKLIST

introduction

The trial balances that follow are provided so that tutors and students carrying out the processing exercises and extended activities can periodically check their progress.

Where trial balances are provided in the text of the chapters they are not reproduced again here.

trial balance Chapter 6, end of Task 2

Pronto Supplies Limited
Period Trial Balance

To Period: Month 2, February 2001

N/C	Name	Debit	Credit
0020	Plant and Machinery	35,000.00	
0030	Office Equipment	15,000.00	
0040	Furniture and Fixtures	25,000.00	
1100	Debtors Control Account	45,965.30	
1200	Bank Current Account	12,450.00	
2100	Creditors Control Account		32,510.00
2200	Sales Tax Control Account		17,989.30
2201	Purchase Tax Control Account	26,600.00	
2300	Loans		35,000.00
3000	Ordinary Shares		75,000.00
4000	Computer hardware sales		85,376.00
4001	Computer software sales		14,900.00
4002	Computer consultancy		2,520.00
5000	Materials Purchased	69,100.00	
6201	Advertising	12,400.00	
7000	Gross Wages	16,230.00	
7100	Rent	4,500.00	
7103	General Rates	450.00	
7200	Electricity	150.00	
7502	Telephone	275.00	
7504	Office Stationery	175.00	
	Totals:	263,295.30	263,295.30

final trial balance Chapter 6, end of Task 4

Pronto Supplies Limited
Period Trial Balance

To Period: Month 2, February 2001

N/C	Name	Debit	Credit
0020	Plant and Machinery	35,000.00	
0030	Office Equipment	15,000.00	
0040	Furniture and Fixtures	25,000.00	
1100	Debtors Control Account	47,666.70	
1200	Bank Current Account	12,450.00	
2100	Creditors Control Account		32,510.00
2200	Sales Tax Control Account		18,242.70
2201	Purchase Tax Control Account	26,600.00	
2300	Loans		35,000.00
3000	Ordinary Shares		75,000.00
4000	Computer hardware sales		86,040.00
4001	Computer software sales		15,564.00
4002	Computer consultancy		2,640.00
5000	Materials Purchased	69,100.00	
6201	Advertising	12,400.00	
7000	Gross Wages	16,230.00	
7100	Rent	4,500.00	
7103	General Rates	450.00	
7200	Electricity	150.00	
7502	Telephone	275.00	
7504	Office Stationery	175.00	
	Totals:	264,996.70	264,996.70

final trial balance Chapter 7, end of Task 3

Pronto Supplies Limited
Period Trial Balance

To Period: Month 2, February 2001

N/C	Name	Debit	Credit
0020	Plant and Machinery	35,000.00	
0030	Office Equipment	15,760.00	
0040	Furniture and Fixtures	25,000.00	
1100	Debtors Control Account	47,666.70	
1200	Bank Current Account	12,450.00	
2100	Creditors Control Account		43,698.35
2200	Sales Tax Control Account		18,242.70
2201	Purchase Tax Control Account	28,266.35	
2300	Loans		35,000.00
3000	Ordinary Shares		75,000.00
4000	Computer hardware sales		86,040.00
4001	Computer software sales		15,564.00
4002	Computer consultancy		2,640.00
5000	Materials Purchased	77,862.00	
6201	Advertising	12,400.00	
7000	Gross Wages	16,230.00	
7100	Rent	4,500.00	
7103	General Rates	450.00	
7200	Electricity	150.00	
7502	Telephone	275.00	
7504	Office Stationery	175.00	
	Totals:	276,185.05	276,185.05

final trial balance Chapter 8, end of Task 5

Pronto Supplies Limited

Period Trial Balance

To Period: Month 2, February 2001

N/C	Name	Debit	Credit
0020	Plant and Machinery	35,000.00	
0030	Office Equipment	15,760.00	
0040	Furniture and Fixtures	25,000.00	
1100	Debtors Control Account	8,991.00	
1200	Bank Current Account	19,224.35	
2100	Creditors Control Account		11,797.00
2200	Sales Tax Control Account		18,242.70
2201	Purchase Tax Control Account	28,266.35	
2300	Loans		35,000.00
3000	Ordinary Shares		75,000.00
4000	Computer hardware sales		86,040.00
4001	Computer software sales		15,564.00
4002	Computer consultancy		2,640.00
5000	Materials Purchased	77,862.00	
6201	Advertising	12,400.00	
7000	Gross Wages	16,230.00	
7100	Rent	4,500.00	
7103	General Rates	450.00	
7200	Electricity	150.00	
7502	Telephone	275.00	
7504	Office Stationery	175.00	
	Totals:	244,283.70	244,283.70

final trial balance Chapter 9, end of Task 3

Pronto Supplies Limited
Period Trial Balance

To Period: Month 2, February 2001

N/C	Name	Debit	Credit
0020	Plant and Machinery	35,000.00	
0030	Office Equipment	19,760.00	
0040	Furniture and Fixtures	30,000.00	
1100	Debtors Control Account	8,991.00	
1200	Bank Current Account	29,762.45	
2100	Creditors Control Account		11,797.00
2200	Sales Tax Control Account		28,620.20
2201	Purchase Tax Control Account	35,267.75	
2300	Loans		35,000.00
3000	Ordinary Shares		80,000.00
4000	Computer hardware sales		132,180.00
4001	Computer software sales		28,724.00
4002	Computer consultancy		2,640.00
5000	Materials Purchased	93,362.00	
6201	Advertising	22,600.00	
7000	Gross Wages	33,010.00	
7100	Rent	9,000.00	
7103	General Rates	800.00	
7200	Electricity	308.00	
7502	Telephone	585.00	
7504	Office Stationery	515.00	
	Totals:	318,961.20	318,961.20

final trial balance Chapter 10, end of Task 5

Pronto Supplies Limited
Period Trial Balance

To Period: Month 2, February 2001

N/C	Name	Debit	Credit
0020	Plant and Machinery	35,000.00	
0030	Office Equipment	19,760.00	
0040	Furniture and Fixtures	30,000.00	
1100	Debtors Control Account	8,991.00	
1200	Bank Current Account	30,174.98	
1230	Petty Cash	4.20	
1235	Cash Receipts	9,740.75	
2100	Creditors Control Account		11,797.00
2200	Sales Tax Control Account		30,150.75
2201	Purchase Tax Control Account	35,281.02	
2300	Loans		35,000.00
3000	Ordinary Shares		80,000.00
4000	Computer hardware sales		138,980.00
4001	Computer software sales		30,214.00
4002	Computer consultancy		2,640.00
4904	Rent Income		456.00
5000	Materials Purchased	93,362.00	
6201	Advertising	22,600.00	
7000	Gross Wages	33,010.00	
7100	Rent	9,000.00	
7103	General Rates	800.00	
7200	Electricity	308.00	
7501	Postage and Carriage	30.00	
7502	Telephone	585.00	
7504	Office Stationery	571.00	
7701	Office Machine Maintenance	19.80	
	Totals:	329,237.75	329,237.75

final trial balance Chapter 12, end of Task 5

Pronto Supplies Limited
Period Trial Balance

To Period: Month 2, February 2001

N/C	Name	Debit	Credit
0020	Plant and Machinery	35,000.00	
0030	Office Equipment	19,760.00	
0040	Furniture and Fixtures	30,000.00	
1100	Debtors Control Account	8,991.00	
1200	Bank Current Account	36,334.98	
1230	Petty Cash	4.20	
1235	Cash Receipts	9,740.75	
2100	Creditors Control Account		17,957.00
2200	Sales Tax Control Account		30,150.75
2201	Purchase Tax Control Account	35,281.02	
2300	Loans		35,000.00
3000	Ordinary Shares		80,000.00
4000	Computer hardware sales		136,980.00
4001	Computer software sales		32,214.00
4002	Computer consultancy		2,640.00
4904	Rent Income		456.00
5000	Materials Purchased	93,362.00	
6201	Advertising	22,600.00	
7000	Gross Wages	33,010.00	
7100	Rent	9,000.00	
7103	General Rates	800.00	
7200	Electricity	150.00	
7201	Gas	158.00	
7501	Postage and Carriage	30.00	
7502	Telephone	585.00	
7504	Office Stationery	571.00	
7701	Office Machine Maintenance	19.80	
	Totals:	335,397.75	335,397.75

final trial balance Chapter 13, end of Task 4

Pronto Supplies Limited
Period Trial Balance

To Period: Month 3, March 2001

N/C	Name	Debit	Credit
0020	Plant and Machinery	35,000.00	
0030	Office Equipment	19,760.00	
0040	Furniture and Fixtures	30,000.00	
1100	Debtors Control Account	9,978.00	
1200	Bank Current Account	36,334.98	
1230	Petty Cash	4.20	
1235	Cash Receipts	9,740.75	
2100	Creditors Control Account		17,957.00
2200	Sales Tax Control Account		30,297.75
2201	Purchase Tax Control Account	35,281.02	
2300	Loans		35,000.00
3000	Ordinary Shares		80,000.00
4000	Computer hardware sales		136,980.00
4001	Computer software sales		32,214.00
4002	Computer consultancy		3,480.00
4904	Rent Income		456.00
5000	Materials Purchased	93,362.00	
6201	Advertising	22,600.00	
7000	Gross Wages	33,010.00	
7100	Rent	9,000.00	
7103	General Rates	800.00	
7200	Electricity	150.00	
7201	Gas	158.00	
7501	Postage and Carriage	30.00	
7502	Telephone	585.00	
7504	Office Stationery	571.00	
7701	Office Machine Maintenance	19.80	
	Totals:	336,384.75	336,384.75

trial balance Extended Exercise 2, end of Activity 5

Interlingo Translation Services
Period Trial Balance

To Period: Month 2, August 2001

N/C	Name	Debit	Credit
0020	Office computers	5,000.00	
0030	Office Equipment	2,500.00	
0040	Furniture and Fixtures	3,000.00	
1100	Debtors Control Account	6,636.68	
1200	Bank Current Account	7,085.00	
2100	Creditors Control Account		2,646.00
2200	Sales Tax Control Account		1,202.68
2201	Purchase Tax Control Account	754.25	
2300	Loans		5,000.00
3000	Capital		15,000.00
4000	Translation services income		5,908.00
4100	Sales of language books		456.00
4101	Sales of language tapes		950.00
5000	Purchases of books	864.75	
5001	Purchases of tapes	1,500.00	
6201	Advertising	550.00	
7000	Drawings	2,000.00	
7100	Rent	250.00	
7103	General Rates	129.00	
7200	Electricity	61.00	
7501	Postage and Carriage	86.00	
7502	Telephone	275.00	
7504	Office Stationery	471.00	
	Totals:	31,162.68	31,162.68

trial balance Extended Exercise 2, end of Activity 8

Interlingo Translation Services
Period Trial Balance

To Period: Month 2, August 2001

N/C	Name	Debit	Credit
0020	Office computers	5,000.00	
0030	Office Equipment	2,500.00	
0040	Furniture and Fixtures	3,140.00	
1100	Debtors Control Account	2,636.68	
1200	Bank Current Account	7,668.75	
1230	Petty Cash	1.70	
2100	Creditors Control Account		1,446.00
2200	Sales Tax Control Account		1,417.58
2201	Purchase Tax Control Account	1,003.10	
2300	Loans		5,000.00
3000	Capital		15,000.00
4000	Translation services income		6,306.00
4100	Sales of language books		920.00
4101	Sales of language tapes		1,780.00
5000	Purchases of books	864.75	
5001	Purchases of tapes	1,500.00	
6201	Advertising	1,150.00	
7000	Drawings	4,000.00	
7005	Wages - Casual	240.00	
7100	Rent	500.00	
7103	General Rates	258.00	
7200	Electricity	145.00	
7501	Postage and Carriage	167.60	
7502	Telephone	461.00	
7504	Office Stationery	633.00	
	Totals:	31,869.58	31,869.58

notes

INDEX